HOW NOT TO MAKE IT
IN THE POP WORLD

(Diary of an almost has been)

JOHN BARROW

For Kim, Rhett and Nile with love.

Many thanks to :

Gaz Birtles, for technical support and direction. Dean Sargent, Mark O'Hara and all the musicians that I have had the good fortune to work with over the years.
Also thanks to Caroline Hutton for support and encouragement, and to Jimmy Mooney for his help.
Cover layout by Gaz Birtles from an original idea by Martin Patton and Steve Taylor.

© Copyright 2003 John Barrow. All rights reserved.

No part of this publication may be reproduced, stored in a retrieval system, or transmitted, in any form or by any means, electronic, mechanical, photocopying, recording, or otherwise, without the written prior permission of the author.
Contact the author at: johnbarrow@lineone.net

Printed in Victoria, Canada

Note for Librarians: a cataloguing record for this book that includes Dewey Classification and US Library of Congress numbers is available from the National Library of Canada. The complete cataloguing record can be obtained from the National Library's online database at:
www.nlc-bnc.ca/amicus/index-e.html
ISBN 1-4120-1413-1

TRAFFORD

This book was published on-demand in cooperation with Trafford Publishing.
On-demand publishing is a unique process and service of making a book available for retail sale to the public taking advantage of on-demand manufacturing and Internet marketing. On-demand publishing includes promotions, retail sales, manufacturing, order fulfilment, accounting and collecting royalties on behalf of the author.

Suite 6E, 2333 Government St., Victoria, B.C. V8T 4P4, CANADA
Phone   250-383-6864   Toll-free 1-888-232-4444 (Canada & US)
Fax 250-383-6804   E-mail sales@trafford.com   Web site www.trafford.com
TRAFFORD PUBLISHING IS A DIVISION OF TRAFFORD HOLDINGS LTD.
Trafford Catalogue #03-1791   www.trafford.com/robots/03-1791.html

10   9   8   7   6   5   4

CHAPTERS

1. Beginnings — page 6
2. Sister Big Stuff - Is the world ready for this? — Page 11
3. Enter Dean — page 18
4. Sammy Day - Marvin Dyche - Stuart Mc Millan - Welcome — page 27
5. New Faces — page 30
6. Sister Big Stuff - The end — page 35
7. Picking Bananas in the funky jungle — page 38
8. Top of the Pops — page 47
9. Scotland - Lock up your daughters — page 56
10. Jean- Paul Barrow — page 62
11. A day at the Palace — page 65
12. Bernard Manning's straight man — page 69
13. No woman - No cry — page 78
14. Moonlighting — page 82
15. The Peel session — page 92
16. The independent label — page 94

17. Swinging Laurels are go   page 96

18. The A & R man   page 105

19. Decadent Berlin   page 107

20. Team 23   page 112

21. Publishing - Albion we love you   page 115

22. Mark & Dean - Come on down   page 121

23. The Hope & Anchor   page 160

24. Miles Copeland (How does it
    feel to be rich?)   page 166

25. Top Of The Pops revisited   page 179

26. Rodeo - Name the guilty men   page 192

27. Boy George – Make way for the
    Lonely Boy   page 205

28. Goodbye Mr.Warner -
    and his Brothers   page 227

29. Happy Records   page 238

30. The Radio One road show   page 243

31. Rhoda   page 250

32. Crazyhead & the Space
    Bastards   page 259

33. The Telephone Always Rings -
    The Beautiful South   page 270

34. Istianity - May we dominate you?   Page 281

For Kim, Rhett and Nile with love always.

Many thanks to;
Gaz Birtles - Mark O'Hara - Dean Sargent - Nick Murphy - Kev Bayliss and all the musicians that I've had the good fortune to work with down the years. Also thanks to Caroline Hutton for encouragement and to Jimmy Mooney for his help.
Cover lay out by Gaz Birtles from an original concept by Martin Patton and Steve Taylor.
Thank you to all the photographers that have graciously granted permission to use their work. All reasonable efforts have been made to contact contributing photographers. Please contact the author with any information relating to photographers not credited.
Contact the author; johnbarrow@lineone.net
www.myspace.com/johnbarrow
www.theswinginglaurels.co.uk
www.myspace.com/theswinginglaurels

FOREWORD

The misconceptions that surround the workings of the pop industry are many and varied - one misguided belief chief among them is that if you've strutted your stuff on Top of the Pops you must be rolling in it! Nothing could be further from the truth. I am living proof of that. I am one of those unfortunate journeymen of pop, always on the periphery, never quite hitting the pay dirt.

The industry exists by allowing gullible kids to believe the myth. It's a dream machine that feeds from its own legend.

Throughout my misguided quest for unlimited world wide fame and fortune, I strutted my stuff with two bands on Top of the Pops,

Black Gorilla in 1977 and the **Fun Boy Three** in 1982.

There is **NO** Lear jet in my driveway!

During twenty-five years in the fairyland that is the pop world, I can point to over fifty record releases. I have worked and recorded for many major and independent record labels and signed megabucks recording and publishing deals - associating with world-name pop icons and producers.

There is **NO** Lamborghini in my driveway.

This is the sorry tale of my stroll through the labyrinth of dreams that is the pop industry.

Answer this? What makes an outwardly level headed chap don leather trousers and bare his soul on stage in front of thousands of screaming pre-pubescent females? I can perhaps point to pivotal crossroads. In 1964, as an eight year old, I watched the Kinks performing You Really Got Me on Top of the Pops - the hairs on the back of my neck still bristle on hearing those urgent opening chords. I pleaded with mum to let me have a pair of Cuban heeled boots - the kind favoured by another hero of mine, John Lennon. I begged her to let me discard my Bryl-creeme plastered short back 'n' sides haircut for a Beatles mop top. I didn't get the boots and I didn't get the hair do!

The sixties were good. The Brits were taking on the pop world and winning. England even won the football world cup. Could it really get any better than that?

As a kid I had my own band. We were fuelled by Mersey fever and inspired by the sixties scene. We slaughtered Beatles covers - banging cardboard boxes for drums in the street. I saved my pocket money up to buy a guitar and it cost me a princely £2 pounds 11 shillings and sixpence. I never could play it.

In 1972 I was blown away at a Roxy Music concert at the De Montfort Halls in Leicester. That night a spellbound nineteen-year-old was introduced to the very wonderful saxophone playing of Andy Mackay. I was smitten. I desperately wanted to be that cool sax player who received the adulation of the crowd that night.

Another stunning night came in 1973 at a Faces gig at the Birmingham Odeon - They were awesome. Surely, one of the best ever GOOD TIME rock n roll bands.

In my time in pop I've achieved almost everything apart from having my own hit. I played on other people's hits, undertook major tours, and appeared on top-flight television and radio shows. One journalist once described my failure to make it with the line,
'Like a goal line clearance, in the last minute of a play off final at Wembley.'

There is no such thing as overnight success. People automatically assume that when band notches up a first hit, they are newcomers. What they fail to see are the years of graft, disappointments and endeavour to get things up and running.

Most books on this subject focus on people that have achieved mega star status - never on the poor stiffs like me, who have come so agonisingly close.

Chapter One

BEGINNINGS

Music is a hugely emotive medium. Hearing a track from the past can transport the listener back to first clumsy gropes with the opposite sex, or to some other memorable experience from years before. A few brief seconds can promote euphoria or sadness.

The music industry holds a total fascination for me - the recording process, promotion, the lot. Even my sons are named after record producers - Rhett is named after Rhett Davies and Nile after Nile Rogers. My interest was surely inherited. Dad was a singer on the Leicester club circuit in the fifties and I remember having yellowing black and white photographs thrust in front of me as a child. He was very handsome in his stage tuxedo.

I was no stranger to the adrenaline rush of live performance - I had hammed it up in end of term shows and plays at school. Music had a prominent place in the Barrow household. Dad rigged up a primitive speaker system in the bedroom that I shared with my brother Paul and he piped music to us on Sunday mornings. The first Beatles album, Please Please Me was a particular favourite. Dad had extensive collection of old 78 rpm records and I never tired of listening to them on a clapped out red and crème Dansette record player with plastic legs. It had an arm that should have dropped records one at a time but sometimes annoyingly released several. Records by, Elvis Presley - Little Richard and Frankie Lymon & the Teenagers. As I said The Kinks were a tremendous influence on me and I remember 1964 as an exciting time - even for an eight-year-old. British bands were at the forefront of world pop and the Brit invasion was well under way in the US - there was very tangible feel good factor.

We used to watch the New Musical Express music awards on our tiny black and white television set at home. Bands like Billy J Kramer and the Dakotas - The Searchers and the Dave Clark Five, who always seemed to be accompanied by hoards of hysterical knicker wetting girls screaming so loudly that the music was all but obscured. 'I could handle some of that,' I thought. I later witnessed similar scenes for myself on tours with Boy George and Culture Club in the '80s.

In the 60s dad was a bread rounds man and one of the drops on his route took him to a music venue in Derbyshire. During one delivery he walked in to find a young band that were sound checking for their evening show. They were the Rolling Stones. They had just enjoyed their first top twenty hit, Not Fade Away and the follow up It's All Over Now was inching up the charts. Dad got them to scribble their autographs on a paper bag for me and I was delighted.

I soon came to realise the power of such an item. Sue Neal, an older girl who lived round the corner, was a real Stones fan and she gave me a big kiss because I tore off a tiny piece of my prized possession and gave it to her. God knows what she would have done for the whole bag! As to its value now, who knows? The signature of Brian Jones, who died in tragic circumstances in 1967, is on it. Perverse I know, but death means money in the auction room.

In 1974 I purloined my first saxophone from a music shop in town called Humbuckers. It should have really been called 'I saw you coming enterprises.' They specialised in cheap second hand instruments which was good because cheap was all that I could afford. With some financial assistance from my dad, I stumped up twenty pounds in exchange for a battered old Selmer C melody - a member of the saxophone family most used in the dance band era of the forties. Unfortunately for me it was by now obsolete and not used at all in the era of loon pants and pork chop sideburns. I was sold a pup!

Never-the-less I was in love with that instrument, with it's multitude of pressy things that surely no one had enough fingers to accommodate. I loved its shape, form and even the chipped lacquer and dents. I can still recall the smell from the musty interior of its case. The only real problem was getting a sound out of it! My first efforts sounded akin to the desperate cry of an elephant seal with piles.

One of my best mates at the time was a lad called Gaz Birtles - we'd met at Emgas where we were gas fitting apprentices. He was an easy going; gangly youth and we hit it off straight away. Life as a gas fitting apprentice was a plumb job for a teenager, the hours were short - the pay wasn't that bad and we spent hours idling in greasy spoon cafés talking about music. One day he announced to me with some conviction that one-day he would be famous.

Gaz's mum had an old upright piano in the back room of her council house and we had a couple woeful of jamming sessions - Gaz torturing the keyboard and me trying to get a half-tuneful wail out of my sax. It was like Les Dawson meets Zoot from the Muppets! Gaz eventually bought an alto sax and it complimented my tenor perfectly - we didn't realise it at the time but our careers in music were to run an inexplicable tandem course.

When reality hit and I passed my City and Guild exams - fearing the responsibility I promptly left and hung on to a series of stop gap jobs, all the time day dreaming about breaking into the world of music.

My playing started to come on bit by bit. I would blow my saxophone into a wardrobe full of clothes to deaden the noise. May, the old lady next door used to bang frenetically on the wall - the most annoying thing was that the poor old dear had no sense of rhythm! Practice sessions were never a wow with mum either. Here was history repeating - when I was ten I was delighted when my uncle gave me a drum kit - it mysteriously disappeared only a few weeks later.

I would religiously watch live bands at the Leicester De Montfort Halls, among them - David Bowie, Cockney Rebel and Sparks. After the show we would hang out at the Holiday Inn in the hope that some of the stars would be staying there. I met the Mael Brothers of Sparks and Roxy Music and I got Andy Mackay's autograph and chatted to Bryan Ferry.

On another occasion we managed to blag tickets for a celebrity promotion at the Horsefair Club in Leicester which was attended by a number of luminaries including legendary Leicester City footballer Frank Worthington and celebs from the world of pop. Among them were Jim Cregan and his wife

Linda Lewis. Jim was a guitarist with Family and Cockney Rebel (it is his instantly recognisable guitar solo on their No 1 hit, Come Up and See Me - Make Me Smile) he later spent many years playing guitar with Rod Stewart. Linda Lewis had a successful recording career too with hits that included, Rock a Doodle Doo in 1973.

We spotted them together at the bar and nervously sidled up to bend their ears. We wanted to be musicians, we explained - could they offer any advice? The reply was both stark and succinct -'PRACTISE LIKE F**K!!!' - Blunt as it was, it was advice that I never forgot.

A guy called Karl Hirst held regular jamming sessions at his flat - I used to sit next to him in school but in those days he managed a trendy clothes shop called the Gear Shop in Leicester City centre. Karl was a technically adept guitarist and had already been playing his Gibson gold top for a number years. I made the huge mistake of telling him that we played saxophones and to my abject horror he invited us up to his flat for a blast. God only knows what we sounded like - we were completely out of our depth. The session was recorded on a reel to reel tape recorder for posterity and for years after he took sadistic delight in telling us that if we ever made it he would reveal the recordings to the world!

As my playing improved it was high time to invest in a real saxophone, so I purchased a spanking new Czechoslovakian copy by Guban. £200 was a hefty sum in 1974 for a teenager, even if spread over endless months of 'easy' repayments.

By this time, Gaz and I had a few lessons from a guy who played in the resident band at the Talk of the Town cabaret club in Nottingham. It helped, but he got us to practice really banal songs from the A Tune a Day sax tutorial book for beginners. 'Home, Home on the Range!' did not appeal – when all the time we were aching to get stuck into something meatier.

Chapter Two

SISTER BIG STUFF (is the world ready for this)

The circumstances that led to my first job in a working band were a series of quirky co-incidences, and as so often happened later, outside influences played a big hand in bringing it about. A local semi-pro band called Sister Big Stuff advertised for a sax player in the local rag. My girlfriend of the time, Colleen, phoned without my knowledge and arranged an audition. In retrospect I don't know if, without her well-meaning intervention, I would ever have applied under my own steam. I'd reached a point in my development where I could have quite easily have given it all up as a bad job - that lump of metal squealed to rhythms of it's own but this gave me the kick start to take things a vital stage further. I felt sick to the pit of my stomach at the prospect of the audition. Sister Big Stuff were a seven piece soul / funk band, with a name on the local scene and they had an agent with real clout - he booked them gigs throughout the Midlands and East Anglia - mainly at night clubs and Air Force bases.

When the fateful day of the audition crawled around I was a snivelling bag of nerves. I was collected in a Porsche by Graham Tom, guitarist and bandleader. Being a motor-phobe, I only found out what a Porsche was when the girl from the flat above probed, 'Who do you know that can afford a Porsche then?' It was an extremely smooth, quick drive for the fourteen miles to the rehearsal room at Bardon, Coalville.

Graham, a myopic, bespectacled curly haired twenty-year-old, was not exactly deficient in the money department. His family owned quarries - like you do! Bardon Hill where the rehearsal room was sited was one and Graham was a company director. The Tom's originally came from Cornwall where another of their quarries was situated.

The rest of the band, including the departing tenor sax man Dick, renowned for his bad breath, were waiting as I was ushered into the rehearsal room. The room was far enough from the house not to cause a disturbance, the gigging band's ideal.

The band comprised of Martyn 'Stalky' Gleeson (drums), Nick Thompson (trumpet) Graham Tom (guitar) Dave Van (keyboards), Vince Fernandes (bass) Melda Farrell (lead vocalist.) They whizzed through a lightning set of numbers, in an attempt to scare me or to give me an idea of what they were all about. I was squirming, they were dammed impressive, but perhaps the intimidating atmosphere made them sound better.

Sister Big Stuff were a covers band, but their canny choice of material set them apart from competition operating in the same market. Their set list included instantly recognisable soul and funk standards but they were not afraid to tackle more challenging tracks by the likes of Mandrill, Average White Band and Frankie Miller.

Most band members were in their early twenties and had been about. As sixth formers, Stalky, Dave and Graham were in a band called Medusa and they had a real rapport. Sax player Dick was also an excellent, fluent player which didn't make me feel any better. Vince was a resolute bass player who would boast proudly of his Portugese-Goan extraction to anyone that would listen and Dave was the most technically adept musically. What he didn't know about chord structures wasn't worth knowing. He was widely acknowledged to have a genius IQ and was once actually turned down for a job because he was too clever!

I took an instant liking to drummer Stalky. His cheeky, smiling face helped to ease some of the tension and little did I realise at that initial meeting, that we would become such good friends. Stalky worked in the mining industry, which went some way to explain his muscular Hulk Hogan arms. He boasted the very loudest bass drum in the Western Hemisphere, and took huge delight in thumping it hard at sound checks, when least expected - thus scaring the shit out the populous in a ten mile radius. It always amused Stalky no end.

Sister Big Stuff blasted through a gutsy rendition of (Your Love Keeps Lifting Me) Higher and Higher, which was originally a hit for Jackie Wilson in 1969. Led by the dynamic vocals of Melda and held together by Stalky's tight drumming,

I was wishing that I could render myself invisible at that point. Next the classic Knock on Wood was followed by Mr. Big Stuff a Betty Wright song, which lent its title to the name of the band.

It was then suggested that I have a go. The intro to Knock on Wood struck up. I was BAD! And I mean BAD! I struggled with the key and the spotlight of attention, while all the time Stalky grinned at me like a P.G Tips monkey from the sanctity of his drum kit.

As the noise in the room subsided there was a deafening silence that could have easily lasted ten years, before someone broke it with, 'Never mind, we'll try another.'

Years after this traumatic event I am reminded of words once said to me 'If you never try, you'll never know what you are capable of.' When I achieved a little more success, I'd repeat this to young kids seeking my advice. I firmly believe in having a go and aiming high. If you don't get off your backside and pitch in you'll never know what is possible in life. If asked, 'How did you get into playing the saxophone?' - 'How did you manage to join a band?' my stock reply would be, 'I just got up and did it - you could do it too.' A lot of people are in love with the idea of playing but many never do anything about it.

I consoled myself with the thought that at least I'd had a go as I struggled manfully to play along to more material. I left Coalville convincing myself that I'd well and truly blown it, Graham zipped me home in super car with the leaving words, 'We'll let you know.'

Two weeks elapsed before the call came. I hadn't thought much about it in the interim and I hadn't confided my experiences to many, so convinced was I that I hadn't made the cut. The words I heard were a total shocker. 'Do you want to join the band?' Did I ever? My lips said yes in auto pilot mode, and I prepared myself for the onset of unlimited world wide fame and fortune, and all the sex a young man could possibly handle!

In a bar some years later Stalky and I discussed my audition. 'I still can't believe that you picked me,' I said. Stalky retorted in his forthright, no-nonsense trademark way,

'We had to have you, NO ONE ELSE APPLIED FOR THE JOB!' Great, this made me think, if a kazoo playing chimpanzee had turned up it would have been snapped up instead of me!

There I was again in Coalville, now a member of Sister Big Stuff. Sax player Dick stayed on to teach me the brass lines and breathe more bad breath on me. I had to memorise over twenty songs in two weeks! Some brass lines were straightforward, others were particularly brass heavy - Average White Band's Pick up the Pieces for example. Sax solos littered the set so I really had my work cut out.

The old lady next door took to banging on my bedroom wall in an increasingly manic fashion though her sense of rhythm had mercifully improved, but then the poor old dear got a lot of practise, as I blew until my cheeks were sore! I often wonder if I was responsible for her eventual move into an old people's residential home! I visualised her on her commode whistling Betty Wright tunes and tapping out a wicked rhythm to the bewilderment of her fellow residents. The trendiest octogenarian ever.

It wasn't easy getting to grips with all those songs; I had to launch into some extensive practise sessions. I didn't read music, so I adopted a method of committing song formats to memory. I spent hours in that bedroom tooting away into my wardrobe. There was little choice, my debut live performance loomed ever large and the prospect seemed more scary as each day passed.

Several rehearsals later I started to find my level with the other members of the band, which is not as easy as it may seem. With any working group of individuals, strong relationships form - these guys had known each other for years. A pretty elaborate sense of humour permeated the set-up and trying to fathom out some of the running jokes and jolly japes took some doing. The humour was ruthlessly cruel and wicked.

My first live gig was at RAF Cranwell in Lincolnshire, sax player Dick came along for the ride. I felt as if my insides belonged to someone else but I'd taken the precaution of packing a spare pair of underpants in case of emergency! It was Saturday and the band travelled together, squashed like sardines in the back of one of Graham's quarry vans with the equipment piled high and packed tightly in the back.

The weird thing about RAF bases is that they all look the same. They were obviously built to some perverted master plan, if you've been to one - you've been to them all. I got to play lots of them - they all seemed to promote the same atmosphere. Saturday night was 'THE night out' for the inmates and with the base being stranded out in the wilds, coach loads of girls were bussed in from outlying towns and villages for the young RAF lads to have a go at.

We were expected to perform two forty five-minute sets of material, sandwiched by a disco operated by one of the RAF lads. If all the bases looked the same, then by the same token so did the characters that peopled them. The DJ invariably sported an unfashionable forces issue short back and sides haircut. He generally wore raised seamed trousers with too many buttons and pockets on them and teetered around on platform shoes resplendent in flowered shirt with lapels large enough to make a hang glider jealous! Despite this, he still somehow fostered the belief that he was irresistible to the opposite sex.

Local girls, obviously sensing that the RAF DJ was a go-getting, jet-setting rebel, threw themselves at him, usually in return for playing any thing by K.C. and the Sunshine Band!

Show time was a blur to me. I remember feeling nausea, and experiencing an almost out of the body experience. Dick bailed me out with timely interventions when first night nerve endings jangled. Trumpet player Nick, barely ever put a foot wrong but then he was classically trained and was an outstanding sight-reader. His once won BBC's Young musician of the year collecting a natty, engraved instrument in a presentation case as his prize. During the first set the audience were fairly subdued, but after Mr.RAF DJ man did his magic, and the effects of alcohol kicked in, the crowd warmed to us. We even did a couple of encores as DJ man surrounded himself with a gaggle of giggling girlies. All things considered the gig went well - a successful debut. Exhilarated, I knew I'd have to be back for more.

Now that I was a real blow monkey I felt it was high time that I broadened my musical listening tastes. For some perverse reason I believed that, because I played the saxophone, I ought to be sampling the delights of jazz. Rightly or wrongly, I thought you can't be a real sax player and not like jazz! I trawled the record stalls of Leicester market for anything jazz related on vinyl. I didn't know much about the jazz field, my first purchase, an Archie Shepp album, had more to do with my attraction to the cool, monochrome, arty 60's sleeve than anything else!

A Lester Young album was also snapped up for 15 pence and I rushed home to enlighten myself and groove away to a new music medium. Apart from being pretty badly scratched, the Archie Shepp album was difficult on the ear, a succession on of saxophone wails and screeches. Obviously my ear wasn't educated enough to appreciate it - neither were my dad's. He came into the room as I was playing it with the words, 'What's this bleeding row?'

The Lester Young album was more mainstream and melodic and I got to quite like it in time but it didn't move me enough to want to don a turtle necked sweater, smoke a pipe and wear sandals. I did listen to more jazz, I still like it when the mood takes me, but at the time it didn't have much relevance to the world of funk.

Sister Big Stuff were on the books of a Peterborough based booking agent, Steve Allen Agency. They operated over a fairly large area, mainly East Anglia. Our bookings were vetted by Graham but because of his time consuming career and the fact that he was rolling in it, he felt inclined to limit us to two or three engagements a week.

Sister Big Stuff were very good at what they did but they never actually showed an interest in seeking record contracts or publishing deals. This again was down to Graham's influence; he saw the band as a nice little diversion, a vehicle to get him out of the house at weekends. He would never have jeopardised his career. With good reason, when last I heard, he was living on his luxury yacht, moored off Tenerife. Occasionally he flits across to Marbella, for a change of scenery. Nice work if you can get it!

As the time passed by the band were clocking up a considerable number of live outings. Most of the venues were large night-clubs like the Top Rank or Baileys chains that catered for up to two thousand punters, seeming mainly to consist of inebriated over lockers. But the more live work we undertook, the tighter and more assured we became as a unit.

It was at this time that I embarked on my very first recording session. It came about when our agent tempted us with a summer residency in the Canary Islands. It was the summer of 1975. Along with the obligatory publicity photographs, the promoter wanted to hear what we sounded like, so a session was hastily arranged at Drum Beat studio which was a four-track facility in Leicester. The recording studio was a mind-boggling new world to me, though it was tiny in every respect to the studios I would frequent later on.

The whole process was a real eye opener and I enjoyed the session despite making some nervous errors. We recorded four tracks to showcase what we were about live. The downside was that Melda had a throat infection which dulled her unique vocal style but in the final event, we lost out to a rival band called Evolution.

The first major bombshell since my arrival in the band was the departure of trumpet player Nick, who quit to take up a music scholarship in London. No one begrudged him this well-earned opportunity - he had the talent and ability to go far. Replacing him with some one of the same musical calibre and pedigree was the problem. We advertised in the local paper.

In the days when there was still a mining industry Coalville was a mining town complete with colliery brass band. It was a product of this tradition that was to turn up in the shape of our new trumpet player.

Chapter Three

ENTER DEAN

Dean Sargent was a fresh faced, sixteen-year-old youth straight from a colliery brass band and school! He looked younger than his years and if I was a bag of nerves at my audition, it was nothing compared to him. That kid with the trembling digits was to become a life long friend and brass partner.

It was immediately obvious that Dean could play and like Nick before him, was an excellent sight-reader. Our only misgiving at that first audition was what Stalky quaintly termed his 'Coronation Street warble!' It was obviously a legacy of his brass band background, but a problem that could be addressed, given time and practise. Funk music demands a very sharp, incisive brass delivery for riff work.

When Dean was asked to join we had to ask the permission of his parents, and we felt like child snatchers! It was with some trepidation that they agreed. It can't have been easy for them to see their young son climbing into the back of a dirty transit van with us reprobates. Despite everything, we were responsible people and took him under our collective wing. Melda especially looked out for him, probably out of some form of mothering instinct. Melda was a West Indian girl and a unique character. As far as anyone could tell, and she wasn't telling, she was in her late twenties and had a very versatile singing voice.

Her downfall was her time keeping. Many times we had to flush her out of an amusement arcade to arrive late at a gig. Stalky would say that her greatest plus point was her shapely behind - he had the best view of it because she stood in front of his drum kit on stage.

Dean's opener was at the Le Chaumier club in Coventry. It was not unusual for us to take to the stage at midnight so that meant finally falling into our beds in the early hours. Most of us were struggling to hold down day jobs, so it could be exhausting. Dean blew like an old pro, but as was obligatory the new recruit was the butt of some pretty viscous mickey taking.

'You'll be late for your paper round in the morning.'

I'd been there. I suffered a similar baptism a few short months before. Dean's parents waited up for him. It came as a shock to learn that our new horn player was too young to buy a drink at the bar!

One pain in the arse aspect of life on the road for a struggling, unknown band was setting up and breaking down equipment. The further up the ladder to success you go, the less you have to worry about such mundane matters. When success comes there is a road manager and road-crew. All you do is turn up, sound check and play.

Being perched on the lowest rung of the ladder means these things need executing by the band, but I've heard successful musicians speak fondly of the early days when everything was such a struggle. I defy anyone to fondly remember loading a transit van, in the early hours of a dismal Glasgow morning, in sub-zero temperatures with the knowledge that a warm bed is 400 miles away!

Rounding the band up was a test in itself because band members lived over a large area. Loading the van was an art form too but Stalky had it off to a tee. Everything had its designated place, speakers, and amps, drum cases; one item out of place made it impossible to fit everything in. At the venue the equipment was manhandled to the stage area and set up. Keyboard player Dave's Fender Rhodes piano weighed a ton, especially if several flights of stairs had to be negotiated. One venue in particular, HMS Nelson, a naval base in Portsmouth, had a crippling eight flights and we would try to leave the dreaded monstrosity to someone else. After humping the thing, the veins in your neck stood out and your knuckles trailed across the floor! Funny but I didn't see Dave struggle with it often!

Vince's Orange bass speaker cabinet fell into the same category; it was a cumbersome behemoth and he would rear up if he thought it wasn't handled properly.

Sure, setting up the gear was no breeze but the loser by some distance was poor Stalky, his task was so much more involved. I always believed that drummers were a bit puddled anyway. They hit things!! Packing away my saxophone was a snip; you put it in its case - job done. Stalky on the other hand, had to break down a whole drum kit. It's just as well he had a degree in Meccano!

I never quite got to grips with the mechanics of wiring and all things related - jack leads - guitar leads - multi-cores - all were a mystery to me. It wasn't for the want of trying. At sound checks I made awkward attempts to help but was invariably told, 'Just leave it John.'

Travelling in the van could be a humbling, character building experience. A lot of bonding took place, given the close proximity. Often you'd travel perched precariously between drum cases and Vince's beast of an Orange bass cabinet. If you've never travelled a few hundred miles, to a one-horse town in the middle of nowhere, in a filthy quarry transit van, wedged between equipment, on a freezing cold night take from me you haven't lived!

We had some great laughs on the way to gigs when band humour came to the fore. Serial jokes and general out and out piss taking was the order of the day. Anyone who'd been fraternising with a 'monster from the deep' of a girl or uttered something out of place was shot down in flames. You got away with nothing and such ammunition was used in relentless fashion.

One example saw the hapless Graham as ammunition provider in chief. A feature of our live show was to invite a couple of girls from the audience onto the stage to sing along with us. When the usually half-cut, giggling girlies were in place, Graham took the microphone to sing the line they were expected to perform with us.

' NA-NANA-NA-NANA-NA- NANA-NA'

A bit of audience participation - in best 'come on - put your hands together' tradition. We launched into the number and when we reached the point where our fledgling Bananarama came in; Graham grabbed the arm of the girl nearest to him to prompt her but the sleeve was empty. The poor girl had only ONE arm!

What actually came over the sound system was something like,

'NA-NA-NANA-AAAAAARGGHHH..SHIT!'

'One armed girl' jokes peppered conversations for the next few months.

Through the expediency of slogging around the clubs and air bases Sister Big Stuff, saw their earning potential and the calibre of work improve dramatically. A gig would pay anything between £80.00 and £125.00, which wasn't bad in the seventies. Graham obviously wasn't interested in the money. He wore a pair of dirty green overalls for loading and setting up, in the top pocket of which was a pristine, crisp ten-pound note. He was very proud of the fact that the money remained in that same pocket for months. He got a kick out of not spending but by his own admission, he was worth a quarter of a million pounds!

On one occasion we played support to a band called The Foundations. They had enjoyed a string of hits in the late sixties. Most famous was Baby Now That I've Found You, a number one in September 1967 and Build Me Up Buttercup a number two in November of the same year. As was usually the case the support act took to the stage first to build atmosphere and break the ice for the top of the bill act. We were into our show when a deep rasping sound gave me a start. It was a mighty booming baritone saxophone played by the Foundations sax man who had jumped up on stage to join us. It was not just any old brass man, but Raphael 'Raff' Ravenscroft, a top session player who was playing with The Foundations to finance his passage through Music College.

He is now universally known for his haunting, atmospheric saxophone work on Baker Street a massive and classic hit for Gerry Rafferty in 1978.

We blew through a few numbers together; the warm tone of the baritone made our sound more meaty and substantial. After encores we retired to the dressing room and Raff spent a good hour giving me tips and advice. He told me that he practised for eight hours each day. If I had tried that, there would have been no time for sleep!

It was refreshing that a top session musician would deign to pass the time of day with a young upstart like me. I was to find later that this wasn't always the case with performers of his standing. Traditionally support bands and headlining bands share an uneasy alliance. Support acts are seen as a minor irritation and at times are barely on nodding terms with the top dogs.

Through 1975 plumb engagements came our way and we supported a number of chart acts which gave us a valuable insight into how successful outfits worked. We opened for singer Jimmy Helms at RAF Conningsby near Lincoln. Jimmy scored a hit with Gonna Make You An Offer You Can't Refuse - a top ten in 1973, later resurfacing as vocalist with Londonbeat enjoying a series of hits in the early nineties, the biggest of which being I've Been Thinking About You in 1990.

We opened for 5,000 Volts. They had a top five hit in 1975 with I'm On Fire - their lead vocalist Tina Charles had eight solo hits between 1976 and 1978, the biggest being the number one I Love To Love in 1976. We also kicked off for a Tony Hatch produced band Sweet Sensation. Their big hit came in 1974; a number one called Sad Sweet Dreamer.

A year before all of this I wasn't even in a band - now here I was rubbing shoulders with pop stars.

I came to realise that Sister Big Stuff had limited expectations and aims. Their game plan never involved seeking publishing or recording deals. With no original material, a publishing deal was a non-starter anyway. I was content at that point just being in a band and I used my time to experience different facets of the industry for the future. I was having a wail of a time. It was FUN. What could beat travelling, meeting people and feeling the pure high that is playing in front of a live audience? The young nymphets and the money was a bonus!

I watched with interest how booking agents operated and soon came to realise what a lucrative business it could be. Agents with a decent roster of acts were literally coining it. Most agents had a well-defined area of operation, as if they'd carved up a map between them. Most placed acts on a rotational basis, charging between 15% and 20% of the booking fee. An agent with sizeable roll call of acts could make a comfortable living. Some bands commanded a much higher asking price; a hit record hiked a booking fee dramatically. It was not unusual to be out on the road three or four nights a week so it's easy to imagine why Mr.20% was grinning from ear to ear. Some agents sub-contracted bands to rival agencies for a split of the commission. The downside of this arrangement was the spectre of double booking - more than once we arrived at avenue to find that another band had already set up.

We still made the occasional forays into the twilight zone! - American air force bases. They sprang up as a legacy of the US involvement in the Second World War. Anyone that hasn't visited one has missed a unique experience. Once you drove through the checkpoint you were subject to US law - everything that was an accepted part of American life was exhibited there. Getting into the base and past the perimeter gate was an intimidating process - armed servicemen barred your way. We played USAF Greenham Common many times and at the time the base housed an arsenal of cruise missiles. Life in the complex was a microcosm of US life - there were monstrous American cars and hyper markets full of American brand name goods. The bars served up beers like Slitz - Budweiser and Miller, drinks barely heard of in the UK at the time.

Pounds sterling had to be converted into dollars and hearing American accents everywhere gave you the distinct impression that you were in a foreign land. Other bases that we appeared at were - USAF Conningsby - Chicksands - Lakenheath and Bentwaters. They were a pleasure to play because you were well looked after and the fees were generous, but one downside was having to perform three forty-five minute sets. Like at the RAF bases, girls were bussed in from outlying areas but when it came to the 'capturing stakes' US serviceman won hands down. All they had to do was turn up! It is a documented fact that English girls go weak at the knees over an American uniform - I can confirm that from my experience, it is true.

One master of ceremonies sported a white tuxedo and Graham thought that he looked like Colonel Sanders on leave from KFC duties. Much like in the RAF bases the punters seemed more interested in the disco - I sometimes wondered why we bothered, when a jukebox in the corner would have sufficed. Once we played at USAF Upper Heyford when there was a security alert on and a lot of the servicemen were in battle dress. Status bikini red they called it. I didn't much like the fact that the audience had guns because I thought that it gave them an unfair advantage.

Back in the real world, an amusing incident occurred in the dressing room at Bailey's night club in Derby 1976. Baileys had a chain of clubs dotted around the UK - all were large cabaret venues. There was one in Leicester and acts as diverse as Tommy Cooper and Suzi Quattro appeared there. Sexist though it sounds now, in those days it was not unknown for clubs to feature topless Go-Go dancers. Baileys featured three on that night and their dressing room was next to ours backstage.

Their dressing rooms were state of the art, with showers and all amenities. Dean discovered a hole in the wall through to the dancer's dressing room and the temptation was too much - we lined up to peep at the unsuspecting girls, who were in various states of undress. We all had a good eyeful; Stalky was last in line. As he pressed his eye to the opening he was oblivious to that fact that his wife Denise had walked in. The rest of us dispersed, busying ourselves and pretended to get ready for the show. Suspecting that something was amiss, she yanked him away from the wall to see what the fuss was about. She stormed out of the room with a face like thunder and relations were a tad strained between the two for sometime. I hadn't seen her that angry since Stalky had photographed his backside in a passport photo booth at the La Fayette club in Wolverhampton.

Keyboard player Dave Van was one of the most complex characters I've ever met. Once, after playing Sadies club in Derby, he went AWOL and we trawled the surrounding area for him before we finally gave up and went home. Dave had gone back to the home of a married mother of five who was at least twice his age. After Sister Big Stuff folded, he played in Geoff Overon's band the Rent and figured in the wonderfully named, Snot Vampires during the punk era.

As work increased we embarked on longer stays away which created problems for those of us struggling to hold down day jobs. Once we played a gig in Torquay which is around 350 miles from Leicester. I left work early and went all the way to the 400 Club in Torquay - we played a one hour set and I got back to Leicester the following morning just in time to leave for work! I knew people that saved up all year to go to Torquay for their holidays! It was shattering at times and seemed pretty bizarre to anyone not connected to the music game. We took a weeklong residency at Madison's Club in Middlesborough. It was like a school outing, full of pranks, wheezes and womanising. We shared bunk beds in a grotty room at a bed and breakfast dive - no Holiday Inn for us.

People often asked where I summoned up the courage to step out on stage. I would be terrified at the prospect of singing at a Karaoke, but have no qualms about playing in front of thousands or doing live television. The worst scenario for me would be a small venue in my hometown, which was full of friends because the pressure to perform is so much greater. A show miles away in Newcastle, before a few thousand strangers is a less daunting proposition - nobody knows you and you can let yourself go, similar to the way that you shed your inhibitions on holiday.

An absolute pre-requisite of life on the road was the motorway service station, or 'Greasy Joe' transport café. Why anyone willingly subjected their stomach to a fry up after miles of travel and quaffing copious amounts of beer is a mystery. On long journeys, you had to stop somewhere, if only to relieve the tedium and the in the early hours your choice was limited.

These establishments were littered with half knackered musicians and tour entourages recharging batteries and returning to base on one engine. From a money angle the transport cafes were cheapest because you got a substantial plate full of grease for your money. Motorway service stations were so expensive - you needed a mortgage for an extra sausage! No place, for a struggling bunch of pauper, musicians. Many an after gig post mortem was conducted in a Little Chef or Happy Eater in the twilight hours. I often contented myself with a strong mug of coffee but these pit stops were essential, long monotonous motorway miles could be potentially dangerous for a tired driver.

While we are dispelling myths of terminology, the term 'dressing room' is the loosest descriptive label in the cosmos. Substitute the words dressing room with; the toilet - the manager's office - cupboard - that tiny storage space behind the stage where the guard dog sleeps and empties its bowels, and you are approaching a more accurate description. Especially in London, dressing rooms at rock venues are often spaces of telephone kiosk dimensions! For a young musician dressing rooms were an Aladdin's cave of musical nostalgia. It was the done thing to leave your mark, and in some there were monikers of bands that had gone to make it big. Toilet facilities in many cases also left an awful lot to be desired too. Times I have seen a poor unfortunate soul pee into an empty beer glass, out of sheer desperation, because of the lack of amenities. Rock 'n' Roll, Hey? This is symptomatic of the whole rock 'n' roll ethos, the lower down the chain of fame you are, the more you have to put up with. True, as you make a name for yourself things radically improve, but no one is excused this learning process.

We played a pub rock dive in Sutton in Ashfield called the Golden Diamond and the dressing room was littered with messages left by musicians who had played there before. At my impressionable age I was in awe to be treading the same boards as some of those guys who had gone on to make it, but not before leaving their mark on those walls for posterity. At that gig, struck by the lack of paying punters, I said to a waitress, 'Where is everyone tonight?' quick as a flash she growled 'You'll not get many in here tonight love - Raymond Froggatt's on down't road!'

Chapter four

SAMMY DAY/MARVIN DYCHE/STUART McMILLAN - WELCOME

When Melda decided to leave I doubted if the band would survive. Since my arrival we had played well over a hundred shows with her as lead vocalist and focal point. We frantically searched for a replacement. The cavalry came in the guise of Sammy Day, a man-mountain, with as many aliases and scams as get rich quick schemes. We approached Sammy who hailed from Derby and he agreed to come to see us perform. When we arrived at the venue there was no Melda! She had pulled one of her, by now, infamous disappearing stunts but this one really dropped us in it. The venue was a huge hanger at an equestrian centre called the Hazelwood School of Equitation. Stalky had been to a wedding and arrived under his own steam. When it was discovered that we were minus a lead vocalist, Graham agreed to take on two or three songs and we had a few instrumentals to buy time with. Denise, Stalky's wife, still in smart wedding attire, volunteered to tackle a couple of numbers.

As the paying public started to arrive in numbers, we caught our first sight of Sammy Day - it was a sight for sore eyes. He breezed in, driving a US army jeep, his gargantuan 6 ft 4 inch frame topped by a totally shaved head. He wore a huge gold gypsy earring. He stepped into the fray and literally saved us. It wasn't an ideal way to audition someone, but the way he dealt with the pressure showed what a true professional he was. That night we performed on a trailer, which had been decked out for the show. It wasn't stable and when Sammy stamped his great size twelve feet, the whole thing rocked. Poor Denise, wearing a LOW, low cut dress, nearly gave the front row something to cheer about, each time Sammy got excited! Outwardly Sammy projected the appearance of a thug - but with time I realised that you couldn't make a more prejudiced opinion about someone if you tried. Chances are that if you passed Sammy in the street, you'd cross over to the other side, but he was one of the most genuine, REAL people I have ever met. Sammy was a loveable rogue, a rough diamond if ever there was one - but with a huge heart. He used many aliases - Sammy Day - Marvin Dyche - Stuart McMillan, are just three that I know about. He was a real 'Del boy' and truly believed that one his scams would make him rich one day. However implausible some of his schemes were, he had a knack of making things happen, against the odds. I literally cried with laughter over some of his ludicrous ideas. In the late 70s he hatched a scheme to play at the San Quentin prison in the US for the inmates. People scoffed at this plan, but he pulled it off in a blaze of publicity. He got television coverage and press interest and even managed to speak to Country and Western icon, Johnny Cash, on the telephone, to ask his advice! Outlandish I know, but this was a typical Sammy scam.

Sammy was also involved in a number of shady deals that it was wise not to ask too many questions about. He devised a way of relieving telephone booths of their takings by adapting a Black and Decker drill and by using the light fitting for power he drilled out the lock on the cash drawer! He also used this method to relieve fruit machines of their booty. It was not unknown for him to siphon diesel from other vehicles to top up the band van.

Once a neighbour of Sam's in Derby complained to the Electricity people about his excessive power bill. After investigating an engineer discovered that his mains supply had been branched into. Sam had crawled through the roof-space and tapped into his supply, borrowing his power for band rehearsals two doors away!

One time at CAD Kineton army training base near Warwick, we played to a rowdy bunch of young soldiers who were fresh from a tour of duty in Northern Ireland. They were intent on some release and this manifested itself in a drinking frenzy. Dean and I were tuning up in a corridor outside the dressing room when a huge serviceman forced his head out of the television room to complain about the noise. On hearing what was going on, Sammy came out of the dressing room, levelled an evil glare at the soldier and said,

'WIND YOUR NECK IN!' The guy, who was no wimp, melted back behind the door.

Chapter Five
NEW FACES

Some months before joining Sister Big Stuff, Sammy had made an application for a New Faces audition while with another band in Derby. It took time to process, so when the letter of acceptance came through, Sammy had already left that outfit. New Faces wasn't a show that any of us would have considered. It wasn't us, but Sammy talked us into it. 'It'll be a good crack!' he said, so we reluctantly went along with it. His application was made under one of his aliases, Marvin Dyche.

To anyone reading this, who is fortunate enough NOT to remember New Faces, let me enlighten you. New Faces was a television talent show - I guess the closest modern equivalent would be the X Factor. It occupied a prime time Saturday evening viewing slot and was a long running success. The idea of the show was to promote new talent and through a combination of votes from the studio audience and people at home and they selected a winner on a weekly basis. The acts were made up of a variety of entertainers, from comedians and dancers to pop groups. A panel of celebrity guests, who were supposed to offer encouragement and advice, often ridiculed the acts, and then had the nerve to give them marks out of ten! Don't give up your day job mate!

The show was very popular with the little old ladies at home in TV land, and was responsible for catapulting a huge handful of acts from obscurity, to some form of stardom. Among these were Showaddywaddy and Les Dawson.

I personally had my doubts as to the benefits of appearing on such a show. The groups they featured tended to be very safe, middle of the road outfits with nice haircuts and matching stage suits. It seemed that in the main, cabaret acts prospered from it. Many a working men's club or summer season theatre boasted - New Faces winner - As seen on New Faces - such was the mileage to be had from a television appearance.

Auditions were held regionally and our nearest centre was Birmingham. Ours was at the Dolce Vita in the city centre - it was a huge, cavernous night club. We trundled to the gig, through the congested streets in our mucky quarry van - at one point losing equipment out of the back door, which had mysteriously opened itself in New Street. I retrieved microphone stands from the road, risking life and limb in the busy rush hour traffic.

Once at the venue we were ushered into a cellar bar downstairs. The main stage area was upstairs and had been set aside for solo vocalists, comedians and magicians. Two other bands set up with us in the same area, and we were expected to perform one song to a panel of judges. We chose a Kate Brothers song You Can Change My Heart, a popular track with our audiences live. It was a rocky number with a nice soulful edge to it and lent itself well to Sam's vocal style.

The song selection was error number one. Error number two was not poncing ourselves up to the nines in flashy stage gear! Sister Big Stuff were not about satin jump suits and wide, floppy hats. We let our music speak rather than our appearance on stage, the co-ordinated matching stage suit thing was never for us. The other acts did ponce themselves up to the nines and for them and the ageing judges it counted for a lot. The average age of the judges, the people who were supposed to searching for the next big thing, was forty plus! We should have done a Frank Sinatra medley! We performed well and were even applauded by the other bands looking on and by a couple of judges.

The atmosphere was very cold and clinical and as far removed from the usual live ambience as you could get. One of the female judges confided in us afterwards that we had missed the cut by just one vote. They stood at the back of the room with clipboards, ticking and crossing. One of the older judges had dismissed us out of hand, purely on appearance, as I'd suspected.

In my opinion it was all for the good. I hadn't told people about the audition, out of sheer embarrassment. Most of my friends were into the fledgling punk movement at the time and would have considered New Faces uncool in the extreme. When our part in the proceedings was over, we hung around to witness some of the other poor sods auditioning on the main stage upstairs. Some of them were woeful. One poor chap in particular, a young comedian, had an absolute nightmare. Every joke he attempted was minus a punch line - he kept forgetting them! One of the judges told him to calm down and start again, but it had little effect. Eventually his face puckered up and close to tears, he bellowed down the microphone as he gesticulated to the panel of judges, 'Let me tell you one thing - At least I'm still young, right!' With that he stormed off to a stunned, silent auditorium. I often wondered if he ever made anything of himself.

Out of all of the artistes baring their souls that day, only two subsequently made it to the show proper on television. One, a young black vocalist, auditioned downstairs with us wearing a painfully loud, green satin suit with trousers a mile and a half wide. He finished third in his heat on TV. The other one did rather better, a comedian / impressionist called Lenny Henry who hasn't done too badly for himself since!

Dean settled in well on trumpet. He was great fun to be with, always chirpy, offering cheeky chappy quips that were impossible not to laugh at. One of our regular engagements was at Scamps Club in Leicester. Being local we played in front of an audience that generally included family and friends. Before one show I walked in on Dean engaging in an act of extreme friendliness with his girl friend in the backstage area. I thought, 'He'll have someone's eye out with that!' He never realised I was there.

Another time Graham booked us into a club called Adam & Eve in Chesterfield. It was a showcase for an influential agent, who travelled a fair distance to see us with a view to signing us. It was Dean's birthday and he had taken the celebrations a bit too seriously. He was as pissed as a fart! He could hardly stand. Backstage we frantically fought to sober him up before the show. No way could we consider pulling out of the gig, there was too much riding on it. I spent almost the entire show with one hand gripping Dean's shirt from behind to keep him upright. After hearing the bum notes flying out of the end of Dean's trumpet, I was reduced to shouting, 'Mime, you twat!' It didn't do a lot of good, we never heard from the agent again. Graham was livid.

Occasionally Sammy brought his red setter along for the ride, usually it slept in the van while we performed, but at the Grenadiers Club in March, Cambridgeshire, the dog saw fit to empty its bowels in the middle of the smart parquet dance floor. Sam begrudgingly disposed of the steaming mountain of evidence before the paying public arrived.

The Grenadiers club was memorable for a design feature seldom implemented in modern night club design. A stairway led us down to the dressing room and half way down a beam of light sprayed torch like from behind a series of pipes down the wall. On the other side were the ladies toilets. Squinting through the gap, it was possible to see a succession of female behinds, flashing at you from twelve o'clock high at seat level behind the cistern! It caused a fair amount of merriment - obviously I didn't look myself!

On a long, long journey to Dorchester, Dave brought along puzzles and brainteasers to occupy us and to relieve some of the boredom. One was three-dimensional noughts and crosses. He asked if anyone fancied taking him on. Dave was a brain box and nobody wanted to give him the satisfaction of letting him humiliate them. Dean eventually volunteered to a few sniggers, saying, 'Show me what to do, I've never played before' Dave ran through a series of complicated rules and they started to play. A few minutes passed and Dean said, 'I'm not sure, but I think I've won?' "'You can't have' stuttered Dave, incredulously. He snatched the book away from Dean and scrutinised the evidence. When the dreaded realisation came that Dean had in fact won, he threw a paddy, slinging the book to the floor. He hardly spoke all day - his pride well and truly dented.

As I mentioned earlier, some clubs back then had dancers who were often topless. A phenomenon strange in this day and age was so common then that you hardly batted an eyelid. The Cats Cradle in Retford, Nottinghamshire, was an old converted church, and they had a topless dancer, who gyrated wildly in an alcove high above the dance-floor. No one took much notice.

I was in the dressing room alone as she minced in looking flushed after her stint. I was a naive twenty-year old; she was naked apart from a skimpy gold G-string and a smile. She chatted to me as if it was the most natural thing in the world - she was totally oblivious of my discomfort. You could have lit a cigarette off the side of my face! I stuttered out a pathetic excuse and scarpered like a scared rabbit.

Chapter Six

SISTER BIG STUFF - THE END

Within a relatively short space of time Sammy, Graham and Stalky all moved on and were replaced. Graham bowed out to mounting career pressure, though he still acted as an intermediary between band and booking agents, and still allowed access to his rehearsal room which was a God send. Rehearsal rooms were not easy to come by; not many people were prepared to put up with the noise. They were often pokey little rooms in pubs or cold church halls. You paid for the privilege of using them and were expected to take your equipment with you when you had finished. This was a real bind because setting up and breaking down the gear diminished valuable practise time.

We replaced Sammy with a black guy called Hubert, an excellent vocalist with real pedigree. His claim to fame was being signed to Decca records in the late sixties and he actually had one of his records featured on the top television pop show Juke Box Jury. He was a smooth operator with a confident stage presence, a silky smooth vocal style and a larger than life professional approach. He brought with him a more laid-back funk delivery in the Johnny 'Guitar' Watson and Commodores mould.

We all had an incline that these were our last days as a working band. It was early 1977. I married my long time girlfriend Colleen, in March. Most of the band came to the wedding - it was an unremarkable day, and it was a rather unremarkable marriage too, lasting barely over a year. It would be easy to blame my involvement in music for the failure but I was away a lot, and that can't have helped.

Gigs were taking us much further away from our native Leicester. We went as far as north Peterhead in County Durham and down to the south coast, but strangely we never played London. This was due to the fact that London gigs were very hard to come by because the agents there had real power. It was very difficult for a band to make a breakthrough there.

We undertook our longest series of consecutive of live dates - eight in all, which were;

Lincoln - Wolverhampton - Wisbech - Warwick - Portsmouth - Hereford - Peterhead and Skegness. It really did feel like life on the road, juggling the hours to hang on to my day job. I couldn't wait for the time when I could hand in my notice to play full time.

When the end came for Sister Big Stuff I had an overwhelming feeling of sadness. For eighteen months the band had provided me with purpose, shown me new horizons and introduced me to some great characters. Some have remained good friends to the present day. It's difficult to explain to any one who hasn't been involved but a real camaraderie is built up between people sharing the collective experience of life on the road. It isn't just the playing - it's the interacting, the humour and seeing places that you would never see if you were tied down in a humdrum, nine to five life. The only survivor from my audition was Dave Van - there had been a lot of casualties on the way.

Dean and I had built up a solid working relationship and we'd developed into a tight brass unit. It was Dean who suggested that we advertise for a new band and I was all for it, I had caught the bug BIG TIME. After my initiation I couldn't imagine not being involved in music - I'd have played every night given the chance. It was back to the good old Leicester Mercury wanted column.

SAX & TRUMPET - SEEK PRO MINDED FUNK BAND

We sat back and waited for a response but little did we realise that when it came it was to ultimately lead to our first Top of the Pops appearance.

It was 1977 - the punk / new wave explosion was at its height and it was like a breath of fresh air. Although I played funk music, I still appreciated the ground swell of fresh attitude that the movement created. I was very open to it, though the music I was playing was light years away. You see it's a question of quality and the essence of quality cannot easily be defined. It is a subjective feeling specific to each individual; diversity is a great cleansing mechanism. With punk, the music was never accomplished but that wasn't the point, it was raw, pushing back boundaries, and forcing you to re-evaluate the norm. It wiped the slate clean. All that had come before wasn't devalued in any way but it stretched musical parameters and provided an alternative energy. Surely angst and energy is what it's all about, isn't it?

My mate Gaz Birtles was playing sax with a new wave outfit called Disco Zombies fronted by the mercurial Dave Henderson, who was to have a huge influence on the Leicester scene and also later in London, with his independent record label. It was during this period that I was instrumental in getting Gaz his first chance to flex his vocal chords in public. I was talking about my future plans to ex Big Stuff keyboard player Dave Van at a party. Dave was putting together a new band and was looking for musicians - the only missing component was a lead vocalist. 'Gaz can sing,' I told him. A get together was arranged and the rest is history. Gaz and I saw each other a lot socially - in pubs, at parties, also live gigs, and we determined that we would one-day work together in some capacity, but at that point we were operating on opposite ends of the musical spectrum. One thing that Sister Big Stuff had done for me was to give me the feeling I belonged. During my time with the band I met a lot of other musicians. I now felt that I was part of the club.

Chapter Seven

PICKING BANANAS IN THE FUNKY JUNGLE

Dean had an early response to our ad from a Leicester funk outfit called Fascination. They were made up of; Sylvester Dowe (drums) - St.Clair Harris (vocals,) - Fitzroy Clarke (vocals) - Vernon Hughes (bass) Martin Potter (guitar) - and lead vocalist Dianne McDonald. Dianne had a chequered musical past, once being on the verge of signing to US soul label Brunswick records. She had been whisked away to the States, given five star pampering and ferried around in Limousines all to get her signature on a recording contract. She recorded a series of demos, one it is said, with the legendary Marvin Gaye. She flew home without signing the deal because she missed her mum!

Her voice was magical. She should have been snapped up years before, but I don't think that she was ever really aware of the talent that she possessed. She was quite content to dabble. Sadly, she died in July 2003.

We auditioned in a function room above a Leicester pub called the Tudor. It was much less of an ordeal than my first audition. I was a more confident player and I had Dean to bounce my nerves off. We were offered the job there and then - We said yes.

Fascination were signed to the Barry Collins agency in Southend. They had access to many areas, London being a very significant one. Graham had wilfully limited Sister Big Stuff live engagements, St.Clair, who handled Fascination's bookings, was the exact opposite. He would turn nothing away - A one-night stand in Glasgow wouldn't phase him. He would have agreed a gig in a public urinal, if the money was right. Fascination commanded bigger booking fees too - £150-£200 was an average fee.

Learning the brass parts to the songs proved every bit as difficult as with Big Stuff and it was a hard slog committing the parts to memory. The live set included Earth Wind and Fire numbers, which were very challenging from a brass perspective.

We debuted at the Top Rank Brighton and when the fateful day arrived we travelled down in a decrepit transit van which was worse than any of Grahams quarry vans. These guys would hire any thing from 'bloke next door car rentals' - as long as it had four wheels. It was little wonder that in the next couple of years I was to spend hour on hour on motorway hard shoulders, waiting for breakdown recovery men.

Amazingly we made it to Brighton but some of those veteran vehicles in the London to Brighton car rally looked in better shape! Great icebreaker though it was, the cramped travelling conditions had changed none; we were virtually sitting on each other's laps. It was the first of many visits to Brighton and I immediately fell in love with the place. The Top Rank was a large imposing building sited on the sea front with a capacity approaching 3,000. It had a sweeping balcony and an expansive dance floor area.

It was the biggest stage I'd set foot on and it looked mighty impressive from the vantage point of the balcony. When the doors opened, the public streamed in and it looked even more intimidating. Strangely, the audience comprised of hundreds of Scandinavian girls, there are a lot of English language schools in Brighton. Our eyes were on stalks!

The lads in Sister Big Stuff were not that predatory when it came to chasing the opposite sex, but these guys definitely were. The words 'rat up a drain pipe' spring to mind! The black guys in particular seemed to view the chase as a standard component part of the gig. They hunted in packs! Don't get me wrong, Big Stuff wouldn't turn away a spot of extra curricular cabaret, but they didn't pursue it with quite the same zeal and enthusiasm. Those poor Scandinavian girls were sitting ducks.

All this debauchery rubbed off on the new recruits, it became a part of our mind set. Playing in a strange place, miles away from home, where nobody knew you, gave you licence to be as outrageous as you liked and get away with it. It's like being on holiday - Problem was - we were averaging three holidays each week! It was purely the numbers game, if one girl wasn't interested, we'd move on to the next and there was certainly plenty to go at. It was very rare not to 'capture' at each live outing - they even kept a league table.

The gig itself was great; we went down well, and at the end there were lots of young girls dancing on stage alongside the band. I thought - 'I could get used to this'

The guys in Fascination were a scream. Drummer Sylvester - 'snatcher'- was a chubby chap with a permanent ear to ear grin, and an afro hairstyle in best Super fly or Shaft tradition. He had the unhappy knack of breaking bass drum pedals, live, in front of thousands of punters. Also he had a penchant for young paper round girls! This is where he earned the nickname.

St.Clair had an incredibly complicated personal life - the stuff soap operas are made of. He was band spokesman and dealt directly with management and booking agencies. He worked with a Caribbean steel band when he wasn't working with the band for pin money. Vernon, the oldest member of the group was an engineer by trade and had played in a number of Leicester bands. Fitzroy was Mr.Smooth, a flash playboy type, a slick dresser with a sex on wheels - pulling car. He was an affable, intelligent guy who later went to work in Libya.

Guitarist Martin Potter was a fluent, dextrous player. He worked in a large music shop in the city centre and was our window to gossip flying around about rival bands. Because of his job he lived and breathed music but he worked long hours including Saturday, a day that didn't really exist for us; it was rare not to have a gig on a Saturday. It was the busiest day in the shop too and the proprietors took a dim view of him bunking off - difficult to understand when you take into account that it was part owned by one of the guys from Showaddywaddy.

Our rehearsal place at the Tudor pub was a function room; usually used for wedding receptions and parties and we had to moderate the volume. Unlike Graham's room this was in a residential area which resulted in someone calling the noise police. Environmental health emissaries descended to investigate. We saw a guy outside gazing intently into a gizmo in true 'beam me up Scotty' tradition. He gave the landlord a written warning.

The Tudor was handy too because Pat, the landlord, let us leave some of our gear in the bottle store in the courtyard at the back and there was always an after hours drink on offer. Luckily, I lived within easy staggering distance.

Fascination were a covers band, but unlike Sister Big Stuff they had ambitions to write their own material and were interested in securing some sort of recording contract. The standard of gig was better too, gone were the air force bases to be replaced by large night clubs.

St Clair contacted a London booking agent, Dingbat Music who had an office at Camden Lock, opposite the renowned rock venue Dingwalls. They got us a gig at the prestigious soul and funk venue, the Q Club in Praed Street, London. The Q Club was frequented by world famous black recording stars and it was not unknown for Stevie Wonder, the Four Tops or the Commodores to be among the paying public. The club was small with a smoky, intimate atmosphere.

It was open all night and we went on stage at 3.am. Having a conventional job, it was a case of getting home and shooting straight to work in zombie mode. We said our first hellos to Mike Oberman from Dingbat Agency. He cut a striking figure, rather rotund, dripping in bling, with black floppy hat and trademark antique walking cane. In his career he had looked after a number of name chart acts, one being the Sweet and he regaled us with stories of how he sent them out for £100.00 a night - even when they were several hit records to the good.

Dingbat Music was an agency that we needed to impress to push our case for more London work, so the Q Club was an ideal showcase. Beer prices were astronomic but I don't suppose Stevie Wonder worried about that too much! In subsequent visits we brought drinks with us. The dressing room was in the broom cupboard category but the gig was a brilliant success; everything clicked and fell into place. Oberman was suitably impressed and he promised us lots of work. Ironically Fascination had managed to achieve more in a few weeks than Sister Big Stuff had in eighteen months.

After another stint at the Q the manager of Boney M came into our dressing room and offered Dianne a contract. Dianne said, 'No thanks, I'm with these boys.' Despite our protestations, she wouldn't budge. That is how she was.

Mike was as good as his word and more London work came our way. Playing there for the first time had been a psychological milestone for me. I had been to London many times before, but playing there was special. It was the place to play. Everything in the music industry revolves around it; you were more likely to get noticed by someone that counted.

The other gigs were of excellent quality too; we played Traceys in Ipswich, Annabelles in Sunderland, Olivers in Folkestone and the Doncaster Outlook club. The night before we played the Doncaster Outlook club a band called the Spots appeared there. The Spots were a pseudonym for the Sex Pistols. Mr.Rotten and co. took to touring under an assumed name because no one would touch them due to their notoriety. After our show I chatted to a bar maid, she told me that Johnny Rotten was 'a very polite young man.' That wouldn't have done his street credibility much of a favour if publicised.

Dingbat put us into another prestige London gig called Gulliver's sited in Bridge Street, behind the Playboy Club in Park Lane. It attracted celebrities in the same way that the Q Club did. Michael Jackson and Mohammed Ali were among the famous patrons. It was another late gig and playing so late sapped your strength, with work the next day to consider.

My work-mates often asked where I had played the night before, they found it hard to understand that I had travelled to London, taken to the stage at 3 a.m. and still managed to make it to work the following day, when they had stayed at home watching Coronation Street!

The DJ at Gulliver's had a show on London's Capital Radio and the club, although small, was one of the places to be seen on the London soul/funk scene. One time there was a private party upstairs and it turned out to be album launch bash for Showaddywaddy. They were trumpeting the release of their latest platter - Red Star - we were invited to join them when we had finished our show. Showaddywaddy are from our native Leicester, drummer Romeo was in some way related to St.Clair, so we bumped into him from time to time. It was my first record industry party and was quite an eye opener, free booze and all the trimmings of record company excess.

Before some gigs, we would meet in a pub called the George, opposite the clock tower, in Leicester City centre. It was a thriving, busy pub with a handy central location for all of us. Romeo used the place too and one lunch time we chatted as he propped up the bar in his usual spot. He asked us where we were playing and we in turn asked him where he was off to. He told us that he had to fly to Germany to record a television show. He flew to Germany, recorded the show and was back in the George before last orders! Such is the whirlwind existence of a pop star.

All this playing away was not having a beneficial effect on my marriage. Most weekends I was away from home and was never being able to accept invites to social gatherings like weddings. It was rare not to be away on a Thursday, Friday and Saturday. It put a serious strain on a number of relationships within the band.

In late July 1977 a strange turn of events led to a bizarre chapter in my career and changed my life completely. At some point in your life there will come a crossroads or a decision that will change its course completely. Mike Oberman was an astute operator with an eye for an opportunity and it was his intuitive curiosity that carved out a major chance for us. He noticed that a record called Gimme Dat Banana, which was moving chart-wards, bore all the hallmarks of a manufactured session man affair. The record was a summer season club success across the country and he suspected that the band credited on the label was a front for enterprising session musicians. It was picking up healthy Radio One airplay and looked every bit a potential hit.

Mike spoke to Response records who had released the record and his hunch was spot on. It had been recorded by

German session musicians and released in the UK to capitalise on its club success. The main honcho at Response, Mike Clare, wanted to find a band to promote the record in the event it was a hit.

Dingbat asked Fascination to take on the identity of the band. The track was something of a novelty song by a band called Black Gorilla. None of us had heard it and were not keen in promoting a record that would plunge us into deepest, darkest Joe Dolce, Wombles or Weird Al Yankovic territory! Response asked us to think it over.

We bought the single and what we heard didn't impress. We were split down the middle in deciding what to do; it was light years away from the material that we were performing - but what had we got to lose? Response promised us a recording deal and after promoting the record any subsequent release would be entirely down to us. At the very least we were guaranteed some form of national exposure if it was a hit, as everyone expected.

The adventure that we were about to embark on would haunt me for years to come. We thrashed it out between us, eventually deciding to go with it. It was a majority decision but Dianne hated the song and was dead against. We felt that if we could benefit from the project long term, it would be worth it. Response wanted to see us perform the song to be sure that we could carry it off.

Dingbat arranged a daytime showcase at Dingwalls at Camden Lock in London. The venue was a stones throw from the agency offices and Oberman knew them well. We had a scream trying to copy Gimme Dat Banana from the disc and there was an awful lot of piss taking in the attempt. When we knuckled down to it we finally worked out a version that would pass for the original.

Radio One's Tony Blackburn made it his 'record of the week' which was a major coup at the time as most of his choices achieved chart status. He hosted the flagship breakfast show which boasted huge audience figures. As we headed down to Dingwalls the single was sitting at number 50 in the national chart. Setting up in an empty day time Dingwalls seemed unnatural but we had time for a couple of dry runs before the record company people turned up. The other song we were to perform was a Gladys Knight and the Pips song called Midnight Train to Georgia, which was made for Dianne and never failed to get her a standing ovation live, such was the power of feeling she put into it.

Oberman arrived with Mike Clare in tow; we made our brief acquaintances and then got on with it. They were suitably impressed but strangely no one said, 'the job is yours,' they just explained what was coming up and how best to handle it.

We were now Black Gorilla and we didn't know what we had let ourselves in for. Mike Clare was happy to let us be the public face of the band. Under the deal we were to promote that surrogate single and any subsequent release would be performed by us. Naff though it was, we planned to milk its success and benefit from the publicity it generated as a springboard for a follow up.

They fully expected the single to make the top 20 and advised us to prepare for a Top of the Pops appearance. Spooky to think that the dream I'd had as an eight-year old was in danger of coming to fruition. At its height the record was shifting 8,000 copies a day and coupled with the exposure on the Tony Blackburn show, the signs looked more than promising.

As we drove home that day none of us fully realised what was in the offing. Dean and I had left Sister Big Stuff in July - only two months before - now here we were looking at a possible chart band association. So much depended on what was to happen in the next two weeks.

The new top 40 came out each Tuesday in those days on a lunchtime Radio One show. All the new entries were played from number 30 up in reverse order. When the next chart was released Gimme Dat Banana had eased up to number 37, still no chance of Top of the Pops - they only screened the top 30. There was a significant happening in that week that was to adversely affect the progress of the record - Elvis Presley popped his clogs! The death of Elvis 'the King' Presley signalled a plethora of re-releases and most of them made a chart showing. There seemed to be millions of them! Seven separate top 30 entries flew in that week, which meant an agonising wait until the next chart, on the following Tuesday.

There was a radio in the despatch area at Bearing Service where I worked and when the next chart rundown was broadcast, I made an excuse to be hovering around it. I still hadn't said anything it to my work-mates for fear it might incriminate me and I was getting an increasing amount of stick for my days off. When the show started I knew that if we had made it would be played as a new entry.

'A new entry at number 30,' the jock announced - it wasn't us. It was Black is Black by La Belle Époque. The next song, 'Straight in at number 29,' the unmistakable strains of the Tarzan call intro on Gimme Dat Banana blasted from the radio. Even if by default, we had a hit on our hands. The song had barely faded from the radio, when a call came from our management; we were to record Top of the Pops the next day.

Chapter Eight

TOP OF THE POPS

People at work didn't believe me - I didn't even get the chance to tell many of my friends and family. The itinerary involved, re-recording the track in the morning and then zipping over to BBC Television Centre to shoot the show in the afternoon.

In those days an act recorded the whole track again and then mimed to the re-recording on the show. Now it has all changed, but the reason for what seemed like a crazy waste of time, were Musicians Union rules. It is impossible for an artist to re-record a track in a few short hours, when the original might have taken weeks. At least we were able to say that it was us playing on Top of the Pops that week, which gave us some consolation. The real problem was in the recording itself; we were leaving ourselves open to some embarrassing questions by the producer. We were not involved in the original session, so there were technical aspects that we couldn't possibly know about.

We collected our gear from the Tudor pub to be greeted by landlord Pat,

'Where is it today then lads?' He normally asked us where we were playing, St.Clair casually countered, 'Top of the Pops,' he thought we were winding him up.

The record didn't have any saxophone parts on it so I was drafted in on backing vocals. No problem - I sang backing vocals anyway. We crawled down to Utopia studios in super van. It was my first time in a major London recording studio and I was bristling with apprehension. The recording went surprisingly well and we came away with a passable version of the song. Before we left the studio Mike Oberman came over clutching a recording contract from Response. We'd never seen a record contract before, it might as well have been written in Russian!

Recording contracts contain some wacky clauses and it is difficult to wade through the jargonise. It is not enough to be contracted world wide now, these days artistes are stitched up universe wide. This clause apparently came into being after Apollo astronauts sang Fly Me to the Moon on a moon mission which caused all sorts of copyright problems. Another bizarre clause is the infamous sanity clause. This absolves the record company of any responsibility, should the artist suddenly lose the plot and is committed to a lunatic asylum! It happens! Is it any wonder? All these clauses, however crazy they sound, are there for good reason.

The contract from Response promised us control over future output but we had to agree to keep the Black Gorilla name. We gave the contract only a cursory glance because we had more pressing matters to deal with.

We loaded our rust bucket of a van and headed for Shepherds Bush and the BBC Television Centre. The closest any of us had come to it before was watching Blue Peter as kids. The BBC building façade is one of the most instantly recognisable in the country so to see it for the first time in real life was weird. We raised a few eyebrows as our battered old van phut-phutted past the security guard to the car park, coughing a cloud of fumes.

We checked in at reception and were allocated a dressing room. Recording a Top of the Pops was an organised, well-structured procedure; everything was run like clockwork. When you consider what they crammed into a show, it was hardly surprising. In the afternoon there was a preliminary run through, which involved miming to the track for lighting and camera angles. Late afternoon involved a full dress run through in stage gear. The show was recorded in the early evening to be broadcast on the following night which in those days was a Thursday.

There was little room for error. Apart from the bands that were appearing, there were promo videos and dancing girls - Legs and Co. to cater for. The interior of the BBC contains a labyrinth of circular corridors, all inter-connecting and the dressing rooms lead off of them. Each floor is numbered and colour coded, for directional ease. Our dressing room was next door to the Blue Peter dressing room. Get down Shep - Here's one I made earlier - type jokes abounded - Oh for just one sighting of Val Singleton. Starstruck - me?

This was a totally unreal world. I walked down one of the corridors and a short, balding chap held a door open for me. It was actor Arthur Lowe - Captain Mainwaring in Dad's Army. Everywhere you looked there was a recognisable face. We sauntered to the studio for our first impressions. The first surprise was how small it looked. Inside there were three stages with very limited floor space and a pen for the studio audience. When filming began each band was afforded a stage area and after each performance studio crew feverishly set up another, while a promo video was shown. This rotational system helped to create the illusion that the studio was much bigger than it actually was. Peering skywards presented you with an incredible array of lighting banks.

Before our first dry run we watched another young band going through their paces. The Boomtown Rats were enjoying their first appearance with their debut hit, Looking after No.1. They were fronted by a youthful, energetic vocalist, Bob Geldof - so lively that he demolished a part of the stage. He leapt from a drum riser to snatch his microphone and brought a section of stage crashing down. This caused panic while studio carpenters hammered away to make good.

All is not what it seemed in the Top of the Pops studio. What looked like glitzy and substantial stage settings on TV screens at home were basic wooden frames. Lighting hid multitude of sins. Our dress rehearsal didn't run smoothly - we needed two attempts. The first shot almost resulted in Fitzroy losing his teeth! As we ran through the song a boom camera zoomed in and failed to apply its brakes in time causing it to crash HARD into the stage. The velocity of the boom catapulted Fitz's microphone back into his face. Proceedings were halted while he was looked after - fortunately he suffered no long-term effects.

Before filming proper there was a break. Some of us adjourned to the BBC bar on the top floor of the building, and this heralded another celebrity spotting exercise. A strange theatrical atmosphere permeated - there were people mincing about in period costume. Just like one mega fancy dress party gone wrong! Nerves were beginning to jangle and Dianne had a few stiff drinks. I phoned my wife to update her, 'I saw the guy from Dad's Army,' I told her, she didn't seem that impressed - I guess you just had to be there.

A pint of Ruddles County was the right medicine. Straight from the bar we were herded into make-up. No vanity - studio lights were so intensely bright that make-up was an absolute necessity. This was relaxation personified - a young female applied slap and pampered you. I sat next to a couple of cards from the band - the Motors. One, named Bram Tchaikovsky, led the girls a merry dance. They were there to perform their hit Dancing the Night Away. They had obviously been there before. Also there were girls from dance troupe Legs & Co. Dean thought that they were too skinny for him, the fact that half of the male population of the UK drooled over them each week, meant nothing.

For our big day we'd had some snazzy stage gear put together, I shudder at the thought now. ME? A white satin suit! It showcased my wedding tackle in a bit too graphic detail which didn't much please my wife. Surely, once in a while, we are all allowed a BAD POSE! When it came to filming we were all nervous. For some inexplicable reason when we took to the set, I had been moved to Dianne's place. Being our token bit of glamour she had been afforded lots of camera close ups. Standing in her place I copped for them all. Not a pretty sight in that suit. Dean had the job of miming the conga part on the intro; his timing was all over the place and his bottom lip trembled visibly - he was still only seventeen. Radio-One disc jockey, David 'Kid' Jensen was the presenter.

Tracks also featured included, Oxygene by Jean-Michel Jarre -Telephone man by Meri Wilson and top of the pile was - surprise-surprise, Elvis Presley with Way down. The whole thing went very well. In the studio monitors played the track at low volume making the atmosphere seem subdued and the audience were herded around as if in some bizarre sheep dog trial. What I also found strange was having a camera shoved inches away from my face and trying not to flinch.

Après show we zipped across London to perform at Gulliver's club - a good example of management getting their pound of flesh. When we collected our van from the car park, a vehicle even more write off-able than ours cut across our path and caused us to brake sharply. As it drifted by, pressed against the front passenger window was a very bare bottom. The Boomtown Rats departing in style!

We were all pretty tired but running on adrenaline as we scooted across town. I had a really warm feeling after achieving a lifetime ambition. We played Gimme Dat Banana in front of a live audience for the first time and it stood out like a sore appendage. From that day on it was written into our contracts that we had to perform 'our hit!' live. WHOOPEE! We did anything to avoid playing it and sometimes we even got away with it.

When we got home it was the early hours of Thursday; I caught up on scant sleep, went into work, and promptly handed my notice in. It felt great.

I was apprehensive all day. Top of the Pops had a regular 7.30 pm slot on Thursday evenings on BBC1. I arranged to watch it with my wife at my parent's house. Colour television was a luxury not afforded to me in those days; we only had a small black and white set in our flat. Family members had congregated to watch with us and it was a weird sensation seeing myself on the goggle box acting the prat in that ridiculous satin suit. I got a lot of close-ups at the expense of Dianne, and I took real stick.

After the show we popped out to a local pub to celebrate with a few brews. I was shocked at the reaction that I got from the locals. They talk about the power of television, but I was totally unprepared for the response. Top of the Pops commanded a viewing audience of between eleven and thirteen million and judging by the kick back, everyone in the pub must have been watching. Some one asked for my autograph - I had a lot of best mates all of a sudden.

We were under strict instructions not to breathe a word about our little arrangement with Response records. When probing questions came I tried to be economic with the truth, but I did tell those closest to me. In the days after our television debut everyone wanted to know us. Offers of gigs and press interviews - they all crawled out of the woodwork. When we returned to the Tudor to rehearse, it was like the return of the prodigal son - landlord Pat milked it. A welcoming committee greeted us, and bar profits were definitely up that night.

Another example of the power that went with a Top of the Pops appearance afflicted poor St.Clair. His ex-wife had watched it and she went hot foot to her solicitors, for more maintenance money. Everyone imagined that we had become millionaires overnight.

Another consequence of our new found fame/notoriety was the way we were billed - our gig posters trumpeted - As seen on Top of the Pops and agents capitalised on our 'chart band' status. We were booked into a top London photographic studio in Covent Garden for a series of long overdue publicity photographs.

Perhaps the most marked change was felt by young Dean, living as he did in a small town with a very insular, close knit community. Lots of people knew each other and he was pestered to death, especially by young girls, and I don't think he was prepared for it. One night he was enjoying a drink in Blooblos club in Coalville and some meat head took exception to the amount of attention he was getting. He split his lip. Coalville - where men are men and sheep are nervous. For a trumpet player it is crucial to look after the lips, we had a lot work coming our way.

Blooblos night club was owned by Graham Tom - money bags of Sister Big Stuff. He imagined that owning a club would be a bit of a wheeze and went into partnership with his brother. The venue was way far ahead of its time and was wasted on a small provincial town like Coalville. Graham introduced some cracking live music to the small venue. He lured XTC - Siouxsie and the Banshees and Steel Pulse away from the metropolis for, as he was to brag for many years after, only £100 a show! He almost secured the Stiff tour for £300 - a package that included Elvis Costello and Ian Dury. What a coup that would have been. He was only thwarted by minimum stage size specifications that the venue couldn't accommodate.

Blooblos once hosted a beach party night in which Graham had tons of sand brought into the club - another wacky idea was the 'bring a can of baked beans' night - for months afterwards Graham was lumbered with hundreds of tins of Heinz 57 varieties!

Black Gorilla Vocalist Fitzroy and bass man Vernon both worked for a large Leicester engineering firm called Jones and Shipman. Fitzroy in his infinite wisdom decided to throw a sicky on the day that we recorded Top of the Pops. He was well and truly carpeted when he went back to work; he obviously underestimated the power of the show.

Mike Oberman had been busy behind the scenes, suggesting that we find a manager to oversee our day to day business - it was getting all a bit too hectic for St.Clair. A business associate he knew, a Scot, Murdo Macleod was a night club owner from Dundee who had expressed an interest in meeting us. Murdo was seriously rich; one of his clubs, the Barracuda in Dundee, was his flag ship and was rated as one of the best in all of Britain.

Dingbat booked us to play the Barracuda as a part of a much bigger tour that would take us up the country, culminating in a series of Scottish dates. We acquired our very own sound engineer and what a luxury that was. Nigel was a professional and could only commit to one tour at a time. His regular pay dirt came from rock band Judas Priest, who were then a massive world wide metal act. He was paid retainer so that he was available at the drop of a hat to service their needs. Working for us gave Nigel a bit of pocket money. Exotic trips to the States and Japan with Judas Priest were the norm, so he treated work with us as a stopgap until the next call came.

Murdo Macleod managed another young band with chart pedigree called Dead End Kids, they had a number 6 hit in March 1977 with a cover of the Honeycombs former No.1, Have I the Right. They were being touted as the new Bay City Rollers - but they never were.

When the dates were announced, at three of the towns we were booked to play two venues in a night. Performing one was exhausting enough and the thought of two filled us with trepidation. The tour took us to;
Stockton-on-Tees - Chester-Le-Street - Newton Aycliffe - Darlington - Ayr - Glasgow - Cumnock - Dundee - Falkirk - Bannockburn.

For this jaunt we availed ourselves of a more comfortable mode of transportation, a blue long wheel based Ford van. It was like living in the lap of luxury compared to what we were accustomed to. The only problem was that when fully laden it was a struggle to achieve 50 mph, which on a long haul north, put hours on the journey. It had two rows of aircraft seats fitted in the front driving section and a generous space in the back, which was partitioned off for the equipment. Those seats saw some action in the coming months as unsuspecting female punters were lured inside. No more perching precariously between drum cases and speaker cabinets. This was the big time! The seating in the front section was like being in a small cinema - all that was missing was the usherette. This beast actually looked like a band vehicle and the comfort was great.

There was also a change in the way that we were treated too at gigs. Food was laid on, drinks were set out in the dressing room and we didn't have to lug equipment around ourselves - we had a Rasta roadie called Wayne - it gave us more freedom to party. Enjoy ourselves we did too.

When the next chart was announced, Banana had slipped to No.30. This flew in the face of all predictions and was definitely due to the glut of re-released Elvis Presley records that peppered the top 30. Banana had apparently sold more records than it had in the previous week. Any other time it would have reflected in an upward movement.

The following week we were pleasantly surprised to see that the single had retained its position. It was quite unusual for a single at the lower end of the top 30 to do that - but it was still picking up healthy Radio One airplay. We had no doubt that if Elvis had eased off on the cheeseburgers for just one more week or so; we could have been looking at a top 10!

We started to appear more in the media, press and teen magazines. We featured in Weekend magazine as Radio One disc jockey Stuart Henry's featured artist. Also in Pink, a little girlie type publication, along side a feature on David Essex who was a real heartthrob at the time. After playing at the Castaway club in Plymouth, Fitzroy caught a train to London to record an interview for the Radio One news magazine programme Newsbeat.

In all these meetings with the press, we were at great pains to emphasise that this song was a total departure from what the band were really about. This was a conscious attempt to distance ourselves from it and sow seeds for the future.

Chapter Nine

SCOTLAND - LOCK UP YOUR DAUGHTERS

The next chart saw the record drop to No.37 - the following week to 50 and the next No. 75. In all our albatross of a hit had spent a total of eight weeks on the chart.

Our stage shows were proving to be livelier affairs and because we had much more time to ourselves, we treated each gig like a night out. Not having a day job helped. Gone were the problems associated with getting up for work - we could now sleep in which meant that we could drink and party.

Our first trip to Scotland took us to Glasgow Shuffles in Sauchiehall Street. This was a large alcohol free, venue full of post-pubescent girls. For some inexplicable reason Scottish audiences really took to us. We were mobbed and often pestered in the street. Although we enjoyed a generous and friendly reception in Scotland, we found ourselves on the sharp end of their criminal fraternity. Meeting Murdo Macleod was very important for us so for the show at his Dundee club, we had spanking new stage outfits tailored. To our horror, after the Shuffles show we discovered that our van which was parked at the rear of the club, had been broken into. Thieves smashed a window and stole a number of items. Our new stage gear was in the van - pristine and still wrapped in cellophane. What on earth could anyone possibly want with those? We called the police and they asked us to make an inventory of what was missing.

At first it seemed that not much had been taken, then came the dread realisation that the stage gear was missing. Here is the list of missing items; seven red and blue satin kung fu style stage suits, with dragon motif trimmings on neck and cuffs! One pair of hideous white platform shoes belonging to Martin (we actually cheered when we heard that these had been stolen!) - One camera - one of Dianne's stage dresses and a travelling bag. Fortunately for us, our instruments were still inside the venue.

We made a statement to the police, got the van window fixed, then trundled off to our next engagement. Some weeks later St.Clair had a call from the Glasgow constabulary. They had arrested a suspect that they believed was responsible for the robbery. Picture this if you can? This guy was spotted in Glasgow City centre sporting one of our red and blue satin kung fu style stage suits - with dragon motif on trims and cuffs, wearing Martin's bloody hateful white platform shoes, with a camera around his neck! How not to draw attention to yourself! The words 'sore' and 'thumb' spring to mind.

St.Clair had to travel back to Glasgow to identify the goods and stay over for the court case. Where is the justice - Martin got those hideous platform shoes back! I had serious misgivings about wearing one of those satin suits on stage, how someone in his right mind could mince around Glasgow City centre in one I'll never understand.

Girls screamed at us, which just didn't make much sense to me. It wasn't as if we were Robbie Williams or something. One time after performing at Glasgow Shuffles, as we filed off stage there was quite a bit of screaming and groping from young girls in the audience. Stage security people formed a cordon to allow us through to our dressing room but a number of kids forced a way through and started pawing at us. It wasn't a major problem; they were only very young. Bouncers roughly manhandled these poor girls, throwing some to the floor. One girl took a full blooded punch to the face. These were big guys, as bouncers usually are and I felt physically sick. Back in the dressing room we made a complaint to the club management. The worst that these girls could have done to us was scratch or tear clothes. Unfortunately the club management were powerless to act because these guys were employed by an outside agency. I appreciated that the security people were only doing their job but to me it was blatant over reaction.

Live offers were flooding in; we were able to command four times the fee that Fascination did. Sonor, the drum manufacturer approached Sylvester, and asked him to play one of their kits live. In return he got a new set with all the accessories for free. Press ads wherever we played proclaimed 'Straight from Top of the Pops' or 'Hit recording artists,' but this had a hollow ring to it for me. The way we were paid was haphazard. It was regular money to begin with, but fees became more and more spasmodic and since quitting our day jobs the band was our only means of income - this put a further strain on my marriage.

Since the profile of the band had been raised my wife had been taking stick from the girls work. She laughed it off at first, but eventually it started to rankle. They would say things like,
'Where is he tonight then? You know what they say about musicians.'

I told her that it was a fallacy - that they were winding her up, but it didn't change her mind. So to show her, I arranged for her to come along to the next gig. It was at the Porterhouse in Retford, Nottinghamshire. The club was known for attracting up and coming bands and a few name bands had passed through on the way to the top. The gig was a stormer - it was a packed, appreciative audience. Immediately after the set we adjourned to the dressing room as our girlfriends waited outside along with a group of fans waiting for autographs. That was where my problem began. A girl standing next to my wife said,
'Which one are you waiting for? I can't wait to get my hands on the sax player!' My wife was furious - 'I'm his wife!' she snapped.

Typical - I got the frosty, silent treatment for the remainder of the night. An uneasy trust existed between us each time that I went away to play after that episode.

The contract that had been offered to us by Response records was dodgy and we didn't sign it. It was restricting and would have tied us down for about a million years. The dilemma was that without a legally binding agreement, we were in great danger of being taken for a ride.

We were once threatened with legal action over breach of contract. At times like that you need the muscle of management to sort such problems out. We were scheduled to play at the Mayflower Club in Southampton and during the

trip south the inevitable breakdown happened. By breakdown standards this was serious - the van needed a new engine and that was an expensive exercise. We were stranded, in winter, half way to the venue and were forced to sleep on the floor of a pub for the night.

There was no way we could get to the venue to fulfil our contractual obligations and the agent tried to sue us for the fee, plus compensation. The new engine cost £700 and the gig fee was £450, with expenses thrown in; this would have cost us dear. A compromise was finally agreed on. We played a number of shows for less than the normal asking price. All together a nice little loss making exercise.

We had an on-going joke - whenever we approached a town, someone would shout,

'Lock up your daughters, the Gorillas are in town!'
The way they performed, it should have been, 'Lock up your daughters - and their mothers!'

We played shows at Dundee Samantha's club and The Barracuda both owned by Macleod - both impressive. We were forced to perform in our reserve stage gear, because that twisted old fruit in Glasgow had relieved us of our new glad rags but Macleod liked us. He offered us a management proposition there and then. He sounded like he knew what he was talking about - he seemed to know the business inside out. Signing a management deal was a necessity, everything had got pretty much out of hand and we needed someone to steer our business dealings. It is beneficial to have someone detached from the band to make objective decisions - band members are too close to it all to make good long-term game plans.

Scotland was great. The tour took us to pretty out of the way places. The black guys in the band were treated as something of a curiosity when we got as far north as Inverness - there were no coloured people there. For one gig we lodged in rooms above a pub and as I enjoyed a drink I was subjected to a venomous verbal attack from a Scottish nationalist. He was worse for wear and was banging on about some obscure battle in the fourteenth century when the Scots turned the English over. I thought, 'it's probably that long since they beat us on a soccer pitch too.' I was surprised by his zeal.

Hamilton was one of our stop off points. I met a blonde girl after the show and I used our usual, 'I've got some band photos back at the hotel' ploy to impress her. It worked. As we walked back to the hotel from the club, a light dusting of snow covered the ground. It was damned cold. We were half way up the stairs leading to my room when the battle-axe that called itself a landlady barred our way. She leapt out at us like a spider,

'Where do you think you're going? - Strictly no girls in the rooms' it said. Great, I thought. But the girl said,

'It's all right, you can come back to my place, and it's not far'

We started to walk and the snow was getting thicker. We walked and walked and walked some more. She kept saying 'It's not far now' - but it was far now! By the time the snow was up to my shins our route had taken us out of town into countryside where the snow had started to drift. At one point a snow plough passed us and I was frozen to the bone. My ardour had well and truly cooled. Coupled to this, the effects of the alcohol had worn off and I only had a thin coat on. It was miles, and I mean miles. When we finally arrived at her house I looked like a snowman but the best was to come - her MUM answered the door! I thought shit, what have I done to deserve this. She was a nice lady - she thanked me profusely for seeing her daughter home on such a mucky night and stuck me in front of a raging fire with a mug of hot tea. The girl said,

'Don't worry you can sleep in my bed' - WHEY - HEY, there Is a God, I thought - she quickly added, 'I'll jump in with my sister'

There are times in life when you really wish hard that you were somewhere else and this was one of mine. Next morning I was given a hearty breakfast and stuck on a bus to town to find my hotel. On the bus journey back it became apparent how far we'd walked; the snow was still really thick. When I met up with the rest of the lads I got stick? All that effort, for a peck on the cheek. Fitzroy managed to steel a girl into his room, no doubt using the band photo scam, and enjoyed a rampant night. How he managed to evade that pit bull terrier of a landlady, is beyond me. He must have used a ladder.

Another time we played in Hereford. As happened on a fairly regular basis the van broke down mid way to the venue. After much grief and delay we got hold of a courtesy vehicle and transferred all the gear from our van only to arrive late. The replacement vehicle was the box type van with a sliding shutter door at the back. It had no windows which meant that those of us travelling in the back with the equipment had no idea where the hell we were.

All this was pretty disorienting travelling back because it was pitch black in there. Arriving home in Leicester at dawn, the slow process of dropping each band member off in turn began. Vernon lived in a narrow street of terraced houses and as we drove down it there was a tremendous jolt followed by a high pitched tinkling cacophony.

All that we could hear were irate, muffled voices. When the shutter door came up it was like the last days on earth. We had clipped a milk float and the lot had gone. I couldn't believe the amount of damage, the float was a crumpled heap. Broken bottles were strewn across the street and a river of milk flowed down the gutter. By this time people in dressing gowns were appearing on doorsteps, to see what all the commotion was all about. I took my saxophone, picked my way through the pile of broken bottles and made my way home. The argument still raged as I went, but I was so dog tired I didn't care. Our insurance sorted the whole mess out in the end.

Chapter Ten
JEAN-PAUL BARROW

Some bright spark from our management company decided that I looked French or Italian. I probably do, it has been said to me often. I have been mistaken for a Turk, a Greek, an Italian, a Frenchman and most hurtful of all, a bloody Colombian! It may well be something to do with the nose. Having a token Frenchman in the band would be a good promotional tool, so I became Jean-Paul. What an icebreaker. I would pretend to speak very little English and the girls were suckers for it. The down side was getting my mum to understand the idea. Mum is no nonsense, down to earth, Leicester woman. She raised my brother Paul and me up to respect the female gender. She would have no part in covering up, or lying for us to girls on the telephone.

Once a girl from Bagshot found our telephone number - she called mums and enquired, 'Can I speak to Jean-Paul please?' This confused mum, she knew that she had two sons, one called John one called Paul. Which of these sons did this girl want? She finally said,

'Make your mind up, which one do you want? John is out and Paul is still in bed!' - The girl never called again. Giving telephone numbers to girls on the road was a definite no-no. Members of the band experienced horrific predicaments because girls had found out their number and plagued them at all hours of the day and night. Dean experienced a real 'fatal attraction' incident when a girl found his address. A girl he had been friendly with, down on the south coast turned up at his mum's door totally unannounced, claiming to be pregnant. Dean was away on tour so it was a tricky situation for his parents to deal with. It turned out that she wasn't pregnant but believed that he would run away with her if he thought that she was.

Another bizarre incident happened to one of the guys at the Ocean bar Bognor Regis. It was early on in the night; not many people had filtered into the club by then. We were assembled in the bar area chatting and enjoying a pre gig drink. A guy came in with a young girl - his daughter. He came over to us and demanded to know who had slept with her. One of our guys sheepishly came forward and they went to a corner to chat.

It transpired that his daughter had contracted a nasty little condition since our last visit and he felt duty bound to let him know. He was taking a huge chance. Not a lot of men would happy with such a revelation. It was all rather civilised; our guy thanked him for his honesty. It turned out that he needn't have bothered, after a check up back in Leicester he was given the all clear.

Bognor Regis was a place that we played on numerous occasions. The Ocean bar was situated on the end of Bognor pier in a complex that included the night club. For some reason we always went down really well there and It was a kicking, lively place even out of season. It was a strange experience setting up there because we had to back the van along the pier for access, across a wooden walkway where you could see the sea heaving away below through the slats. When the weather was inclement in winter it was blustery and freezing cold on that pier end.

For some unknown reason Bognor was a happy hunting ground for the Gorillas; we very rarely failed to capture there. With our stage show over one night, Dean, Martin and I went on the prowl, the place was always packed. The band photo scam worked and I ended up taking a girl back to the hotel with me. Our room had three single beds which we shared, once inside I locked the door. When Dean came back he found the door locked and on hearing noises inside, got on his hands and knees to peep through the keyhole. As he did a big guy came out of the room next door and seeing Dean on his hands and knees said,

'Can I help you mate?' Dean said, 'I think I've lost my keys' to which the guy replied 'Why don't you ask your mate to let you in, it sounds like he's enjoying himself in there!' I was completely oblivious to the fact that Dean was outside. It must have been noisy though, for some reason this girl kept screaming 'JESUS - JEEEEEEEEZZZZUUUUUUUUUS' very loudly. This was strange. To the best of my knowledge Jesus wasn't even staying in the same hotel! Another time in

Bognor Dean and I saw a couple of girls who worked in a Bognor seaside rock factory and it is fascinating how they get that writing down the middle but it was bloody cold on that sea front with your trousers round your ankles.

Chapter Eleven

A DAY AT THE PALACE

I never thought I'd hear from Sister Big Stuff again so when I got a call from Graham Tom it was a pleasant surprise. He called to see if Dean and I would be interested in helping with one of Sammy's mad schemes. The idea of working with those guys again appealed and I said yes without hesitation. This episode was to prove to be every bit as embarrassing as the Gimme Dat Banana debacle.

I hadn't seen Stalky for some time. He was drumming for a band called Pinkertons Assorted Colours. It was a prestige job; they'd had two hits, the biggest of which was Mirror Mirror - an international hit in 1966 and the band toured on the back of that reputation. When I got more details of Sammy's master plan I cringed - a lot. Sammy had seen Prince Charles on a newsreel dancing the Samba in Rio and decided to write a song to capitalise on the publicity it had caused. He called the song Soa Ula Samba and he wanted Sister Big Stuff to reform to record it.

It all seemed like a bit of a giggle and Dean and I went into the project without telling any of the lads in Black Gorilla. The first rehearsal back in the little outhouse at Graham's pile in Coalville was a scream. It was almost the original SBS line up assembled, with the exception of bassist Vince, who for some obscure reason declined the offer. I wonder why? One addition was female vocalist Gloria Charlz, who like Sammy was from Derby. The other was Martin Vandelis who stepped into Vince's shoes on bass.

The full line up was; myself (tenor sax) Dean Sargent (trumpet) Graham Tom (guitar) Sammy Day (vocals) Gloria Charlz (vocals) Martyn 'Stalky' Gleeson (drums) Dave Van (keyboards) Martin Vandelis (bass)

The song was a commercial soul song and Sammy had cajoled Penny Farthing Records into considering its release. Raising funds appeared to be no problem and the project was rushed through in double quick time. Beck studios in Wellingborough were selected for the recording and after several rehearsals we knocked the song into shape. The rehearsals were great fun and all the old band banter resurfaced. One armed girl jokes included. Recording the track provided no major headaches although keyboard player Dave had to get a cab for the forty mile trip from Leicester because he missed his lift! It wouldn't have been a Sister Big Stuff enterprise without a comical mishap. The song was an upbeat soul thumper with brass riffs and a fine timbale drum break from Stalky. Sammy had a knack for penning commercial songs.

Local radio gave Graham and Sammy their first interview just days after the song was recorded, but the best was to come. Sammy had contacted Buckingham Palace and apparently Prince Charles was more than happy to receive the first pressing of the record. It was a typical Sammy blag. The plan was to go down to 'Buck' house and present the record to a member of one of Prince Charles's household staff. Apparently the Prince himself would be away parachute jumping. Any excuse to avoid meeting Sammy!

Sammy went into overdrive arranging for the press to cover the project, and he got it too. National newspapers showed an interest but I suspect that like me, they reckoned Sammy was not the full ticket. Promotional copies were pressed, one in a snazzy presentation frame for the Prince and a day was arranged for the trip. Friday April 28th 1978 was D-day and we met in Derby for a civic send off by the Lord Mayor. He was kitted out in all his regalia - chain and all, flashing cheesy grins at the press and struggling in the breeze to tame his Bobby Charlton comb over. Definitely twilight zone stuff! We made the front page of the Derby Evening Telegraph.

Next it was to Leicester for a rendezvous with the Leicester Mercury who took a tacky photograph of us hanging out of a telephone box, Sammy in the foreground proudly holding the presentation single aloft. If this all seemed a bit much to take on board the best was yet to come. Our transportation for the jaunt to London was a mini bus bedecked with home made posters proclaiming, "We're going t'at Palace.' What Sammy was trying to convey with that curious phraseology was lost on all but himself.

He had rigged up a loud hailer system and attached speakers to the roof. This was to treat members of the general public to a sneak preview of the track, at about a million watts as we travelled. He also had a microphone and as we drove along he would shout, 'All right missus?' at deafening volume. We saw more than one poor woman stooping to pick up spilled shopping. We hadn't even got out of Leicester before a motor cycle policeman - Sergeant Tichmarsh, pulled us over to have a word. I felt for him - he was lost for words, and all he could say over and over was, 'You can't do it. You just can't do it!' We explained the nature of our enterprise to him. I got the impression that he was trying hard not to laugh. He walked back to his motorcycle still shaking his head. He let us off with a warning when surely he could have charged us with something, even if it was aggravated gross bad taste!

As soon as the policeman was out of earshot Sammy resumed his one-man mobile DJ act. If belting out our music was an acute embarrassment in Leicester, picture the amount of squirming that went on in Piccadilly Circus and The Mall in London itself. Stalky, Dean and I crouched down low at the back of the vehicle in an attempt to shield us from the public gaze. Sammy parked right in front of those famous iron gates outside Buckingham Palace and was admitted into the Palace forecourt. It was all very stiff and official; a member of Prince Charles's household staff accepted the record on the Prince's behalf. Unfortunately the bevy of national newspaper hacks that we were told would be waiting didn't show. That miffed Sammy.

All in all I can quite honestly say that I've never laughed so much in my entire life, mainly out of nervous embarrassment. We made the front page of the Leicester Mercury but the recording deal didn't materialise and the single was never available on general release.

Sister Big Stuff left London for home but Dean and I stayed on, Black Gorilla had a gig at The Castle Club in Richmond. We were eternally grateful to be able to get out of that mini bus. When we arrived at the club a welcoming committee of Gorillas met us. St.Clair was clutching a copy of the Leicester Mercury; with us splashed across its front page. They feared that we had joined another band behind their backs. We explained that it had been just a bit of fun, perhaps we should have been a bit more up front about it. I hurt from all the laughing that I had done that day.

Chapter Twelve

BERNARD MANNING'S STRAIGHT MAN!

Some of the gigs that we took on with Black Gorilla were dubious to say the least; there was one at Roots club in Chapel town, the red light district of Leeds. I remember feeling very apprehensive - there was a real feeling of menace, and I for one was glad when we were out of there. St.Clair seemed afraid to turn work away and sometimes that led us into tricky situations. One such engagement was at the Painted Lady night club at a place called Kirby Bellars near Melton Mowbray. There was absolutely nothing wrong with the venue itself; it was quite a nice cosy cabaret club. For our sins we were on the same bill as Bernard Manning. Venues refused to book him because of the racist and sexist content in his material. Black Gorilla had five West Indian guys in their ranks so I was surprised that we took the gig on. We did two forty-five minute spots and Manning took the slot in between. When we played our first set he hadn't even arrived.

We were towelling down after our opening stint when he deigned to turn up in his Rolls Royce, hot foot from a show elsewhere. Manning was swearing a lot. He slipped into a pair of shiny patent leather shoes, pinned on a red, velvet clip-on dickey bow, grabbed a microphone and took to the stage. I went out front to watch and stood on the balcony with guitarist Martin. He was scathing but very funny and some of the audience took real stick. It was then that I became an unwitting fall guy for Manning's razor wit. Spotting Martin and me leaning over the balcony he bellowed,
'F**k me, put that pair back to back and they'd look like a f*****g pick axe!'

The entire audience stared up and creased. Needless to say, it was a trifle embarrassing. I never imagined that one day I would play straight guy to Bernard Manning. After his show he picked up a cheque for £350, a lot of money in 1978 and disappeared into the sunset back to Manchester in his Rolls.

Through this period my pal Gaz Birtles had joined a band called Wendy Tunes, a new wave power pop outfit based in Leicester. They had a clutch of infectious pop tunes in their armoury and were starting to make waves. Gaz had really found his niche as a front man and was a magnetic revelation on stage - a real live wire. There were a lot of people, who thought Wendy Tunes could go all the way.

There was a vibrant scene in Leicester then. Other bands getting noticed were - Raw Deal - Dead Fly Syndrome - The RTRs - Robin Banks and the Payrolls - Disco Zombies - Farmlife and Sincere Americans. There was definitely a feel of expectation in the City at the time. Wendy Tunes drummer was Gaz's younger brother Phil Birtles, an excellent tight expressive player.

During this period another Black Gorilla record surfaced and again we had no prior knowledge of its existence. Although we'd rejected the deal with Response Records they just carried on as usual. The latest dirge was called Bamboo Child - it wasn't so much of a novelty song but it still wasn't us. The German session guys who recorded these tracks could obviously play, but the material they were producing was so out of step with what was happening at the time. We wilfully under promoted the track, which was difficult as we were still billed as Black Gorilla. Gimme Dat Banana must have earned someone some money, it reached No.9 in Spain, No.12 in South Africa and sold well in Scandinavia.

Here is an example of the sort of trap we were in - In 1980 I visited Berlin and a friend, Mick Mooney, led me to a record store that had a Black Gorilla album on sale. I knew nothing about it and never played a single note on it, but there I was pictured on the front sleeve, in full colour! The album was called Private Collection and was released on a subsidiary to the Phonogram label. I bought the album as a keepsake and for its cringe factor.

Dean and I quit Black Gorilla for a spell, it got to a point where we didn't know if we were going to get paid or not, and it was a real struggle to make ends meet. By this time I had gone back to work for my old company BSL on a part time basis, which suited me down to the ground because

I could play away and not have to get up until lunchtime the following day.

In my brief spell outside the band I did a spot of recording with Wendy Tunes and made guest appearances with them on stage, thus performing with Gaz for the first time. I also worked with a band called Raw Deal. Both outfits were a total departure from the funk field and I found it exhilarating. It was nice not to have the relentless cycle of travel and touring. I'd quite forgotten what a weekend in Leicester with my friends was like. Eventually, Fitzroy tempted us back by guaranteeing a regular weekly wage, and dangling the juicy carrot of a Swiss tour before us. I had never performed abroad before so it sounded very appealing. The Swiss engagement was a two week residency at the Blackout Club, an exclusive night club on the Zurich airport complex. The gig placed us in excellent company alongside name funk luminaries, Light of the World and Beggar and Co.

I flew while the rest of the band travelled overland because I had to beg for time off work. We were given smart apartment rooms close to the club managed by a Swiss/German guy called Klaus. He was priceless. If you could have bottled him as a character for Harry Enfield he'd have been an instant hit. Klaus had a fair command of the English language; but he thought it was cool to swear and that is where his problems began. Klaus used his expletives in all the wrong places, mainly at the end of sentences. He explained the apartment ground rules thus, 'No girls allowed in the apartments at any time, f*****g!' and 'It is your responsibility to keep the rooms clean f*****g!' The poor guy had absolutely no idea why we laughed at him, f*****g!

The club was hi-tech and was the first club I'd seen with a huge video screen that projected visual images of bands as tracks played. Drinks were scandalously expensive but fortunately food and drinks were provided. The club's clientele were well heeled. It can't have been cheap to stay on the air port complex and the club attracted air hostesses and pilots, who let their hair down.

We had a pretty wild time in Zurich, with only the show at night to worry about, it was one big party. Dean met a rich

South African girl who for ages afterwards bombarded his home with long distance telephone calls, begging him to visit her - all expenses paid. Daddy was rolling in it; he owned a chain of restaurants. For her eighteenth birthday he flew a sports car over from Rio to surprise her, the biggest surprise from where I'm sitting is that Dean never took her up on her offer!

There was an Italian girl who developed a desperate crush on me. She turned up every night to see us play and sat right in front of the stage looking up at me with 'I'm available eyes.' I didn't want to know so avoided her like the plague. Bass player Vernon, on the other hand, never one to miss an opportunity, lured her back to the apartments on the pretence that I would be there. I wasn't. Vernon sorted the poor girl out, while the rest of the band watched from every conceivable spy hole. One hid in a wardrobe, one on the balcony, another under the bed! Klaus would have gone mad if he'd known f*****g!

The Zurich trip was successful; we had played a prestige venue coming away with the knowledge that we could hold our own in top class company. We even wrote a couple of songs during the time that we had free, but in a way Black Gorilla were never going to be anything more than a band with a novelty hit record. It was a shame because the band were talented and with the right direction and impetus could easily have succeeded in their own right.

Back in England it was straight back on the tour merry-go-round. We came back with our tails up, but as so often happens in music, we were soon brought back down to earth. Our first gig on our return was at Leicester Scamps Club, it was a mucky Tuesday night and seventeen people paid to see us! The conquering heroes return to one man and his dog, and I bet the dog didn't pay! In the way that things come back to haunt you sometimes, a mate of mine Gaz Bond, was one of those seventeen punters that night. To this day he ribs me about it. It seems hardly credible that after all that I have done in the business since then, Gaz Bond still only remembers that disastrous night at Scamps!

Moss Side in Manchester is not the sort of place that you venture into of your own free will. We played a club there called the Russell Club which was sited in deepest, darkest Moss Side. It was a venue predominantly frequented by Afro-Caribbean punters. We played our set and hung around until throwing out time, when we could get our gear out. Dean had struck up a relationship with a white girl who was there with her West Indian husband. He danced with the girl as her husband glared at them from the sidelines.

I watched a potentially ugly situation developing and tried to warn Dean off. Eventually he left with the girl and was followed by a now worse for wear husband. When everything was packed to go there was still no sign of Dean - we started to get concerned. We trawled the area and those streets looked particularly grim and forbidding late at night. Eventually we had to give up and head back to Leicester.

Getting back in the small hours, it was straight to bed but I was rudely awoken by a call from Dean's mum, she was understandably pretty frantic. I told her what had happened. Dean was stranded at Manchester Piccadilly railway station, with no money to get home. His mum had to negotiate with the stationmaster to secure him a seat on a train. Dean was very apologetic when he realised the upset he had caused.

Probably one of the strangest incidents to befall me happened in Whitehaven, Cumbria. We were playing a weeklong residency at the Zodiac Club and were lodging at a nearby farmhouse. I didn't like Whitehaven much. Too many fields and trees, I am city boy through and through and if I get too far out of town I get nauseous.

Our after show entertainment took Martin and myself to the home of two girls who shared a place together. The girl I was with was a tall divorcee, with a huge mane of tight curls. We had drinks and listened to music and eventually we were asked to stay the night. On the way to our respective rooms I decided to use the bathroom to freshen up. After I did, I entered the bedroom to the shock of my entire life.

MY GIRL WAS AS BOLD AS A COOT!

A slap head! Gone were the flowing tresses, it was a WIG! No explanation was asked for - none given. I was the subject of much ridicule the following day when my fellow Gorillas learned of my little experience.

Bannockburn in Scotland was the setting for a fine little exhibition by Sylvester across the aircraft seats in the band van. The venue was imaginatively called the Tartan Arms in that little town made famous by that battle, all those years before. After our performance Sylvester decided to give an encore of his own. We noticed him creeping out through a side door with a girl in tow. Sussing out what he had in mind, we waited and then trooped outside. It was winter and it was cold, so there was no way he'd be out in the open.

We crept up to the van parked just outside the club; the slight rocking motion confirmed our suspicions. Six pairs of eyes peered through windows and what a spectacle. The poor unsuspecting girl was oblivious to the fact that she was our after show cabaret. Sylvester performed remarkably well in very trying circumstances - worthy of at least eight out of ten on the scorecard. We slipped back into the club before we were rumbled. She looked very flushed when they came back to be greeted by winks and knowing smiles.

Our travels took us to the famous Music Machine in Camden Town, London. Top acts performed there; the Boomtown Rats played the night before us. Celebrities also frequented the venue, Marc Bolan was a regular, although he didn't put himself out to come and see us. The Music Machine later was transformed into the Camden Palace in the 80's by Steve Strange. We played in mid week and the gig was sparsely attended. My saxophone sling broke during the show and I just caught my sax before it crashed down to the stage floor. I scampered to the dressing room for my spare while the band played on. By this time I was playing a 1962 Selmer MKVI tenor with nickel keys, it is still my pride joy and has accompanied me through many adventures in pop land. Through all the bleak times I always resisted the temptation to sell it, but I must admit in the darkest times, I came close.

Playing four or five night clubs a week did have a detrimental effect on my social life. When I did get free time back in Leicester, the last thing I wanted to do was go out to a club. I had seen so many across the country. The facades and décor were different, but in many other respects they were the same. Most had DJs convinced they were God's gift to womankind and played the bloody same records. I swear that I could have written out a play list before entering a club and get it spot on. Big clubs often featured promotional nights where a chart act would appear to mime to their hit; it certainly drew in the crowds. We featured on one such promotional night at Preston Clouds club as a girl called Viola Wills mimed to her hit Gonna Get Along Without You Now, which was a top ten hit in October 1979. It was a blatant mime. She did one song - signed a few autographs and left, presumably clutching a fat cheque.

Another profitable ploy was to invite a guest radio DJ along to play records. Again at Preston Clouds we played on a night which featured Radio Luxembourg disc jockey Tony Prince. He played the same records that the resident DJ would have played, signed a few autographs, gave out a few T-shirts and melted away, also presumably clutching a nice cheque.

Some of the clubs we played in were huge. Sadies Club in Derby was a former cinema; it had three-tiers and from the back performers looked like ants! Fusion club in Leicester was a former bowling alley. We played there once and were allocated space in the bowels of the club to get changed in. The bowling lanes were still in situ; cobweb covered and dusty but untouched. In a scene reminiscent of the famous Spinal Tap 'Enormo Dome' sketch, come show time eight satin suited Gorillas staggered about backstage looking for an entrance into the club. After twenty or so frustrating minutes we were rescued and led to the stage by club staff.

One time we were playing a Thursday, Friday and Saturday stint at Sherry's Club in Brighton. Dean and I went out to sample the local nightlife and enjoy a couple of beers prior to gig time. We visited a couple of sea front bars, grabbed a bite to eat and returned to the venue. We suffered a slight set back when the bouncer refused to let us into the club! 'We're in the band,' we said. 'They all say that' he said. So we spent an eternity outside arguing with him. It was getting close to show time and the situation was only resolved when St.Clair came out to vouch for us.

With all our previous promises reneged on by record company and management the rest of the guys still showed little or no interest in producing original material. The quality of the gigs hadn't diminished though. We supported Tamla Motown act the Elgins at Birmingham Barbarellas. They had scored a big hit in 1971 with a track called Heaven Must Have Sent You.

Preston was a place where my life flashed in front of my eyes. We took on a residency at Clouds club that required us to play each Thursday, Friday and Saturday for a month. We had a lot of free time and Dean and I spent most of it drinking and womanising. After one show I met a girl who asked me back to her place. You'd imagine that by now I would have learnt my lesson, with all the scrapes that I'd got myself into before. No. I'd enquired as to her marital status, she was separated from her husband and being the trusting soul that I am, I believed her. We went back to her small terraced house not far away. We hadn't been there long and it was late when the doorbell rang. She went to see who it could be at that unearthly hour and came back to announce,

'It's my husband!'

Everything from then was in slow motion. She told him that she had company but he wouldn't leave. She said it might be best if I left. TOO RIGHT! I was in complete agreement with her on that score. The problem was getting out of the house. There was only one way out and that meant passing lover boy who was sulking on the doorstep. She uttered the immortal words that were meant to re-assure me,

'He won't hurt you I promise!'

Those words did not re-assure me. The thought of fisticuffs sickens me, I'm not a big guy but I had no alternative but to walk out past him. He was huge and drunk. As I edged past him on the step he scowled at me. I was bracing myself for a bunch of fives that thankfully didn't fly past his wife who was restraining him. I flew back to the club in a time that would have put Lynford Christie to shame. The guys in the band ripped me to bits. Never again.

Stories of life on the road often glamorise it. It isn't glamorous at all because there are long hours of travel and you often wake up in a strange bed not knowing where the hell you are. Some bands are quite content to tour non-stop, that's OK - some earn a very good living out of a suitcase. Without hits to back you the danger is getting stuck on a relentless merry-go-round, playing the same old clubs. We played some clubs many times and eventually you start to ask where it is this getting me? Sure, we had some great laughs and great nights and there were lots of girls, but at some point you have to try to make sense of it all.

Now there is definitely a different morality. Don't forget that at that time there was no AIDS which is a disease that would have seemed like science fiction then. The most inconvenience that could befall you was a slight irritation in the trouser area - easily sorted out with antibiotics. The only problem was with antibiotics you couldn't drink, and it was a dead give away if one of the guys suddenly took to drinking orange juice on tour.

Chapter Thirteen

NO WOMAN NO CRY

My marriage was on the skids at this point and without getting all agony aunt on you - my music was a vital crutch to me. It took my mind off the problem and got me out of Leicester. By incredible coincidence, Stalky's marriage bit the dust at the same time. Synchronised marriage break ups; there's a future event for the Olympics!

I was walking close to my flat one day and a car pulled up - it was Stalky. I hadn't actually seen him for a while so we went for a beer. I told him that my marriage was over and he said, what do you know - so is mine. With one of those pieces of misguided logic that seems so sensible at the time, we decided that we would drink, party and womanise Leicester ragged - in the few months that followed, we certainly gave it a good go.

On the Black Gorilla front there were gigs, gigs and more gigs but this was therapy for me. We played at Annabelles Club in Loughborough. Being close enough to promote the gig ourselves, we had posters printed for fly posting; Stalky helped me to post them. The operation was carried out in the small hours to avoid being nabbed by the local constabulary; billposting carried a mandatory fine. Why we chose the dead of night is one of life's little mysteries, we later discovered that by far the best time to do it is in the day - there are more people about and you can blend in with the crowd. At night you stand out like a sore thumb and are easily spotted skulking in the shadows.

We had a night of drinking and then returned to my flat to collect bucket, brush and paste to descend on the town, giggling as we went. A couple of times we had to take evasive action - ducking out of sight from a patrolling squad car. It was quite a messy job too, one of us pasted, and the other put up and smoothed the poster down. Paste ran down my sleeves. In the following days I saw our posters around town and thought, 'I can't remember putting that one up!' It was not unusual to see them on bus shelters, across doorways and on road signs after a twilight pasting blitz.

Out of town venues would take care of publicity and promote the gig themselves. When it came to major chart acts record companies or booking agencies handled poster campaigns for tours and new record releases. The poster distribution business is very competitive. Stories of rival companies resorting to extreme measures to protect their patch were common place. Territories were carved up between them and they were aggressive in keeping their exclusivity. Record companies would pay a fee for distributing posters across an agreed area but I never understood how they verified that they had in fact been hung.

Deep winter was not a fun time to be touring. Travelling in that slow monster of a van, for long distances was a strength sapping experience at the best of times. But with an ineffectual heater, it was horrendous. On one stint across Scotland we travelled through the night to our next stop and it was bitter cold. We all huddled together for warmth in the seating section behind the driver with our legs covered in blankets and sleeping bags. Feet felt like blocks of ice and you could see the ice forming on the windscreen in those little whirly patterns as we drove. Necessity forced us to pull over at a service station in the middle of nowhere to take on fuel and Sylvester braved the elements to do the job. We set off again, but not for much further; Sylvester had filled up with petrol instead of diesel! To any one not too familiar with the difference, petrol is thicker and it clogs the pipes up in the engine. We shuddered to a standstill and very soon the inside of that van was so incredibly cold it made you want to cry. One of the guys trudged back down the road to the service station and Sylvester went after him - I think he was just glad to get out of the van because he wasn't exactly favour of the month. Eventually the AA came out to purge the engine of petrol. We sat in those freezing conditions for hours with a chill wind buffeting the van. I swear it was one of my most miserable experiences ever.

Sometimes it was possible to grab forty winks in the back of the van as we travelled but in that cold it was impossible - also it depended on the man at the wheel. If it was sound man Russ - everyone forced them selves awake, however tempting shut eye seemed. Russ slung the van around, hitting curbs and steaming through red lights as eight very tired Gorillas stared wide eyed and zombie like at the road ahead daring not to go to sleep. Russ drove on auto pilot staring blankly ahead at the road. Grabbing a nap was essential in the days when I had to get up for work the next morning, but even if I managed one I was like the walking dead next day and could only be contacted by a series of raps and sign language

A third Black Gorilla single materialised and the first we knew of it was when we received promotional copies in the post. The A side was titled Soul Dancer - probably the best yet but it still had little or no chance of seeing chart action. Performing the song live was not so bad because the track fitted in better with our material. However it had deep vocal parts and the only one capable of digging that deep was Fitzroy, who landed the dubious honour of singing it live.

Personnel started to drift away. Guitarist Martin Potter, he of the hideous white platform shoes, bunked out to finish serving his sentence at his music shop. A guy called Victor from Wolverhampton replaced him. Victor was short in stature but reputedly massively over blessed in the wedding tackle department. He spoke in a very broad Black Country accent which sounded strange because he was a West Indian. While we were auditioning for a replacement guitarist, one applicant came all the way from Paris. It must have been a real eye opener for the poor chap; at this point we were rehearsing in a tiny outside room next to the toilets at a pub called the Robin Hood. In the summer there was a permanent smell of urinals wafting through the air, very bracing? The guy didn't land the job and had to travel all the way back to France no doubt cherishing the experience and smelling of an English toilet.

Even though things were strained I still entered into my live commitments as cheerily as I could and there was a lot of it to enter into. It was at the end of a ten-day consecutive run that we played a club in Loughborough and we were all shattered and just wanted to go home. The gig was unremarkable and I looked forward to sleeping in my own bed. I was a couple of blissful hours into my slumber when I was rudely awakened by urgent rapping on the French windows in my bedroom. I peered through the curtains bleary-eyed and in the half-light could just make out a figure that was Dean. I had only said my goodbyes to him outside the club just a couple of hours before. He urged me to let him. It turned out that he had been chased by a police car down the winding country lanes near his home in Coalville. He had been drinking and was understandably reluctant to stop, so he put his foot down. He abandoned his car and organised a lift to my flat. Silly boy.

Talking of brushes with the boys in blue, one night after playing the Exeter Quay Club a girl stayed behind after the show and we offered her a lift on our route out of Exeter. We were some way out when a police car, flashing lights and all, forced us over to the side of the road. A very stern looking officer quizzed us on why we had a fifteen-year-old girl in our van with us. It must have looked suspicious - technically she was a minor and she was in the back of group van with eight musicians. I know that on occasions the Gorillas have plumbed the depths of depravity, but we did have some scruples. Musicians do tend to get a bad press though most of it is totally unwarranted. The police took the girl home. It appeared that some public-spirited citizen had called them after seeing her clambering into our vehicle. She certainly looked a lot older than she was. We had an agreement to throw under sixteen year olds back, except for Dean who would have no qualms about having a go at the mother as well!

Chapter Fourteen

MOONLIGHTING

I started to hang out with a bunch of musicians who made up a crop of new exciting bands coming to the fore on the Leicester scene. A lot of these I met by socialising in watering holes around town. I recorded sax on a demo by a band called Raw Deal at Beck Studios in Wellingborough and went on to play live guest slots with them when I was able. This introduced me to the fine guitar work of Richard Barton and the vocal skills of Craig Marshall, both of whom I was destined to work with in the future.

The Phoenix Theatre in Leicester promoted a series of late night gigs and showcased a number of these new bands. Those nights were really exciting. One regular was Robin Banks, the Payrolls and the Wads fronted by a guy who wrote songs mirroring mundane life experiences - their gigs bordered on pure theatre. Robin was effortlessly nerdish. He took to the stage in a parka and motorcycle goggles and didn't have to try very hard to be really odd. One night I pushed him onto the stage on a toilet on castors as the band played the theme tune from the old classic soap opera Crossroads. Ex Sister Big Stuff guitarist Chris Horlock was a regular on these wild blowouts.

Another band, Dead Fly Syndrome, performed a whole set with their backs to the auditorium while projecting slides onto a screen on stage. These bands stripped music down to its bare essentials and provided a sense of real occasion. This period was also very productive for me from a session work perspective; brass players were in short supply - an endangered species. All things brassy were very much in vogue then.

Bizarre happenings and situations have followed me throughout my years in music. One example has to be the liaison with Laurel Aitken often referred to as the 'Godfather of Ska,' by the music press and media. Laurel had been on the scene for donkeys' years and was a pioneer in the Ska movement from its fledgling days in the late fifties and early sixties. The late seventies saw a revival of Ska music, largely due to the 2-Tone explosion. 2 Tone Records were a Coventry based independent label and in their stable they had bands like the Specials and Madness who were storming the charts. Laurel enjoyed a higher profile on the back of it and even scored a minor hit with a track called Rudi Got Married in 1980. He was based in Leicester and no one really knew how old he was, but he had to be in his fifties at the time. He had a reputation for replacing his backing musicians with frightening regularity and rarely went out on tour with the same faces.

Another disconcerting trait was changing song formats and structures live which threw his musicians into disarray. Spontaneity is healthy and refreshing, but too much can confuse and fragment a performance. For a session player this was frustrating because you never knew what he was going to do next. His new found prominence meant that he was in demand and his renaissance saw him featured in major articles in Melody Maker and New Musical Express. He had asked a number of the Raw Deal lads to make up his backing band for an album that he was recording in London. Gaz and I were recruited on saxophones, Rich Barton on guitar, Pez on bass and Nick Murphy on drums.

We rehearsed material at Drum Beat studios in Leicester and Laurel was up to his old tricks, shifting and changing formats. We would rehearse a number one night, get it spot on and the following session he would have completely changed its makeup and expect us all to telegraph what he was doing. I should have really been warned of what was to come then I suppose. After a number of rehearsal sessions the material was knocked into shape and we travelled down to Gooseberry Studios in London's China town. When we arrived at the studio our worst fears were confirmed. The studio was in a basement underneath a noisy dental practise! I knew enough to realise that a dentist is not the ideal neighbour for a sound sensitive studio environment. Down in the studio drilling was audible as the dentist busied away at someone's choppers in his surgery! A stair well ran down the side of one wall in the studio and periodically the clatter of footsteps could be heard. As we walked into the studio a blind man was tuning a grand piano in the corner. Piano tuning is something that blind people do well with their highly sensitive hearing. There are a lot of them in that profession. As we walked in Rich said, 'I wonder where the toilets are? I'm dying for a pee' Quick as a flash the blind guy, who still had his head buried in the piano said, 'You might as well do it in here mate. Sounds like everyone else has!' We all cracked up at this brilliant spot of sarcasm. He obviously didn't have a high opinion of the studio facilities either.

When it came to recording Laurel decided that we would lay down the backing tracks live in studio, which was a bad move considering the amount of background noise. At one point during the recording a stranger minced into the studio and left by another door. The red 'DO NOT ENTER' recording light was on and we all looked at each other as if to say, 'Who the hell was that?' Nobody knew - he was certainly nothing to do with the studio complex. He'd probably popped in to collect his dentures! The session didn't start well. A track we'd polished over several rehearsals was completely re-vamped by Laurel, and we virtually had to relearn it from scratch. It isn't the best place to do this sort of thing, studio time doesn't come cheap and you can waste a lot of precious time re-hashing material. The songs were Ska beat, which isn't technically difficult to master but because there are a lot of staccato off beat beeps, it requires a lot of application. Repetitive playing can make you light headed and it takes real concentration, to keep up with the track without passing out.

At one point the producer came into the studio area and complained that we weren't achieving the right feel. Hardly surprising given all the grief we had to put up with from outside influences. He sent the engineer in to conduct us as we recorded. The stiff jumped up and down in front of us - flailing his arms about like a demented baboon! Picture a 1970s Swedish disco dancer - the sort you'd see on trashy Eurovision pop programmes, and you've got it! He had a pocket full of loose change that made a God-awful racket as he leapt about. I was dying to laugh but avoided eye contact with Gaz at all costs. Rich turned his back to us too, stifling a guffaw.

Considering that the studio bristled with live microphones, the dental sound effects, footsteps on the stairs, and added rhythmic loose change in pocket effects from the chimp prancing about in front of us, the track must have been peppered with noise. I never heard the finished album but tracks from that session have surfaced on a number of album releases since. In the pub afterwards we cried with laughter, it was worth it just for the memory and I'll never forget that blind piano tuner.

Cargo Studio in Rochdale was frequented by a number of bubbling under new wave bands in the late 70s including the likes of the Gang of Four and this was to be the setting for a series of demo tracks by Wendy Tunes. Dean and I were asked to record brass on a couple of tracks, after appearing live with them. We went up for a weekend session, and on Saturday night we all travelled over to nearby Leeds for a night out. Leeds University was the venue for a leg of the Stiff Records tour featuring Lene Lovich and Reckless Eric (hopeless Eric, as guitarist Martyn Watson called him after the gig!) It was a great night to set the weekend up. The recording went well - Wendy Tunes came away with a clutch of good demos and soon after landed a support slot on a college tour with Beserkley Records act the Rubinoos. Beserkley showed an interest in signing Wendy Tunes too but the elusive recording contract never materialised. They eventually signed a deal with Zilch Records and actually recorded an album but sadly it was never released. It was that deal that was to provide a stumbling block for Gaz when we finally got to work together at a later date.

Wendy Tunes had the potential to go a long way but the breaks didn't come and when they eventually split Gaz joined an outfit born out of the ashes of Raw Deal, called the Newmatics. Also from Raw Deal were - Rich Barton (guitar) Pez (bass) and Martyn Hallett (drums) They worked a lot of colleges and universities. 'Rock against racism' was a much-favoured cause at the time and we did an awful lot of benefits - we rocked against racism two or three times a month! There was always yet another benefit to support; in our time we have saved whales and helped to eradicate racial bigotry - in fact it seemed like we saved everything except one legged, partially sighted, lesbian asylum seekers!

I worked with the Newmatics on the same basis that I had with Raw Deal and Wendy Tunes, as guest sax player. I would play on five or six songs in the set, occasionally doubling up with Gaz on saxophones. Newmatics drummer Martyn Hallett left early on and later went on to work with chart act Transvision Vamp who were perhaps best remembered for their blond female vocal focal point Wendy James. I saw him once on the Des O'Connor television show.

Martin's replacement was Nick Murphy a talented left-handed drummer who also played keyboards. Nick was a bit of a jack the lad in those days, running a nice little sideline misappropriating cycles to order, from late night forays in the streets.

The Newmatics signed a recording deal with an organisation called Sin City from Nottingham. It encompassed studio facilities and an independent record label. It was run by a Greek called Byron, who along with manager Andy Case got them a series of gigs at the legendary 100 Club in Oxford Street, London. The Stones had regularly used the venue for tour warm ups. They recorded what should have been their debut single with them - an original song called Streets on Heat but unfortunately it was never released.

Chesterfield College of Art played hosts to us one night. We had a microphone stand that had a solid circular base and Gaz found that if he pushed it out towards the audience, it would swing round in an arc and then return to its original position. He would do this for effect as he sang. He tried his usual feat of showmanship but misjudged the trajectory of the stand and failed to catch it as it teetered back towards him. It smacked him full in the mouth causing him to swing round grimacing to face Nick on the drums. Nick promptly fell back off his drum stool in hysterics - Gaz's two front teeth were redesigned Dracula style! The blow exposed nerve endings and as he gasped for breath the pain was excruciating. Someone took him to the nearest hospital for treatment while the band saw the set out with a series of instrumentals. He required some pretty extensive dental work to put things right. It is called suffering for your art!

The Newmatics gave me my first chance to play at the De Montfort Halls in Leicester. Seeing bands at that venue had kindled my earliest urges to play music in some form. It was where I saw my idols including Roxy Music - Bowie and Cockney Rebel. I yearned to set foot on that stage in some capacity. The Newmatics had already played there, supporting Talking Heads in 1978 - after the show they were invited back to their hotel room, where they chatted into the early hours. This time they were to support Steel Pulse, a reggae band with hits the previous year, Ku Klux Klan and Prodigal Son. Bedfellow's style wise they were not, but stepping onto that stage meant everything to me - another significant milestone. Our reception wasn't bad and the auditorium wasn't full but in the dressing room after I realised I was on hallowed ground that had been trodden by Sinatra and the Beatles. Woolwich Polytechnic was another venue that we played several times. Once we played a benefit night and the sound system was operated by Neville Staples of the Specials - drummer Brad and lead vocalist Terry Hall were also there. The Specials were several big hit records to the good and were riding the crest of a wave with their 2-Tone Record label.

After the gig we chatted with Brad and he offered helpful advice on setting up an independent label, which was to come in very handy later on. Little did we know then that some of those people were to play a very big part in our lives in the not too distant future. We supported Bad Manners, another Ska chart band at the Dog and Trumpet venue in Coventry. Lead singer Buster Bloodvessel was in good form that night. Quite a few of the 2- Tone people hung out at that venue which was really a large pub. I saw Pauline Black of the Selecter there that night.

After the demise of Wendy Tunes, Gaz's brother Phil joined an outfit called the Sinatras, a band fronted by tenacious bass player/vocalist Tommy Hamilton and lead guitarist Nev Hunt. They were attracting substantial interest from labels in London and Dining Out which was set up by Leicester ex pat Dave Henderson, offered them a one off single deal. They recorded a track called Happy Feeling enlisting me to record a sax solo over an extended instrumental passage in the song. All this led to my first visit to the very wonderful Woodbine Street recording studio in Leamington Spa. It was the studio that was later used to record the classic Specials No.1 - Ghost Town. Woodbine was then situated in a row of terraced houses, not a typical setting for a recording studio. The small studio room was in the cellar and the access was down a steep ladder. Producer John Rivers was a bubbly, incredibly talented, technically innovative engineer who left a lasting impression on me that night.

A lot of independent record labels recorded there, including Cherry Red Records, one of the top indies of the time. The recording went well - I was pleased with my efforts and came away with the strong feeling that I would be back one day. Unfortunately for me, when the single hit the streets it was minus my sax - the track had been re mixed and a guitar part had taken its place. It seemed at the time that using my sax on any recording gave it the kiss of death!

There were some deadly eccentric flakes floating around Leicester at this period - one was a guy called Steph who fronted a manic band called the Wiggly Worms. These guys were MAD-MAD-MAD. Steph was into all sorts. I once saw him on television playing Superman in a play. He later did a spot of male modelling and even appeared in a soft porn film. He was working in a trendy bar in Ibiza when a film crew and a troupe of page 3 type nymphets arrived to film around the pool. It was for the Electric Blue series of erotic films and the director needed extras. He said to Steph,

'Do you want to be in my film?' Steph said, 'What do I have to do?'- The producer said 'Just fondle naked girls!' Steph said 'OK then.'

It was a dirty job but some one had to do it! Drinks were administered to lower inhibitions and with the exotic setting and hot sun beaming down - BINGO. Gaz later rented the video to give Steph marks out of ten, but he was not much in evidence in the final edited version.

Another off the wall musician was a character called Rob Grant who fronted a band called Sticky Bob and the Klingons. He also released material under the alias, Mr.Concept - generally a series of hilarious skits and sketches. It was never a dull moment when those guys were around.

During this period Stalky and I lived the hedonistic life of 'young-free and single' cads. He stayed over at my flat after our nights out on the prowl; it was a pretty wild time. We shared some incredible bingeing sprees. Implausible as it sounds now, alcohol fuelled female hunts were the order of the day, with the agreement that if one of us captured, the other one had to go along with it, for the sake of the other. Overall we came out roughly even over a period of time, so it wasn't a bad arrangement. Waking the morning after a booze fest, squinting over to the other side of the bed, it was either 'Jesus, what did I do!' or 'Whey-Hey that'll do nicely!' After one such booze fest Stalky insists that I was involved in steamy, grounds for arrest, performance in a telephone box opposite the Clock Tower in Leicester town centre. I can't remember - such was the alcoholic haze that surrounded me. If true, it would have provided free late night cabaret for the queue in the taxi rank nearby.

By some tragic error of booking the Newmatics were sent to play at the American air force base USAF Alconbury. A band had pulled out at short notice and they were expecting a soul band - the Newmatics were not a soul band. Most of the guys had never seen the inside of a US base so I filled them in as we journeyed there. The gig was a nightmare and the reception was hostile. This was not the environment for a band that was considered to be new wave.

As we laboured through the set we were barracked and catcalled from a particular section of the audience. This had never happened to me before and it was not the best feeling in the world. It was starting to get to Gaz too. He started to bite and when he slagged the US off a big black guy had to be physically restrained from storming the stage to get at him. In the end the big master of ceremonies, white tuxedo and all, rushed the stage waving like a mad man. Someone pulled the plug and turned the disco on. I was only too pleased to see the sanctity of the dressing room. We still got paid though and spent our ill-gotten gains drowning our sorrows in the bar, downing cocktails.

This period was very productive for me but I was playing with so many different outfits that it got confusing. Craig Marshall former lead vocalist with Raw Deal signed recording deal with Fred Cantrell - the same guy that Wendy Tunes had recorded their album with. He invited Dean and yours truly, to join regular sax man Phil Greenwood, to play on his debut single. The session was at Ramport Studios in London - a studio owned by members of the Who. Ramport had some impressive customers. Hits albums by Roxy Music and Thin Lizzy had been recorded there and the studio walls were full of the sleeves of hit albums it had spawned. Some albums that I had in my own collection graced those walls - recording in the same space as some of my heroes gave me quite a thrill.

With his first advance Craig bought a rather nifty Anthony Price designer suit which must have cost him dear. Price was a sought after designer favoured by rock stars, including Bryan Ferry. The track that Craig selected for his first single was a track made famous by Toots and the Maytals called 54-46 Was My Number. We recorded the track live which is not a method much used in this age of rampant technology. Recording live brings its own problems - getting a take that the producer was happy with could mean many laborious takes and that brings its own set of pressures for a musician. Once the studio engineer was happy with the overall sound there were a series of dry runs to get the right balance. After that it was a question of getting everyone to play the track perfectly at the same time. Like the false start in a sprint race, nobody wants to be the one to make a mistake and cause a re-take. It was frustrating when you felt that you'd played perfectly, but had to do it all again because someone else had messed up.

The results of the recording were pleasing but God knows how many attempts it took before the producer was satisfied. Like the Wendy Tunes album the song was shelved and never released. There goes the curse of John Barrow again! At least I got to ride in Fred's Bentley - I felt like royalty. Craig went on to form a band called Wild Bikinis and in later years Dog Patch Four.

Chapter Fifteen

THE PEEL SESSION

Up to his death in 2005, John Peel was an icon in the world of radio broadcasting. His late night Radio One show was avidly listened to by millions. He championed many bands that went on to have significant careers in the world of music and his opinions were well respected. Bands like: T Rex and the Faces to name just two. The John Peel live session was an institution that had given a first chance to many bands. The Sinatras asked Dean and I to play horns on a Peel session that they'd been asked to do. Apart from Top of the Pops, it was to be by far the most credible thing that I'd been involved with in my career so far. The Peel show was incredibly hip and his endorsement carried real clout, so this was a major coup. The Sinatras were a band capable of breaking into the highest division - all it needed was the right exposure and the breaks.

We were to play on three numbers and we worked hard to make sure that we were as prepared as possible. Recording the session was a one-day enterprise, so you had to be on the ball. They were recorded at the BBC studios in Maida Vale, London - the BBC provided a house producer to oversee the session and our producer was a former member of the Glitter Band. When we headed to London and stopped off at Corby to pick up vocalist Tommy - we were horrified to find that he had his girlfriend with him! Girlfriends and recording sessions do not mix. Sessions can drag for a musician - there are long periods of inactivity while you wait to do your bit. It must be doubly wearing for a spectator who has no involvement or understanding of the processes involved. My worst fears were confirmed. I cringed as she sat in front of the huge mixing console. This was not the time or the place for blowing in ears. She threw inane questions like,

'What does the blue knob do Tommy?' and 'Tommy, what would happen if I press this button?' With precious recording time at a premium, you can do without that. In the end, Tommy sensed the displeasure of the band and despatched her to a corner, telling her to be quiet. She looked bored shitless. Despite this hindrance the session went well. There was a lot of brass work to record but it was a very fulfilling day. We got paid a radio session fee. Session rates were settled between the Musicians Union and the BBC. For professional orchestral players session fees are their livelihood and membership of the Musicians Union was essential - BBC studio technicians and cameramen refused to work with non-members.

The session sounded great on the radio. It was the first time that I'd heard myself on Radio One and it felt good. John Peel gave all the musicians a name check and the session was subsequently repeated. I was pretty proud of our contribution from a brass angle.

During this period Black Gorilla faded away. Dianne had long since left to go back to the cut and thrust of the hosiery industry. It was a sad demise but most precious of all to me was my first Top of the Pops - even if it was in that suit. I still get ribbed about Gimme Dat Banana. It was even a question in a pub pop quiz once and to begin with I thought it was a wind up. Someone told the question master who I was and much to my embarrassment he announced it to the whole pub. I imagined that I would be the only one who got the question right - but another sad git knew the answer. Should get out more!

We were asked to supply brass on the Sinatras second offering for Dining Out and had a rough demo tape to work the parts to. The secret with brass is not to over embellish. In a musical sense it is the icing on the cake, so it is important to use it as an access tool, to lift, bolster and augment the overall sound of the track. Our experience in the funk field stood us in good stead, we were used to stripping songs down to component parts and that gave us a good appreciation of song structures. Some funk numbers were complex and had time signatures that were difficult to grasp but I was always more than happy to play one note on a track if that was all that was required. It's not what you play, but what you leave out that makes the difference.

The single, Seeing Comes Before Words, was played many times on John Peel's Radio One show. It was a real buzz to hear it.

Chapter Sixteen

THE INDEPENDENT LABEL

Independent record labels were incredibly hip then. A backlash against establishment ideals transmitted itself to an attitude towards major labels and the huge conglomerates that controlled them. Small indie labels mushroomed and flourished on the back of the punk movement, cocking a snoop at the EMI's of this world in a David and Goliath way. Their popularity forced the major labels to sit up and take notice and they took the big guys on at their own game and gave them a good run for their money.

Eventually many of these labels were swallowed up by the big boys, or climbed into bed with them. David Henderson's Dining Out label was a shining example of what an indie label was all about. His first releases were basic - with photocopied sleeves and primitive typesetting that gave them a home made feel. It was completely at odds with the typical output of major record companies with their flash, expensive packaging and mega bucks promotion.

Even so most relied heavily on the major organisations for distribution, using their considerable muscle to get product into shops. Many small labels signed licensing deals that allowed them their own name identity. Good examples of this arrangement were Stiff Records and 2-Tone - both very successful in the late 70s and early 80s. By releasing material in this way, small labels kept their alternative appeal to the record buying public and at the same time utilised the awesome financial and promotional power of their wealthy bed partners.

I bought one of Dave Henderson's early Dining Out releases; a track by the Disco Zombies called 'Drums over London.' It was as basic as you could get, and it reeked of a low budget project, but there was something challenging and dangerous about it. Being signed to one of these labels carried a lot of kudos. One real advantage was the control of the output and packaging. Recording for a major often meant loss of control and a much more impersonal development, as I was to find out later for myself. Independent successes forced the Sony's of this world to buck up their ideas and take more note of the ground swell of public opinion.

Many small labels were the targets of take-overs and successful indie bands were poached. Some resisted: Scritti Politti and the Smiths, both on Rough Trade records were a good example, although both were eventually lured away to major record labels. Small labels became a sort of breeding ground; many bands first came to prominence only to be snapped up later by the big fish.

The John Peel show on Radio One was an incredible ally to the independent label network, often showcasing acts and material that had no chance of making daytime Radio One play lists. His show went out at night, so he wasn't subjected by the constraints imposed on daytime programming schedules. Peel championed many up and coming bands that made the transition from indie to major - bands including; UB40 - Echo and the Bunnymen - Orange Juice and Aztec Camera. He took chances while the daytime shows peddled mainstream chart material.

Chapter Seventeen

SWINGING LAURELS ARE GO!

The late 70s heralded an explosion of fanzines and it was no coincidence that the ascendancy ran in tandem with the rising popularity of the independent record label. Fanzines acted as a mouthpiece for the indie record scene and their popularity bore all the hallmarks of that brash and proud energy. Basic packaging and a garage feel was what kids identified with - promoting an anti-establishment stance. Fanzines reviewed bands that struggled to gain national exposure from the likes of NME or Melody Maker. They promoted a healthy underground, alternative view of the music industry. Exposure in a local fanzine was often the only publicity that a band starting out could get, and many contributors worked on them for love.

The Newmatics were still gigging and I made the odd appearance with them when I could afford the time. At one such gig at the Fosse way in Leicester, Gaz and I propped up the bar and chatted afterwards. Gaz was getting increasingly disillusioned that the elusive recording deal never looked like materialising. We talked about breaking away and starting up an experimental project on the side.

Well aware of our limitations, the idea seemed challenging and exciting. A wave of experimental synthesiser based acts were breaking through into the mainstream of music at the time. David Bowie's, Low album was an inspiration and I had been really influenced by the work of Brian Eno. I was fascinated by his collaboration with Robert Fripp on the instrumental album, No Pussyfooting. A couple of years before. I knew I was onto something - playing the album at home elicited the, 'What's this bleeding row?' response from dad, a real barometer that I was doing something right!

We arranged a series of impromptu sessions to see what we could develop. We both played saxophones and Gaz sang. We used a baby mono Roland synthesiser and an Elgam drum machine which was full of tacky bossa nova beats and had a mind of its own. The first results were primitive but there was a germ of something good. I had the keys to the place where I worked and when it was deserted at night we practised in the warehouse. It was spooky to say the least.

We were pleased with the fruits of our early labours. Saxophones in stark juxtaposition with the dinky synthesiser sound, held together by that corny drum machine - seemed to work. At the time no one else was using that blend of instrumentation. Gary Numan and Human League were prominent in the charts of the time.

I bought an Akai reel to reel two-track tape recorder and some of the resulting recordings were bizarre but we started to develop interesting ideas. We practised where ever we could - one time even making use of Dave Van's flat and the obligatory pub function rooms.

We knew that we were onto something - it felt right. Gaz came up with a working name for our 'band' - 'the Swinging Laurels.' He is a talented photographer and it was on one of his forays into the great outdoors, searching for art, that he got the inspiration for the name. While taking photographs in a cemetery (as you do) he noticed a laurel bush swinging in the wind, and the name was conceived. Some years later I discovered that the word laurel means penis in some parts of the Far East! We were about to embark on a career that we hoped would bring unlimited world-wide fame and fortune - oblivious to the fact that in some parts of the world we'd be known as 'the Swinging Pricks!' I can just see the posters, 'Tonight... the Swinging One Eyed Trouser Snakes!' or "Latest album by the - the Swinging Love Rockets!'

When the time was right to commit fledgling ideas to tape, we booked studio time at Woodbine recording studio. I felt that John Rivers was the perfect foil - I was so convinced that he had everything we could want to convert our sketchy ideas into real songs, and I was right. We booked a Sunday session to record four tracks - a tall order given the state of readiness our songs were in. It was a wonderful day. John Rivers was the perfect catalyst for our unconventional ideas and he pitched in great ideas. We slowed things down, speeded things up and the results sounded like nothing I had ever heard before. We were like kids in a sweet factory, and at the end of the day we were buzzing. We were right about Woodbine.

A lot of producers would have scoffed at our wacky, off-the-wall ideas but John was open to them. The tracks we recorded that day were: Are Go - Disco Laurels - Murder Mile and Death Laurels. Afterwards we hadn't a clue what to do with the tape; it was so off the wall we couldn't imagine anyone would be interested in it. It was great to have written and recorded something that was entirely original. Gaz and I formed the songs from nothing although a lot of the initial inspiration for those early efforts came from Gaz tinkering on his synthesiser. With Big Stuff and Black Gorilla, I realised that the only real way forward in the business was with original material, and now we were in a position to produce it. At last it felt like we had achieved something. I wasn't in the least bit bothered that it wasn't mainstream.

That first Laurels recording session taught me a lesson. Since then I have preferred to go into a recording studio with a basic framework that leaves room for experimentation and spontaneity. Pre-conceived ideas of what the finished track should sound like often stunt creativity once ideas have been bounced around in the studio. Now we had something tangible - a professional recording to promote. Gaz put together a compilation cassette - Crying Out Loud. It featured several Leicester bands and provided a useful vehicle for our newly recorded material. It was advertised in Sounds and made available by mail order. Bolstered by the confidence in our project, he approached record companies and cassette copies were sent to independent labels.

Cherry Red Records and Rough Trade Records turned us down saying that they couldn't understand what it was all about - taking into account some of the weird stuff that they released gives you a measure of how radically different our material was. We started to suspect that we might be onto something but landing a deal by sending out unsolicited material was wishful thinking - the odds are lotto big.

Most record companies receive thousands of demos from young, naive hopefuls who haven't got a chance of being signed. Later when we were signed to Warner Brothers Records, I saw boxes filled to the brim with cassettes sent by aspiring rock stars. You may think they listen to every one - they don't. The only certain way to get your material heard is to play it to an A&R man personally. Having said that, there are rare exceptions where a speculative postal approach has paid off. I was told by the head of A&R at Elektra Records that they'd signed Simply Red purely on the evidence of a rough cassette recording of a rehearsal. On hearing Mick Hucknall's voice they immediately descended on Manchester with chequebook in hand.

Against all the odds a positive response came from Lincoln based independent label Dead Good Records. They seemed intrigued and were talking of a deal, so we hastily set up a meeting. It came like a bolt from the blue, when Gaz targeted labels he selected Dead Good only because he liked the name! Dead Good operated out of a small office in Lincoln and had released a number of singles with varying degrees of success. Bands also on their roster included: the Cigarettes - the Whizz Kids and Sincere Americans. We travelled to Lincoln to meet the people behind the operation in a cosy pub called the Wig and Mitre which was a stones throw from the awesome Cathedral.

The two young guys behind the set up were both in their early twenties. Martin Patton and Steve Taylor were real music fans and we discussed every thing except a deal at first. Martin was an ex Uppingham public schoolboy; not you might think the obvious candidate for an aspiring record company mogul. Steve played bass with the Cigarettes and had travelled the country working with the merchandising crew on Buzzcocks tours - he knew what life on the road was all about.

When we finally talked about a deal, it was as informal as you could get. They wanted us to release a 10 inch six track EP. There were no contracts, just a verbal agreement. This didn't worry us - an informal deal with a small independent was an ideal career move for us at that point because our game plan was to release one or two singles and hope to catch the eye of one of the majors.

Driving back from Lincoln we were like giggling school kids - we had landed our first record deal. We got on well with our new managers and felt their youthful enthusiasm would take us places. They shared an infectious love of music and were fans in the way that we were fans. Our arrangement was not what I imagined a record deal would be; some artistes sign away their souls for fifteen minutes of fame. The great advantage was the control we'd have over output and we were not tied down legally if we wanted to move on.

We wrote new material and returned to Woodbine to record three more tracks, taking Newmatics sticks man, Nick Murphy with us. Peace of mind - Swing the Cat and Mourning Laurels were the tracks recorded. Nick was not only a stunning drummer; he was a more than useful keyboard player. Peace of mind was a song strongly influenced by Nick while Swing the Cat was born of Birtles / Barrow doodlings and boasted a rambling synth bass line, punctuated by insistent brass licks.

Swing the Cat was notable for Gaz's lyrics, which recounted a plaintive plea from a sado-masochist for more lashes from the cat o'nine tails across his red raw back. Not a subject often covered in pop music, sadly!

A two-day session at Woodbine studios necessitated an overnight stay so we booked into the Crown Hotel close to a huge wrought iron railway bridge that straddled the main road in the town centre. The hotel was peopled by a weird combination of misfits and we looked for hidden cameras for a time believing we were unwitting extras on a film set. It was good to see John Rivers again; he helped us to shape our basic formats into recognisable song structures. The two principle tracks were definitely the best thing we'd recorded to date. Peace of Mind featured an exciting, extensive timbale break by Nick which only underlined his talent. The session exceeded all our expectations and Dead Good loved the results.

As events moved forward we were oblivious to the movements Dead Good were making behind the scenes with an eccentric entrepreneur called Stevo. The new romantic movement was still in it's infancy and they had started to manage a synthesiser based duo called Soft Cell and a singer/songwriter, Matt Johnson aka The The. They named their alliance Some Bizarre. Stevo was a charismatic character known for his unpredictable behaviour but he had gauged the climate astutely and had major recording companies eyeing his projects with interest.

Once Stevo sat in the plush offices of a world major record company and calmly played with a yo-yo while he was negotiating a mega deal. New romanticism was being touted as the next big thing in music; people like Steve Strange, Boy George and young bands like Spandau Ballet and Duran Duran were starting to create a buzz. In the same way that record companies capitalised on punk, they were anxious not to miss out on the new romantic movement.

Some Bizarre managed to get a compilation album deal with Phonogram to showcase new bands in this new genre, it featured, Depeche Mode, Soft Cell and Naked Lunch. It became difficult to see where this left the Swinging Laurels in the great scheme of things.

Our first press splash appeared in a free trade paper in Leicester called the Trader. It had a column devoted to music, which was imaginatively called the Insider and described itself as 'A regular spot with today's music lovers in mind.' The house photographer took us out in search of a suitable location to shoot pictures to accompany the feature. He decided that a derelict building site was the ideal back drop to photograph a pop band - he was wildly wide of the mark as it turned out. When the feature appeared in print we were show cased perching on what appeared to be a large pile of bricks, gazing wistfully at nothing in particular. All very Ultravox. 'Ohhhh Vienna' The headline read 'Laurels Branch Out' We also made our first appearance in the Leicester Mercury who were altogether much kinder but insisted on photographing us with our saxophones, a tried and trusted local paper old chestnut. Photographers absolutely adore shooting saxophones at any given opportunity.

On the record front the unthinkable happened and it nearly knocked the stuffing out of us. Dead Good decided to shelve the Swinging Laurels project because the Some Bizarre enterprise had taken on a life of it's own, though they assured us that they would secure us an alternative deal. The cruellest thing of all was that our EP had been pressed - we'd even taken delivery of the white label test copies. We took one to the hip Etchies club in Leicester - the DJ played it loud and it sounded huge. A white label is a test pressing with, as the name suggests, a plain white label. They are pressed prior to a major production run so that discrepancies with sound quality can be identified before thousands of units are pressed. These can be very collectable because they are only pressed in limited editions. Some white labels have fetched thousands at auctions and one lucky chap found an early Beatles white label at a car boot sale and collected a small fortune when he sold it.

To have the plug pulled so close to the point of release was so disappointing. This was, as we were to learn over the coming years, was what the music business is all about, 10% exhilaration and joy and 90% utter gut wrenching disappointment. Dead Good records ceased to be as a label identity while Some Bizarre went from strength to strength. The Some Bizarre album made a showing in the album chart and Soft Cell, The The, and B movie, all signed to major concerns. We still felt that being associated with Martin and Steve might yet pave the way for something positive if only we could bide our time. Surely it couldn't do us any harm being associated with these guys, now they were making a name for themselves. Sometimes it is very difficult to see ahead long term when you are so subjectively involved.

In the meantime the Newmatics brought in a guy called Henry on vocals - Nick Murphy assumed the mantle of leading light with the assistance of guitarist Rich Barton. Henry was a totally different style of vocalist to Gaz - his style was more laid back and lent itself to the subtle reggae tracks that they were writing. Nick called me to see if I would be interested in recording brass on a single for Map Records. The track was called But My Love penned by Nick himself. Dean and I agreed to travel to London to do our bit. The backing track was already recorded so all we had to do was punctuate the track with minimalist brass lines. The recording had an incredibly infectious, gentle, reggae groove and featured fine guitar work by Rich Barton. The brass parts were simplistic but added to the overall feel of the mix and we had the feeling that with a bit of luck it was commercial enough to do well. The subsequent single was play-listed by a number of independent radio stations but unfortunately didn't generate enough sales to trouble the chart statisticians.

The Swinging Laurels were still in a state of limbo. Some Bizarre saw their protégés Soft Cell dent the lower echelons of the chart with their first major record release, and were sitting back, watching their meteoric rise. The follow up was called Tainted Love - a Northern Soul dance classic, previously recorded by Gloria Jones. Soft Cell's synthesiser based version with Mark Almond on vocals was a massive hit and reached No.1. I saw Martin in the studio audience of Top of the Pops, looking completely gormless, when they screened it on TV. It was frustrating that our progress had been stunted while they were in the ascendancy.

Martin and Steve still maintained their support and made a lot of very useful contacts. One Friday I took a call at work from an excited Martin saying that he'd got us a recording deal with Decca Records. Hearing the news in my mundane office setting rendered me speechless. An advance of £40,000 was mentioned - they loved Peace of Mind and wanted to meet us. When Gaz called in for his daily 'Heard ought,' news up date, I told him the news and there was whooping and hollering down the phone line!

Decca Records were one of the major players. They had taken a raw young band called the Rolling Stones and transformed them into world-beaters in the 1960s, now they were interested in the Swinging Laurels - a band that had yet to play in front of a live audience! We could hardly believe it. I arranged to take the following Monday off work so that we could travel to London to see A&R head Tracy Bennett.

On meeting Tracy - a man by the way - in his gold disc bedecked office we soon realised that the offer was real but there was an inevitable drawback. He wanted us to re-record Peace of Mind, with Richard Strange producing. This was the major problem; we had recorded the track in such a spontaneous fashion, that it would have proved virtually impossible to recreate. Nick's fantastic timbale solo was a one off and totally unique. We came away to think about it. To me, Tracy had come across as big I am and seemed really pretentious. It was as if he was doing us a big favour talking to us; the deal was on his terms, or no deal. We decided to let the deal go. Martin and Steve assured us that there would be more offers. I came away thinking, 'Never trust a man who has a girl's name!'

Chapter Eighteen

THE A & R MAN

A&R stands for artist and repertoire. It is the job of an A&R man to find new acts for his record company just like a football scout trawls for new players. They really ought to be called 'the lesser spotted A&R man' because they are rarely where they say they are going to be - except if there is something in it for them. Then they hunt in packs.

Most A&R people tend to be frighteningly young, which can be just a little unnerving. Record companies assume that the youth have got their ear to ground and are open to new fads and movements. But the thought of trusting your future career to a ten-year old is a bit disconcerting. In order to get signed you have to come to their attention in some way. You can use the tried and trusted route - record a demo - get a record company to listen to it and if there is further interest- try to cajole them to come and see you perform live. Being the record company ears and eyes, they talent spot for the label.

Herein lays the problem. Most A&R people are in London, as are most record companies, and it is virtually impossible to get a live gig in London, without a record deal. Promoters generally only want signed bands. So it is a catch 22 situation. When you do secure your gig in the capital, you are still at the mercy of the A & R man. It is a lottery if they show up or not. Many times in my playing career I've played London with cast iron guarantees from A&R people that they would attend, only to find after the show that they hadn't bothered and it had been all for nothing. Setting up a gig takes an awful lot of preparation and effort, sometimes weeks and to be snubbed in this way is a very galling experience.

The position of A&R man is a very attractive one for a young person in the bright lights of London; they are feted, fawned over and generally treated like royalty. To get one of these people to travel out of the Capital is another virtual impossibility. An awful lot of talent in the provinces is overlooked because of this policy. Bucking this trend were independent labels such as Kitchenware (Newcastle) Post Card (Glasgow) and 2-Tone (Coventry) who based their operations in their own back yard, so they didn't have to rely on the London music machine. Signing a band to a major long-term recording contract can mean an investment of hundreds of thousands of pounds. So it is understandable that there is pressure to make the right decisions. But no A&R department wants to turn the next Beatles away, as some poor sod famously did in the early 60s.

Chapter Nineteen

DECADENT BERLIN

Berlin was a city that had always intrigued me. Apart from the unique political circumstances that had moulded the place, there was a pervading atmosphere of decadence. The Berlin wall, a tacky concrete graffiti ridden monstrosity, split two communities; on one side depressing dull austerity, on the other bright lights and anything goes hedonism. Gaz and I had friends who lived and worked in Berlin for the civilian side of the armed forces; Gaz had already spent time there and came back with lurid tales about the lifestyle. We spent a week there to distribute compilation tapes featuring a number of Leicester bands. The idea was to generate interest from Berlin promoters and record labels and the compilation featured five Leicester outfits, all of which had already generated interest from UK record companies: Swinging Laurels - Il ya Volkswagen - New Age - Shapiros and the Sinatras.

Rob Grant, then playing guitar for the Sinatras, was also along for the ride. We crashed down in the flat of Leicester ex-pat, Mick Mooney. Also living in Berlin were other friends from home, Joe Keaveney and Tony James. These guys had become acclimatised to life in this fascinating metropolis, and had a good grasp of the German language. Before the wall came down in 1989, flying into Berlin was a spooky experience. All air traffic, including commercial flights had to fly at very low altitude over East Germany to be monitored by the military. The cold war was still very much a fact of life. Low trajectory had a very painful effect on the ears - the East at night was pitch black and as the Berlin sprawl came into view, you saw an island of bright neon, beacon like in a sea of darkness.

The nightlife was an eye-opener. It was a twenty four hour life style. We staggered out of a place called Café Central at 7am as our music pumped out of the sound system. Another night in the Café Gaz spotted Jayne County -

formerly Wayne County of the band the Electric Chairs before her sex change. He sauntered over to her - she was sitting with a famous French transvestite. After their conversation, she pleaded poverty and borrowed money for a taxi fare home and handed over a hastily scribbled IOU. He never did get his money back. Women?

Mick Mooney got us tickets to see the Jam at the Metropole. We also saw punk band UK Subs in a real dive on a rainy night across town. We spoke to front man Charlie Harper who was wandering around the auditorium with a vicious dog straining on a leash. He was very helpful but some of those punks looked sinister and intimidating.

We had an unforgettable day in the East, through Checkpoint Charlie. East Berlin was full of incredible buildings, huge edifices that still bore pockmarks from the shelling in World War Two. Cars were tinny East German production Trabants that rattled around in stark contrast to the flash diplomatic Mercedes that purred around West Berlin. Only a limited amount of money was allowed to be taken over the border and it had to be spent before you returned - the exchange rate was four or five to one. There was such a disparity in exchange rates, that it was difficult to offload it all. We were approached by East Berliners seeking Western currency or Levi jeans.

We were so obviously from the West and seeing us eat at a top restaurant must have really stuck in the craw of the locals. Department stores were pathetically spartan - no special offers - no choice. If you wanted to buy a watch there was one model - one style - advertising was non existent. It was the same for all commodities. Russian conscript soldiers, armed to the teeth, were everywhere. A stark reminder of the plight of poor Berliners came with a forest of little white crosses planted in the soil, close to no mans land at the Reichstag. Each cross signalled a lost life of some wretched Berliner, cut down by border guard machine gun fire in a pathetic attempt to get across the wall. In the East we travelled on the S bahn which is the Berlin equivalent of the London underground network. As Gaz took photographs a woman on the platform became very animated and screeched at us in unintelligible German. A machine gun wielding soldier called us off the train and unceremoniously ripped the film out of his camera!

Seedy Berlin was another side of life that had to be sampled. Mick Mooney took us to a bath show at the unearthly hour of 3am. I spent the majority of my time there staring at the floor in a vain attempt to avoid eye contact. It was a tiny place and the drinks were an extortionate price. Girls cavorted in a state of near nakedness. At a predetermined point the floor peeled back to reveal a frothing bubble bath. The athleticism of those females should be an inspiration to us all - one performed an amazing stunt with a florescent Coke bottle that took some believing. When the offer came for a member of the audience to join the girls in the bath, I stared even more fixedly at my shoes, relieved that a squaddie, sitting next to me, made the bath in record time. He left behind a pile of clothes.

Rob was befriended by an Eastern bloc working girl called Dina. Her job was to encourage punters to part with money for drinks or a bit of the other in cubicles situated behind the stage area. She sat on Rob's knee, practising her English. He got on with her so well that he was even offered a free sample of the merchandise. Rob, being a gentleman, declined. She taught him some pigeon German too, for days afterwards Rob would gleefully say,

'Das isht fantastishun' - it sounded authentic enough at the time!

I came away from Berlin with a determined promise to myself that I would play there one day. I loved it. The trip didn't yield a great deal in furthering our musical aspirations but hearing a Laurels track blast out from a trendy Berlin bar was very satisfying.

Back in Leicester the Swinging Laurels carried on. We were using a rehearsal facility, which was run by two guys, Tom Norden and Joe King. It was a basic space in the basement of a decrepit old hosiery factory near the city centre and it boasted two rehearsal rooms and an eight-track recording set up.

Both guys had been around a fair bit. Joe had been involved with several local bands and ran a recording studio called Drumbeat which the Newmatics had frequented. Tom had a lot of contacts in the business - he had played for the Edgar Broughton Band, who had a couple of hits in the early '70s and Doll by Doll a band fronted by Jackie Leven. Our practise sessions were pretty shambolic - we weren't prolific writers but material slowly began to emerge.

Martin and Steve again got another company interested - Dindisc/Dinsong and once more we went to the smoke to gaze at even more gold discs on the walls of yet another plush office. Dindisc were pretty happening, they had Orchestral Manoeuvres in the Dark on the record label and were involved with Heaven 17. Both bands were at the very vanguard of the new wave of synthesiser music. In the Dindisc office, we produced a reel to reel 2-track recording of a new song we'd written called Lonely Boy. It sounded basic, but we hoped that the potential of the song would be appreciated. They liked it, but came out with the classic line straight from the A&R manual, designed to piss young hopefuls off,

'It's great, but I really would like to hear some more material'

We didn't have any more material. To add insult to injury, they played the forthcoming single by Heaven 17, (We don't need this) Fascist groove thang. It sounded loud, brash and awesome - It made our little reel to reel offering sound mighty tame in comparison.

Martin informed us that there was a chance of a publishing deal from Albion Music based in Oxford Street, London. We kept our fingers crossed and waited for details. An affable Welshman called Dai Davies ran Albion. Dai had managed the Stranglers and had a number of name bands signed to publishing or recording deals. On the publishing side they had Joe Jackson, a world name at the time and on the record label was Hazel O'Connor, who apart from notching up the hits, had just starred in the film Breaking Glass. Also signed to the Albion records were The Members, and punk outfit 999.

We had no idea how interested Albion were and it took a phone call to bring it home to us. I took a call from Dai at work. He asked what we were doing about the proposed deal. I said, 'We've had some interest from Dinsong,' Dai said in an impatient tone, 'Well there is a deal on the table from Albion too, and if you don't make your minds up, "THE DEAL IS OFF" this focused us and we determined to visit Albion as soon as possible to discuss terms.

Chapter Twenty

TEAM 23

We decided to go for the Albion deal. They were even talking about releasing a single on their recording arm to get us on our feet. A meeting with Dai coincided with another session opportunity that enabled us to kill two birds with one stone. The manager of a band called Team 23 from Coventry contacted me. They were desperate to find a brass section to help them out on a couple of prestige gigs. Their own brass men had left them in the lurch so we enlisted the help of my old sidekick Dean on trumpet.

Team 23 were signed to Race Records, an independent label run by Brad, the Specials drummer. The first gig was at Dingwalls in London, where I had been through that bizarre audition for Response Records with Black Gorilla, three years previously. Dean was up for it but we were gluttons for punishment because it meant learning twenty songs in two weeks. I had the distinct feeling that I'd been down that road before. Team 23 played a brand of foot stomping soul music - the sort later made famous by the likes of the Blues Brothers and The Commitments. All were white guys with greased back hair and who dressed in American football jackets, while belting out a set that didn't come up for breath.

We attended a series of rehearsals in Coventry, which is about twenty miles from Leicester. Guitarist Jim came over to collect us - travelling in Jim's car more than eclipsed anything that the 'white knuckle' rides at Alton Towers had to offer! The vehicle had serious steering problems. There was so much slack on the steering wheel that the car veered erratically from side to side as he fought manfully to control it, swinging the wheel wildly one way then the other. He seemed completely unaffected by the experience. I closed my eyes a lot. When we arrived at the rehearsal room my nerves had shot it and I needed time to calm down. A change of underwear please! We worked very hard to memorise our parts though some numbers were familiar to us. Just as we started to get t grips with the material, Gaz's wisdom tooth erupted and he had it extracted days before the gig. This left him swollen and hamster like and he had no chance of playing until the swelling eased.

When the Dingwalls gig came around it was the perfect opportunity to meet Dai. Gaz came down for the meeting and when we met Dai in a pub close to the venue we were struck by his sincerity; he was quietly spoken, not like other loud, brash record company types. We fleshed out the basis for a deal and accepted an offer to release Peace of Mind, the track we had recorded a year before for Dead Good Records. It looked as if our perseverance had finally paid off.

The gig at Dingwalls went well. We were ponced up in American football jackets, to fit in with the band stage image. Being back at Dingwalls was special too, more than once my memory slipped back to that bizarre Black Gorilla audition. We came away from the metropolis happy in the knowledge that things had been resolved on the Swinging Laurels front.

Our next Team 23 live outing was our last. Weymouth was our destination and we travelled down in a real car and thankfully not in Jim's trick circus car! It was a day in my life that I'll never forget. They say that everyone remembers where they when they heard the news of the President Kennedy's assassination in the 1963. A news flash on the car radio announced the killing of John Lennon in New York. The news generated a profound sadness. Lennon was a massive early influence to me, someone that as a kid I stove to emulate. The feeling was of total disbelief as we travelled down to the south coast for the concert. I remember very little of that show - generally my memory is pretty sharp; I can remember very small details surrounding the many gigs I have played down the years, even down to club and dressing room layouts. This day was so soured by the tragic news that we performed like automatons - such was the black cloud that enveloped us.

It seemed crazy to have put ourselves though so much sheer hard work for only two live outings with Team 23, but it was worth it. We enjoyed the experience and it had been a nice little diversion. After our involvement with the band they carried on for a time, but eventually they went their own separate ways.

Out of the ashes of Team 23 evolved another Coventry band called King, fronted by ex Reluctant Stereotypes vocalist Paul King. 'Stunt driver' Jim and drummer Stompy were both involved the new outfit which was later to enjoy success. They scored a No.2 hit in 1985 with Love and Pride on CBS records. King supported the Swinging Laurels at Birmingham University in 1983 and we had a good chat with Jim and Stompy backstage. It goes to illustrate just how quickly things can happen for you in the pop world when the luck is with you. King had five hit records in all which probably helped Jim to buy a car that was capable of steering a straight line! Vocalist Paul King went into television after the break up of the band, as a presenter for music channel MTV.

Chapter Twenty One

PUBLISHING - ALBION WE LOVE YOU

The deal on the table from Albion was both a publishing and recording arrangement - the bigger emphasis being on publishing. By way of a leg up, they offered to release Peace of mind / Swing the cat via the recording arm of their operation. It was a hip label which had already enjoyed chart action with Hazel O'Connor and punk band 999. Our immediate concern was releasing Gaz from a straight jacket of a management deal. Our solicitors, Berger Oliver warned us that the solution might not be a quick one - not the sort of news we needed. There was no way that the Albion deal could be signed until he was released from his five-year deal, which still had three years to run. We had to handle the situation with kid gloves, if his old management team suspected that he was about to sign a lucrative publishing deal, they would want a piece of the action. The last thing we wanted was a long and protracted legal battle. After seeing several deals flash before our eyes, only to be cruelly snatched away at the last moment, we were desperate not to let this one slip away.

This highlights one of the most frustrating aspects of the music business. If it was all just about making music then fine, but when you are saddled with all the legal and contractual technicalities, it gets as far removed from music as you could get. No deal can be sealed without legal formalities of course, but to the uninitiated it can seem bewildering. Once the explosive mix of management deals, recording deals, publishing deals and solicitors are added to the equation, it is enough to knock the creative stuffing out of any young aspiring musician.

Not many people understand what a publisher does. I have to hold my hand up and admit that this included me until I got directly involved. The publisher can be an invaluable asset at the outset of a career in music. Basically a publisher takes original songs and promotes them in any reasonable way possible for the benefit of the writer. This can take many forms, including, getting other artists to cover your songs, film and television sound tracks and advertisement jingles. Also in the publisher can be an ally in securing a long-term recording deal by paying for demos and publicity.

You sign songs over to them for an agreed split percentage cut which in our case was 60/40 in our favour. Each time one of your songs is broadcast, say on Radio One, a fee is paid to the songwriters. The publisher collects this revenue and pays a royalty every six months, taking their cut and giving the balance to the composers. The bigger percentage cut you are able to negotiate the more royalties you are paid. Our 60/40 deal was a very good one for an unsigned band with no track record and who had yet to play live.

A fee is paid for the broadcast of material on radio, film, and television; there are even fees due for jukebox plays. Nightclubs and restaurants pay a licence fee to the Performing Rights Society and those fees are split down and distributed to Society members. In the '80s the fee for a Radio One play was about £80, so you can imagine that a worldwide hit record can generate huge amounts from radio airplay alone. The potential payouts are enormous. It is possible to earn significantly more from publishing royalties than from record sales, which are based on units sold. Visualise the royalties that are paid for Lennon/McCartney compositions each year from the radio alone on a worldwide scale?

Some songwriters compose material to order. It can be an extremely lucrative exercise if your publisher can get someone like Madonna to cover one of your compositions. Other songwriters make a very good living writing jingles for radio and television - they are paid a fee each time their work is broadcast. Tony Hatch has a nice regular earner for writing the theme for soap opera Neighbours, which is shown worldwide. Getting a song played on Baywatch has one of the biggest paybacks there is; the show is one of the most viewed television programmes around the world.

Big names have been known to re-negotiate their royalty percentage after reaching star status. High profile cases have been fought and won in the courts when it has been ruled that the publisher was raking a disproportionate amount. It is rumoured that the Police were initially only on a 50/50 cut with their publisher, even after having several massive worldwide hits. It has become the in thing now for big star song writers to form their own publishing companies and collect their own royalties - Gary Numan did this very successfully. David Bowie sold his back catalogue for a huge fee to a financial institution. The songs of major stars generate huge royalty payments and will still do so years into the future, because of this they can be a very attractive investment proposition.

While all the legal wrangling was going on around us we carried on making plans and rehearsing as best we could. It was during this period that Gaz became a style victim. After seeing a photograph of Jerry Dammers of the Specials gracing the front page of the NME sporting a splendid goatee beard, he cultivated one of his very own. When it first sprouted it was a rare old thicket, reminiscent of a French girl's armpit. Not many people had a goatee then so it became a real curiosity and in time we all warmed to the new look. As time went on the beard became synonymous with the Swinging Laurels 'image' and the beard evolved from Latin girl's armpit to a little slimmed down, Brazilian landing strip, sporty number.

Once it even saved him from an extremely tricky situation. The police phoned me at work to ask if I knew someone called Gary Birtles and could I describe him because they thought they had him locked up in the cells at Charles Street police station in Leicester. It was a simple matter - six feet plus with a goatee beard. There can't have been many people matching that description mincing around old Leicester town, at the time! This satisfied Mr.Plod, the chap they were holding was short, scruffy and comatose. The stiff had broken into a Leicester night-club called Rapunzles and after rifling the tills he decided to imbibe in a selection of spirits from the chemistry set. Police found him rat-arsed and in a heap behind the bar with the burglar alarm blaring. The only form of identification on this reprobate was a membership application card that I'd filled in, when proposing Gaz as a new member.

My beloved saxophone almost tooted it's last after a nasty incident that left me with only the clothes that I was standing up in. I had travelled down to Brighton for a few days. I had always felt an affinity with Brighton since my Black Gorilla days; the place captivated me. When I got back in Leicester I caught a taxi from the railway station to my flat on Beaconsfield Road. As the cab rounded the corner to my horror I saw that my windows were boarded up.

I couldn't believe my eyes; the whole flat was sealed off. While I was away I had been burgled. The jester had not been content to steal my worldly shackles; he also saw fit to torch the place. A neighbour took me in, proffering a large whisky. It was absolutely heartbreaking; my album collection had melted in the intensity of the heat. I lost virtually all of my clothes, furniture, photographs and it was as if my whole identity had been erased. The only saving grace was that my saxophone was still where I had left it - the case was scorched, but the instrument was unscathed. The character that violated my flat left the most valuable material thing I owned, which was sitting there in full view. He was subsequently arrested and sentenced to a nine-year stretch. Police grilled me at first suspecting that I had set the whole thing up as an insurance scam. They also questioned my girlfriend Kim asking embarrassing questions about various girls seen coming and going from my flat. Neighbours had given the police a complete dossier on my movements, which I found really sinister. The whole unsavoury episode made the front page of the Leicester Mercury. I can think of better ways of making publicity!

Back in the real world, Gaz's management contract resolved itself quicker than any of us had dared to imagine. We signed to Albion and were advanced £700 for the first option on the contract, all of which went to pay solicitors fees, for extricating Gaz from his old contract. We signed our deal in an office with gold discs on the walls. In the hustle and bustle of that busy office in Oxford Street, London, as we signed, Nicky Tesco of the Members came into the room; he stuck his thumb up and grinned broadly.

We'd finally done it. It was patently obvious that with a single soon to be released, the pressure would be on us to perform live. Fast on the heels of our signing our first photographic session was arranged. We were despatched to an address in London where we were ushered into a changing area. It became apparent that the studio was used for taking photographs of young girls without vests on - colour transparencies were everywhere featuring girls in soft porn type poses. There was no way I was taking my vest off - I can tell you! The photographer set about making us look like real pop tarts; posing for all we were worth. We had been asked to bring our saxophones along. Photographers love this sexy inanimate object, but have you ever tried to get a saxophone to pout?

They'd give anything for a shot of a spangle of light issuing from your bell end! He had us jumping in the air with our saxophones around our necks and adopting the most ridiculous poses imaginable. Most of the photographic studios I have used seemed to be situated in disused warehouses. Stark white rooms with huge plain paper back drops that draped down from ceiling level. Strong lights change the mood with coloured gels, used to illuminate the set, creating the required atmosphere. Different hues both in backdrop and lighting create a different ambience and a clever photographer can change the overall feel of a scene by slight manipulation of these effects. We leapt about until something in me desperately wished that I was a vest less female. The resulting prints actually turned out well. The Swinging Laurels name and the Albion records logo were printed in the bottom corner and, seeing that Albion records moniker felt pretty damned good. The leaping shots were much favoured by the press though I still cringe looking at them now.

With the single release imminent the drive to involve other musicians became imperative. Playing live was a must and we couldn't do it with just two of us. We set out an agenda - at the very least we needed a keyboard player and a bass player. We elected to stay with the drum machine because its tacky vibe had become an integral part of our sound scape. We weren't anti-drums - in fact Nick Murphy played a conventional kit on Peace of Mind and Swing the Cat - playing in conjunction with the machine to good effect. But it has to be said - drummers are loud, and like to bang things, which is reason enough!

Chapter Twenty Two

MARK & DEAN - COME ON DOWN

Getting to this stage at all, with all our trials and tribulations meant that whoever we did enlist had to be just right - they had to be one of us. Whoever did fill those vacancies would be stepping into a cosy situation - we'd already done the hard part by securing a publishing and recording deal. We were tempted to poach someone from another band; after all we did have a bit of a carrot to dangle. Other bands creating a buzz in Leicester through this period included, Future Toys - New Age - the Sinatras - Electraplexx - Farmlife - Cloud 9 and Mandella. All were destined to release their own material - all had as much chance of making it as anyone else.

We pinned a card on the notice board in the Carlsboro music shop in town, and a reply soon came so we set up a rehearsal at Joe King's Soundlab studio. As soon as we saw keyboard player Mark O'Hara we knew that he was a Laurel. Mark, or 'torn pocket gob' as Gaz was later to affectionately call him, turned up for the rehearsal sporting a painfully loud checked jacket. He had spiky black hair and an insane looking 'here comes Johnny' grin. He was like a smart Sid Vicious. Additional keyboards made a fantastic difference to our songs - Mark was our man. He had previously been with a punk outfit called the Stazers and sometime later he told me, that he had been totally stoned at that first audition. Mark agreed to join, he was an excellent player and our song writing took on a whole fresh, new dimension. We bounced off of each other creatively and our writing elevated itself to a much higher level. Even the existing material took on a new lease of life.

The Swinging Laurels were in a pretty unique position; with a single due in the shops we had never played a single note in front of a live audience. Mark began to stamp his presence on our set, fleshing it out, embellishing it and contributing some fine original ideas. All that was missing was the final piece of the jigsaw - a bass player. After some agonising, I suggested Dean Sargent, my old Sister Big Stuff and Black Gorilla partner in crime. He was first and foremost a trumpet player, but he did play keyboards. Our bass lines were not the most musically taxing; they were pretty simplistic. We got him over for a try-out and the combination worked like a dream. Dean was welcomed aboard the good ship Laurel. The bonus was that we had access to his considerable trumpet playing talent too, so in effect we were getting two musicians for the price of one.

With the influx of synthesiser and drum machine technology came a real sea change in the way music was recorded and performed. In much the same way that punk had stirred things up, this new technology caused some real resentment in the ranks of the traditionalist, bass/drums/guitar/vocals, dinosaur mentality. A lot of musicians - mainly drummers, saw these technological advances as a threat. Change in any form usually meets with resistance, but you have to accept the inevitable or end up being stuck firmly in the past. With our experimental outlook, the Swinging Laurels had no pre-conceived ideas about what was the norm and had no problem embracing new ideas. Nothing delighted us more than trying out some new effect or gizmo.

It was late August 1981 and with the unit getting tighter we aimed to play live in some capacity to coincide with the release of our record in September. Because it was unlikely that we would be able to perform a conventional live set by then; we came up with a hair-brained scheme to get us across to as many people as possible in a short time scale. We decided to perform not one, but four shows in one night! The idea was to play four numbers at each venue and hot foot it across town to the next.

Gaz and I visited likely venues to set up the scam - all were pubs in the city centre. We didn't want the venues to be too far apart because after each show, we would have to dump the equipment in the back of Mark's escort van and scoot to the next. We rehearsed hard and did a spot of illicit fly posting to announce the venture. Although we'd never played live, we were known through word of mouth and had enjoyed quite a lot of local press exposure. There were those that thought that the Swinging Laurels would never get off the ground, after all our near misses. There was a tangible buzz - people wanted to see what all the fuss was about. No other outfit on the scene sounded like us and none used the new technology alongside old brass - that is what set us apart from the pack.

When the dates were confirmed the mini tour looked like this: The White Horse, Oadby (8 pm) - the Town Arms, Leicester (9 pm) supporting The Rent (featuring superb blues front man Geoff Overon and ex-Sister Big Stuff, Dave Van - on keyboards) - the Kings Head (9.30 pm) and finally the Haunch of Venison - now the Orange Tree. (10 pm) -

We really had our work cut out; when the dreaded night arrived we were all pretty hyped up. The first gig was in a pub called the White Horse. One Mr. Gary Bond, obviously not too put off by the disastrous Black Gorilla gig at Scamps, treated us to his presence. It was generally a lively pub, but we performed in front of only a few punters though the reception was encouraging. We set off for leg two with the wind in our sails. The second gig was at the Town Arms, a pub with a function room upstairs; we supported Geoff Overon's band, the Rent, a great blues outfit. Geoff had been a stalwart of the Leicester music scene for some time and very well respected by his peers. Consequently this was probably as close as we could get to a real gig on our inaugural mission. By the end of a shattering night full of giggles, we had a contingent of people following us around. Oddball though the idea was, the exercise had done the trick. We went down really well; those gigs did a great job of promoting the Swinging Laurels. Following the success of this bonanza we repeated the lunacy in Nottingham. We played at the Tavern in the Town, in the city centre, where disinterested bruisers of the lager-lout variety, eyed us suspiciously as we raced through four songs. It seemed like a good idea at the time!

Our record had, after a relatively short space of time picked up some stunning reviews, some of which suggested that we had tapped into a rich vein.

'Watch your backs Soft Cell, these boys have got your number two hit ready to go!' screamed one review.

Management team Martin and Steve in conjunction with Albion started to get us some welcome publicity. The best news of all was that Peace of Mind eventually peaked at No.1 in embryonic independent chart listings. We couldn't help thinking what might have happened had it been released sixteen months previously when it was originally pressed for Dead Good. It showed us how much ahead of its time it was. We scored our first national press feature in a magazine called Disc. They used a photo shot by Steve Pyke, which had been used on our record sleeve.

When I first got hold of a copy of our record I looked at it over and over again. It was the first record that had my name on the writing credits and that meant the world to me. Years of being a real music fan had left me with the habit of scrutinising sleeve credits on the albums that I bought. I believed that everyone on them was a 'someone.' That first night I propped the record up on my bedside cabinet, so it would be the first thing I saw when I woke up.

Anne Nightingale and 'Kid' Jensen played the single on night time Radio One. I heard our record on local radio many times and it gave me a nice, tingly feeling. Any musician who tells you that they don't listen to the radio or read record reviews is a liar. True, when we started to get more radio play you tend to get a bit more blasé about it, but in the early days it meant so much.

Another strange feeling was hearing the record on a Jukebox - it was featured in a few local pubs and it knocked me back at first. John Peel also played it, but in the final event it only sold a few thousand copies. But to come from being unknowns to independent chart recognition with radio plays and the first glimmerings of national music press exposure, in a few short weeks, was far more than we could have ever hoped for.

Some Bizarre eventually parted company with Martin and Steve but lots of the bands from that Phonogram compilation album enjoyed success - Blamanche - Depeche Mode and The The among them. We met Martin Fry of ABC in the buffet car on a train home after one of our visits to London. He was heading back to Sheffield, clutching a Some Bizarre compilation album. ABC soon found success with the hit Tears Are Not Enough, in October of that year. It was released on the Neutron label peaking at No.19. He seemed a nice chap, and our paths were due to cross again in the near future.

When I started playing with the Sinatras in 1980, I made it clear to guitarist Nev that as soon as the Laurels fortunes picked up; that project would take precedence. I suppose it was inevitable that with the Sinatras doing well, the two projects would impinge on each other at some point. Nev rang me at work to say that they'd landed a support gig at the Lyceum in London. It coincided with a Swinging Laurels gig and I told him I couldn't make it. He went ballistic - it was a major prestige gig for them and was set up by Island Records who were interested in signing them. They played the gig minus the brass. Island Records eventually pulled out of the deal and it was only years later that I found out that the band they were support to that night was a young Irish band called U2. Nev went on to feature in a number of bands after the Sinatras, most notably independent chart regulars, the Meteors.

Managers Martin and Steve started to create more live opportunities for us - one of these was at Lincoln College of Art, supporting Neil Innes. Neil had been with the cult sixties band Bonzo Dog Doo-Dah Band who had had a hit in the 60's with I'm the Urban Spaceman.

This was our first ever gig in a concert environment but it was a stinker. The drum machine was constantly too fast or too slow and the sound flew around in the cavernous hall. The last vocal line came back at us in the form of an echo. We were glad to get off, but it taught an invaluable lesson in humility after the heady start to our live career. Our drum machine was not state of the art; Gaz selected the tempo for each song by sliding a control up or down. The calibrations were so tight that a millimetre either way meant that we were saddled with frantic speeds or slow, slow motion. Gaz often tried to alter the tempo with his foot, mid song, which was a sight to behold - particularly if the song we were playing was too fast for us to keep up with. I suppose it wouldn't have been so bad if we weren't prone to giggling - which we were. Neil Innes was good though; God knows what he thought of us.

We did some recording at Soundlab studio in Leicester with Joe King at the controls. This gave us a chance to record some of the new material we'd been working on with Mark and Dean and the results were pleasing. One of the new songs was an instrumental called One of Our Saxophones is Missing. It was a cavalry charge of a number that was to become a live favourite. We got another gig in Lincoln, at a venue called Cinderella Rockafellas. Our set was expanding and we got a sound technician, Neal Quincey, in to record the set live - some of the material later surfaced on vinyl. Our confidence was growing steadily and when our first chance of a gig in London came along, we felt ready and able to take it on.

Albion Records approached us to see if we would be interested in playing a set at their annual party at the Venue in London. We didn't have enough material to fill a complete set, but it was a night that could help further our careers. We travelled down to London with Joe King along to mix the sound. When we arrived we were taken aback by its size and we approached the gig with some trepidation. When we saw the guest list it filled us with dread, Albion were parading us as their latest signing before the great and the good of the recording industry.

Management is crucial in this sort of situation, lots of work behind the scenes is needed to liaise between interested parties and although we had publishing deal and had a record in the shops - we were yet to sign a formal management deal. Things were run purely on trust. Dean christened our managers 'the 10% brothers' - and it stuck.

When we launched into our set at the Venue, at first things went well, then disaster struck - the bass synthesiser went horrendously out of tune. Sweltering heat in the room generated by so many bodies affected the tuning mechanism - it was temperamental at the best of times. We tried in vain to rectify the problem but eventually had to retire, red faced and disappointed.

Some instruments are prone to de-tune in a hostile heat environment; there is little you can do about it and our Roland mono synthesiser seemed especially susceptible to this problem. During the sound check the venue was empty and cooler as a consequence. We were sorely disappointed; the room was full of characters that could have given us a leg up in the business. We were in a dour mood as we left for home. Martin and Steve's ex-Some Bizarre partner Stevo was there, we bumped into him as he hailed a taxi outside - he seemed pretty smug, but he told Martin that we'd make it anyway, which was some small crumb of comfort.

We pitched straight back into writing and recording. It was imperative to pen songs that would arm the 10% brothers in their quest to secure us a major contract. We adjourned to the leafy confines of Wragby in Lincolnshire to Studio Playground where we recorded three tracks with Tom Norden in the producer's chair. Drummer Nick Murphy also came along too. Albion once again footed the bill and the tracks recorded were Pyjamarama (a Roxy Music cover) Same Address, and an instrumental called Bang Bang...is anybody there?

'Bang Bang ...is anybody there?' was pure Laurels. It was a free form instrumental with insistent tribal back beat - swirling synthesiser and brass intrusions making a rhythmic brew. Daytime Radio One it definitely wasn't. Our publishing deal demanded twelve original songs in each twelve-month option. An advance was due at the commencement of each option and the amount increased significantly as each year passed. The search had to begin in earnest for a more substantial, long-term record deal - gigs in London were essential. The 10% brothers were working hard on the live aspect and Albion stumped up the cash for another session at

Woodbine where we put down a further six tracks. The session straddled a three-day period and it was good to work with John Rivers again. We came away with a fair representation of our overall strengths and were confident that we could confront the major labels and make them sit up and take notice. The six tracks recorded were, Lonely Boy - Sensurround - Beating Heart - Rodeo - Go Out and Find Her - Disco Laurels.

The trust in our management pairing developed into friendship, which probably isn't an ideal way to conduct a serious business relationship. Martin had enjoyed a privileged education at Uppingham public school where he boarded as a child. This was interesting because he shared a dormitory with world-renowned psychic Mathew Manning and witnessed many bizarre paranormal manifestations that scared him and the rest of boys witless. I badgered him for details, but he was understandably reluctant to speak of the happenings for fear of ridicule. He had bottled much of it up since his schooldays. Martin told me of nights when objects inexplicably floated in mid-air, beds levitated, writing appeared on walls and objects materialised from thin air. Anxious parents withdrew boys from the school and eventually Mathew himself was moved on. I read his best selling book called The Link in the 70's, the success of which elevated Mathew to a status almost akin to that of Yuri Geller. At the time I found some of the assertions in the book unbelievable, but Martin had been an eyewitness to some of the more incredible incidents. I can understand why he didn't like to talk much about what he had seen.

There was no doubt that Martin viewed the music business seriously, but he used the gold disc he had been presented for Soft Cell's massive No.1 hit - Tainted Love - as a tray when he had his Cornflakes for breakfast.

Steve was a blond haired, bespectacled chap always managed to look dishevelled however hard he tried to dress smart. When driving his car his seat was so reclined that he was almost horizontal. Oncoming traffic probably thought his car was radio controlled, though his driving was not as bad as

Jim's from Team 23. He did however have an aversion to traffic islands, sometimes choosing to ignore them altogether!

Dave Henderson asked if the Laurels would be interested in releasing a four-track EP, featuring early experimental, instrumental material on his Dining Out label. It was a no strings attached one-off deal which at the very least could bring us more welcome publicity. For the project we remixed instrumental Bang Bang...is Anybody There? at Alvic studios in London on a weekday night. Ian Dury had recorded there. We blasted down to London after a hard day's graft and worked through the night. We emerged bleary eyed in the early hours, knowing that we had to face work that same morning. My eyes were bloodshot when I made it into work.

Mark was working for a motor factor and his boss was lenient at first, but it soon wore off. Dean had been working on the market in Coalville selling ladies underwear, a job that suited him down to the ground after spending most of his time helping ladies out of them. He developed a unique line in calls to attract the attention of passing female trade, a particular favourite of mine being,

'Low prices...Ladies pants are down!'

We wanted to make it abundantly clear from the outset, that the EP wasn't a conventional Laurels release, just a platform to show another side to our musical armoury. We called the EP A Taste Of... and came up with a classy looking black and white sleeve with a distinctive early 60's feel. The sleeve pictured us posing with horns and Gaz crooning into an old radio microphone - photograph courtesy of Steve Cooke

The initial pressings sold out pre-release although we did very little to promote the record. Tracks featured were, One of Our Saxophones Is Missing - Death Laurels - Disco Laurels -"Bang bang...Is Anybody There?

The EP garnered very welcome press attention, picking up articles in such publications as, Noise, NME, Melody Maker and Sounds. More offers of live work filtered through. We played a few student fresher's balls, in halls of residencies. These gigs were great fun, but did little to advance the name of the band. We were invariably performing to a hall full of pissed up students, who would be hard pressed to remember their own names, let alone that of the band. London had to be the place to play to attract the record company and press interest.

My brilliant dad **ALBERT BARROW** on the drums - Dad was a fine singer in the working men's clubs of Leicester in the 1950s

Photo; unknown origin

Young John in **BLACK GORILLA** days - in that satin suit.
Fortunately we are not able to see the trousers
Photo; unknown origin

SISTER BIG STUFF 1975

Left to right - Top Nick Thomson - Vince Fernandes - Middle; Dave Van - Melda Farrell - myself Bottom; Graham Tom - Martyn 'Stalky' Gleeson.
       Halcyon days - mile wide flared trousers
          Photo; Neville Chadwick

SISTER BIG STUFF

Top ; Graham - Theresa - Dave - Middle; Stuart Williamson - Dean - myself - Vince Fernades; Bottom front; the awesome Sammy Day - would you mess with that guy ?

Photo; unknown origin

SISTER BIG STUFF; On our way place to Buck House -. Sammy proudly holds our presentation record aloft.
Top; Sammy Day - Stalky - Dean Sargent; Bottom; myself - Graham Tom - Dave Van - Gloria Charlz - Martin Vandelis

Photo; the Leicester Mercury

BLACK GORILLA 1978

Proof that I wasn't exaggerating about the suits!
Back row; Me - Victor - John - Dean
Front row; Sylvester - Fitzroy - St Clair - Vernon
Photo; unknown origin

THE NEWMATICS; I know lets get on top of the tour van and have our picture taken! Left to Right top; Rich Barton - Nick Murphy - Gaz Birtles Bottom left to right; Chris Horlock - myself - Pez

Photo; unknown origin

THE SINATRAS 1981 Live at the Nags Head & Star Leicester - featuring Dean and myself on brass. Tommy is on vocals - backing vocals left are - Maxine and Martin - Nev Hunt is on guitar - far left.

Photo; Steve Cooke

WENDY TUNES Back, Phil Birtles - Gaz Birtles - Martyn Watson - Mark Fowler - Front; Andy Benny

Photo; unknown origin

SWINGING LAURELS; Early days circa 1980
Left to right - myself - Nick Murphy - Gaz Birtles

Photo; Gaz Birtles

SWINGING LAURELS
Early 1981 Albion records promo shot snapped in a studio more used to taking soft porn photography. They had us jumping all over the place - I am on the left, Gaz is on the right - I kept my clothes on.
Photo; unknown origin

The Swinging Laurels   wea

An early WEA records publicity shot. It was a baking hot June day and we spent all day sitting around on barges on the Thames. I am sporting a string vest and leather jacket! - Art, or what?

Photo; Mike Owen

The **SWINGING LAURELS** 1982
Left to right; myself - Mark O'Hara - Gaz Birtles - Dean Sargent

Photo; Jill Furmanovsky

GAZ BIRTLES live at the Hope & Anchor, Islington London

A French girl's armpit is attached to his chin

Photo; Michael Hemsley

MYSELF and **GAZ BIRTLES** swinging the cat at the Hope & Anchor, Islington London
Photo; Michael Hemsley

THE FUN BOY THREE with the **SWINGING LAURELS**
Taken at BBC Television Centre during a break filming
Something Else pop magazine programme for BBC2

Photo; Buster Brown

A Live shot taken in Cardiff on the busking tour of 1982. Bemused shoppers think they are watching the Singing Lorries

Photo; David Rose

The **SWINGING LAURELS** supporting the **CLASH** in 1982
Left to right; Gaz - Dean - myself
Photo; unknown origin

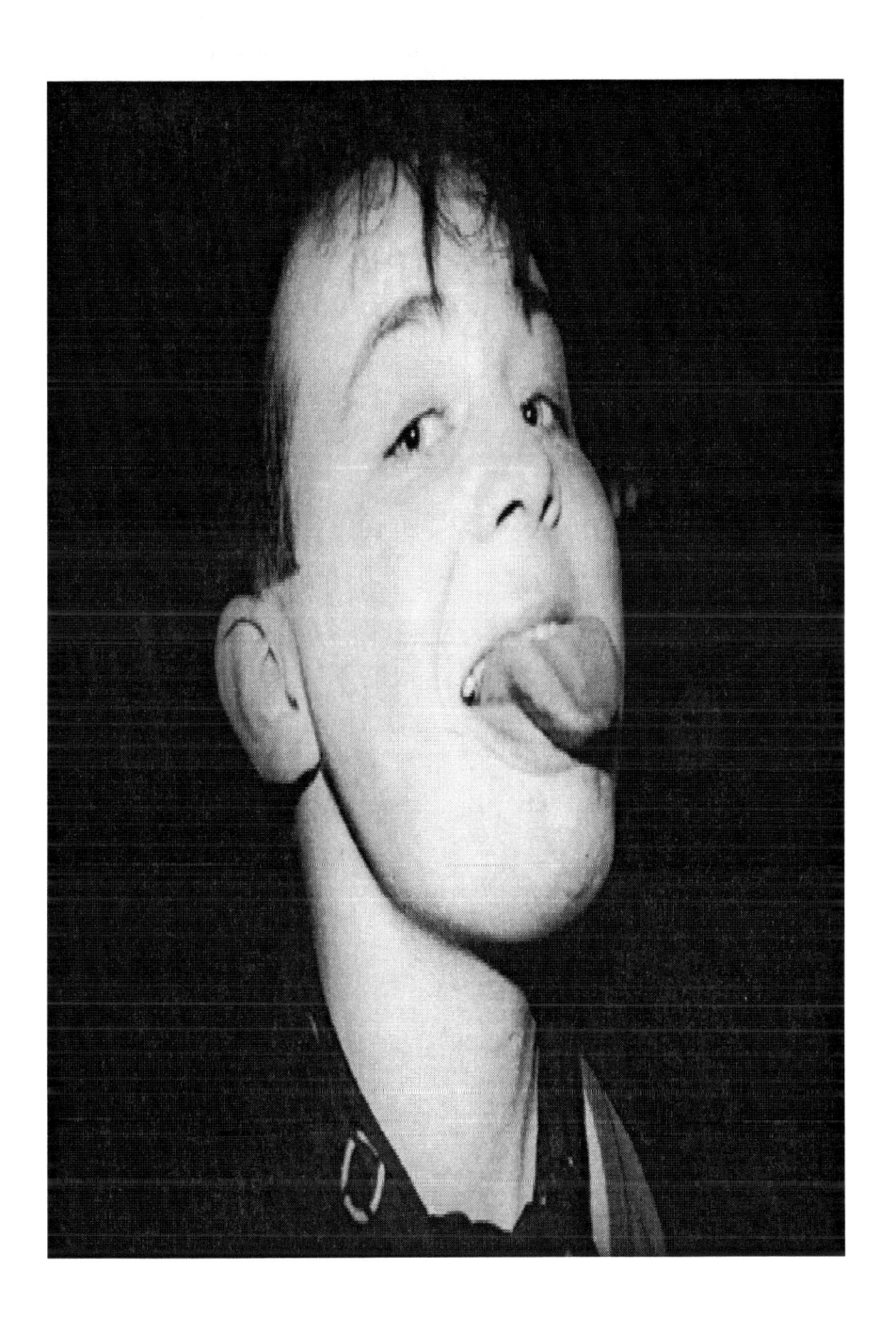

DEAN SARGENT and his amazing dancing tongue
- no wonder the girls liked him!
Photo; Steve Pyke

Still from the **FUN BOY THREE** video for the hit The Telephone Always Rings - **FB3** are in the foreground with **BANANARAMA** behind and Chas Smash of **MADNESS** - The **SWINGING LAURELS** horn section are in the background. The video was produced by **MIDGE URE**.
Photo; Martin Patton

Trying to look macho in leathers - live at Upstairs at Erics Bournemouth in 1984.
Photo; courtesy Coast to Coast magazine

Gaz and myself live at the Abbey Park Festival playing session horns for **RETURN of the SEVEN** in 1994.

Photo; unknown origin

The **SWINGING LAURELS** 1983.
Left to right; myself - Dean Sargent - Mark O'Hara - Peter Harriman - Gaz Birtles - Kevin 'Reverb' Bayliss.

Photo; unknown origin

RHODA DAKAR

Photo; Julio Venezuela

The **BEAUTIFUL SOUTH** featuring the legendary **SAM MOORE** on the set of the **JOOLS HOLLAND** TV show. Brass men are: Kev Brown - Gaz Birtles and Don Owen.

Photo; Phil Cass

CRAZYHEAD

L - R; Ian Anderson - Pork Beast - Vom - Reverb - Fast Dick

Photo; unknown origin

The **BEAUTIFUL SOUTH** brass section:
Left to Right; Tony Robinson - Kev Brown - Gaz Birtles.

Photo: unknown origin

Three older **LAURELS** playing brass for **BABY GENIUS**

Photo; unknown origin

IST and friends taken after the Summer Sundae appearance at Leicester De Montfort Halls, 2005: Left to right; Na'im Cortazzi - John Barrow - Gaz Birtles - Kirsty Wells - Kenton Hall - Kevin Hewick - Kathy Haynes - Brett Richardson - Mark 'Flash' Haynes - John McCourt

Photo; Kitty Valentine

Chapter Twenty Three

THE HOPE & ANCHOR

We supported chart act Shakatak at Leicester Polytechnic. Their brand of light club oriented funk helped them to chalk up fourteen hits and the show was a sell out and it provided us with the chance to play in a sizeable venue on a large stage.

The 10% brothers came up trumps with a London gig that was to change everything - a showcase gig at the legendary Hope and Anchor in Islington, London. The venue quite rightly laid claim to legendary status, it had hosted many bands that went on to become world name acts including: the Stranglers - the Jam - the Police - the Specials and Madness.

The Hope live area was in a cellar with a low ceiling and equipment had to be loaded down from the street outside via a wooden trap door. Capacity was 150 at the most, but that number was often exceeded as a sweaty throng packed in. The Hope had been at the vanguard of the London pub-rock scene in the late 70's, spawning acts such as Ian Dury and the Blockheads, Eddie and the Hot Rods, and many more. I saw live footage of the Stranglers on the Old Grey Whistle Test on BBC2 from the Hope, performing Hanging Around. The intense, heaving atmosphere impressed me. It was a place that could attract record company A&R types and also the music press. They put regular block ads in the national music press as did the Marquee and the 100 Club - another valuable source of press exposure.

When we'd played there a number of times the landlord showed me a page from his bookings ledger. In one weekend in 1979, the live attractions were, Friday night - Madness / Saturday night - the Police / Sunday night- the Specials - all were paid around £20! Until you could command a healthy paying audience, it was more than most likely you would end up in the red after travelling expenses were taken into account. Our first Hope and Anchor gig came in

December 1981- it was cold and there was a light covering of snow of the ground. On the way to Islington we stopped off at Blackwing studios to meet Dave Henderson where his band Worldbackwards were recording an album for Illuminated Records. We recorded brass on four tracks but we only had a limited time. Blackwing was a studio favoured by Depeche Mode, who had recorded some of their earliest hits there. The Worldbackwards album surfaced in February 1982, and we were delighted to see that the Swinging Laurels were singled out for praise in the Melody Maker album review.

'MORE (please) of the Swinging Laurels, who brighten proceedings immeasurably with their zestful brass,' Adam Sweeting wrote.

We played our first Hope and Anchor gig to a less than enthusiastic audience of about twenty. We played well, but debuted on a Monday, one of the most unattractive weekday nights. The manager was impressed enough to offer us a residency of four Tuesdays through February 1982. Not the best night to play but it gave us the chance to establish a buzz and hopefully create a following. This galvanised Martin, Steve, and Albion into action; they had a four-week period to cajole as many industry people as possible to attend. Albion pressed flexi-discs of Swing the Cat and mounted them on natty presentation cards to give them away as freebies. They manufactured snazzy, multi-coloured backdrops, with stylised saxophone and keyboard motifs for our stage backdrops.

Another showcase saw us playing The Barracuda in Bond Street, London supporting Way of the West, a Mercury Records act who had just had a near miss with their single Don't Say that's Just for White Boys, which peaked at No.54. The next time we played the Barracuda we headlined and dozens of complimentary tickets were sent to record companies and press. It's a gig which sticks in my memory; I had to catch a train to London after a hard day's grind, arriving at the venue with barely enough time to change. I have this enduring memory of Slim Jim of the Stray Cats staggering out after the show - inebriated, clutching a Swing the Cat flexi-disc. He was married to Britt Ekland at the time. These gigs were cleverly engineered to attract as much publicity as possible, and they achieved that. We now knew that we could play in the Capital and hold our own; those shows gave us a taste of what it was like. With the Hope and Anchor residency to make plans for, Albion worked feverishly to whip up interest in the band.

To warm up we played a series of small low key live outings to hone our set and kick it into shape. One of these was at a pub called the Railway, in Coalville, Leicestershire. This gig was significant because the promoter was Martyn 'Stalky' Gleeson, my old Sister Big Stuff partner. The place was packed which no doubt delighted Stalky as he counted his door takings.

A Swinging Laurels gig had the air of school outing about it - we piled into a rented estate car with the gear stuffed in the back and a real rapport built up between the four of us. Dean was effortlessly funny; some of his one liners were hilarious. Once at a sound check, in an empty venue, we were 'One two - one two-ing' testing the microphones when a female well blessed in the mammary department waddled across the floor area in front of the stage. Quick as a flash Dean blurted down the microphone,

'The juggler's arrived!'

The poor girl was oblivious - we were rolling about in hysterics. Another of Dean's favourite lines when spotting large breasted girl was,

'Look, there's Norma…..Norma Snockers!'

Mark constantly berated Dean for his overtly sexist outpourings, but it made little difference. In the space of time that we had to kill before a gig, we would visit a local pub and play darts, skittles or table football to while away the time. Gaz and I would normally take on the other two and Mark would chalk up on the scoreboard, 'Stars versus Backing band.' This was Mark's pointed way of having a dig. Up to that point all the radio and press interviews had been conducted by Gaz and me - the Albion publicity photos still only had had the two of us on them.

Swinging Laurels gigs tended to take on a life of their own - anything that could go tits up usually did. Arty backdrops had a habit of drooping or falling down although thankfully by this point we had dispensed with the Elgam beat box with its erratic speed fits and transferred the drum patterns onto reel to reel tapes. My Akai reel to reel tape recorder became Laurel number five - arguably the most talented member. It didn't mean that we were immune to stage gaffs. To compensate for these, a sort of merry banter developed between band and audience. More often than not this was born out of self-preservation. On a good night these off the cuff; throwaway quips made the night and saved us from embarrassment.

I've always found Dudley to be a dark hole of a place. Once we played a dive called JBs club and the audience was on the excited side of apathetic. During our set Mark spotted a group of bruisers at the bar, with their backs to us. He announced over the microphone,

'This song is for the fat beer-bellied bastards at the bar!'
With contorted faces they turned around in concert. Quick as a flash Gaz said,

'We've got nothing against fat beer-bellied bastards!'
With that they turned back to the bar and we quickly lurched into the next song. We didn't let Mark go any where near a microphone on stage after that.

Technology sometimes has a habit of kicking you in the teeth. Due to its inflexibility - If it went wrong live, it was obvious to all. With live musicians, particularly drummers, it is easier to cover up mistakes by improvising through a dodgy spell, but machines limited you in this department because when they stopped - they stopped.

On the first of our quartet of Hope and Anchor gigs the audience was on the sparse side, although we had invited a lot of A & R people along - none showed on the night. The second was better with more people, some press and a couple of A&R types. By the third, the place was jumping with record company representatives including, CBS, EMI, Warner Brothers and Island Records. Also in attendance was the music press, NME - Melody Maker and Sounds.

When we travelled down to London for the final gig there was a real air of expectancy. Several major labels were talking seriously about a deal and the venue was a sweaty heaving mass of bodies. Rival A&R people eyed each other up suspiciously across a room full of bobbing heads. This was precisely what we had aimed for. Once one record company showed interest the others seemed to jump on the bandwagon, scared that they were missing out on something.

In that tiny, pokey dressing room there was a real sense of anticipation. We were entitled to be nervous because it was probably the most single most important gig we would ever play. Backstage we waited apprehensively for our cue that came in the form of a cheesy intro tape. We prided ourselves on our selection of material. We firmly believed that the intro tape was vital to set the scene. We featured tacky 60's music such as, Wonderful Life by Cliff Richard and Street of a 1000 Bongos by the Brian Fahey Orchestra. A wave of nervous energy wafted over us. 'Go for it!' was the usual battle cry.

It was a stormer of a gig. Swing the Cat had the crowd jumping - Beating Heart, a Birtles composition featured cute vocal interplay between Gaz and me - Go Out and Find Her was a luuuurve song with shared vocals and Rodeo culminated in a blistering trumpet solo from Dean. These were lapped up by the throbbing audience. Back in the dressing cupboard, we were all dripping with sweat - all except for Mark that is - in all the years that I played with Mark, I never saw a bead of sweat on him! That night we didn't have to be told that we'd done the business

A gratifying event for me was seeing head of A&R at WEA records, Tarquin Gotch, performing an incredibly silly twitching dance in front of the stage as we played. He looked well out of place with his loud yellow and blue striped blazer and sensible haircut - like your dad at a wedding reception - but he was a major player in record company circles. Afterwards he made it clear that he was interested in signing us.

The live reviews in the music press were so complimentary it was embarrassing. We couldn't have wished for better reviews.

Karen Swayne from Sounds enthused,

'The chances are you've never heard of the Swinging Laurels, but try to remember the name, because they are a group who deserve your attention and adulation. They are the latest of a crop of young bands who are stripping down pop to its essential factors, they offer great songs delivered with a snappy enthusiasm and keep frills and fuss to a minimum. These boys are gonna be big, or I'll want to know the reason why.'

Adam Sweeting of the Melody Maker wrote,

'Is it pop? Is it jazz? They don't know, and nor do I. But only a fool could argue about the efficacy of their brash, swaggering triple horn blast. Then there are the trappings of techno beat-taped drum machine, baby synths - but the Laurels use them as quick-access tools, extracting necessary pulse and texture, and then blowing them apart with their ragingly immediate melodies. See them soon.'

The impetus thrust us towards our record deal and the 10% brothers were fielding offers of work from a variety of sources. Live work poured in - everyone wanted to know us once the ball started rolling.

Chapter Twenty Four

MILES COPELAND - HOW DOES IT FEEL TO BE RICH?

Gaz and I wrote lyrics for a song called Rodeo and it became a firm live favourite. The song was autobiographical and told of our struggle to get noticed in the pop world. One line, written by Gaz asserted,
 'I'm gonna hang on tight to every hand that I shake'
This line was particularly apt in the light of the incredible series of events that were to happen next. We played Dingwalls, Camden lock, London; it was my third visit with as many bands. The gig was ok; we got a nice reaction from an appreciative audience. After the gig a short, chubby, balding American guy accosted me and told me that he was an agent from New York. 'Oh, sure' I thought. He begged me for Swinging Laurels material to take back to the States with him. I gave him a copy of Peace of Mind and a biography and I watched him, clamber into a cab. He didn't look like an agent type, but what does an agent look like? He said he'd be in touch. I took that with a pinch of salt, it wasn't unusual to be approached after a show by someone claiming to be your saviour.
 Days later Martin was rudely awakened at 3 a.m. at his Streatham home by a transatlantic phone call. The guy turned out to be an agent called Rick Shaw and back in New York he very strongly recommended us to his boss. The voice on the other end of the phone said to the still half-awake Martin,
 'How does it feel to be a rich man?'
 The caller was none other than Miles Copeland, manager of the Police, at that time one of the hottest bands in the world. Miles, father Police drummer Stuart Copeland, ran US record label IRS. He explained that he thought the Swinging Laurels were going to be huge and wanted us over in the States as soon as possible. A support tour of the US and Canada, with Squeeze was mentioned. Martin was rendered speechless by this call - Copeland tracked us down through our publisher, Albion. We didn't find out about it until the chance had passed us by. The 10% brothers - in their

infinite wisdom decided it would be best to 'crack' the UK before embarking on speculative forays to the States! Speaking for myself, I wouldn't have minded a stab at being rich. Given the youth and relative inexperience of our management team, perhaps this offer from one of the most powerful prime movers in rock, spooked them - but we were more than a little miffed when we discovered that this priceless chance had gone begging. In the music industry, like life itself, chances need to be grabbed with both hands. One thing is sure, when they pass you by; there is no second chance.

One great thing about any London gig is that you never know who is in the audience. Our meeting with Miles Copeland's emissary at Dingwalls proved that. Name venues attract all sorts of people, including people closely connected with the business itself. It was another of these chance encounters that was to ultimately lead to our most exciting adventure yet.

Martin called me at mum's house on Sunday March 14th 1982 with some astonishing news. The manager of the Fun Boy Three, Rick Rogers had been in the crowded audience at our last Hope and Anchor gig and liked what he saw. It transpired that the Fun Boy Three were on the look out for a brass section to play on their next single; Rick wanted us to do the honours. As Martin spoke the import of what he was saying dawned on me and my imagination began to race.

The Fun Boy Three were formed by breakaway members of the Specials - Terry Hall, Neville Staples and Lynval Golding. They had already charted with The Lunatics (Have Taken Over the Asylum) - which reached No.20 November 1981 and It Ain't What You Do It's The Way That You Do It, a No.4 in February 1982. The latter of these elevated girl band Bananarama to stardom by giving them equal billing on the recording credits. Potentially this could be very big if it worked for us in the same way,

With our Warner Brothers deal seemingly going through, this was just what we needed - a successful liaison with the Fun Boy Three could make all the difference. With their high profile we expected that the single would at least make the top twenty and when I put the telephone down my head was swimming. I dashed over to Gaz's house in a taxi with the good tidings; we jumped about in the street with excitement.

The track, The Telephone Always Rings, was from the debut album - Fun Boy Three, where it appeared minus brass. We caught a train to London and made our way to T.W. studios in Putney. It was there that we first met Terry, Lynval and Neville. It was all a little awkward at first, but we soon broke the ice and got down to business. Mark's services were not needed, but he understood that success with the project could ultimately mean a leg up for the Swinging Laurels. The track was simplistic and the brass riffs were basic but then the Fun Boy Three stripped songs down to bare bones, the results were both pleasing and successful. Dave Jordan was producer; he relayed our parts to us and they were committed to tape. Dean blew a fine, improvised trumpet solo over the middle eight passage in the song. They were pleased with the results so we packed up, said our goodbyes and ordered a cab to take us back to St.Pancras railway station. Terry Hall sat next to me in the back of the taxi; he was going to Euston station for his journey back to Coventry. Some quarters of the press labelled Terry as a glum deadpan character but in reality he has an intuitive and mischievous wit. I asked Terry how well he expected the record to do - he had been associated with seven Specials hit singles and he told me very candidly, that as long as it sold 100,000 copies, he didn't care! But he expected to crash into the top 75 from advance sales alone.

Back home we planned how to benefit from the inevitable press coverage that we would attract when the single surfaced. At work I was hauled over the coals for my absenteeism. I deserved it - surely it was only a question of time before I was given an ultimatum but I resolved to keep my head down for as long as possible. We played another show at the Hope and CBS, Island records, Warner Brothers and EMI were all in the frame of interested parties, but now more than ever before, it was all about timing. After a wizard show we all adjourned to an eatery in Covent Garden to discuss contracts with the 10% brothers and solicitor/friend Nigel Pearson of the London firm, Berger Oliver. Dean had other ideas. He had captured a whale of a girl - a real monster from the black lagoon and seemed intent on dragging her along with us. Dressed in black with purple hair, she lumbered along, while gripping him in a fearsome arm lock and gazing intently into his eyes. At one point she stepped out into the road and was hit by a passing black taxi cab! She picked herself up, dusted herself down and walked on as if nothing had happened! It was a collision that would have put a rhino out of action, but it barely affected her. Dean later disappeared with Moby Dick and appeared at the hotel the following morning looking sheepish. I'd have rather spent the night with a crew of Russian trawler men! He took some stick, especially from Mark.

When we'd finished playing one time at the Hope and Anchor I was stopped by a punter, as I pushed my way through to the bar. One endearing feature about the Hope was the close proximity from stage to audience, but given the choice of talking to him or pulling out my toenails with white hot pliers, the latter option would run a close second. He went off on one and accused us of destroying the fabric and integrity of the music industry. Why? Because we had no drummer or guitarist. I explained that it was a conscious and a well considered decision. Here was a typical example of rock 'n' roll dinosaur mentality. Some people are incapable of embracing ideas that are against the norm and I find that attitude one dimensional and stifling. Our conversation got quite animated. If it was up to him, every band would be Status Quo! We agreed to disagree and I escaped thinking, 'Hang on a minute. You paid to get in mate!'

With the influx of synthesised music technology, a real sea change in the way that music was played and recorded evolved. In much the same way that punk had stirred mainstream music up, new technology caused real resentment in the ranks of some traditionalists. A lot of old school musicians saw technology as a threat. Change of any kind often meets with a luddite-like resistance and early 80's records are littered with the sound of the drum computer. It stands out so obviously listening to it now. The Linn drum computer was much used. Very few producers of the period were disposed to recording a live drum kit because real drums could often take an eternity to set up. With the drum computer you could programme songs before setting foot in the studio, thus saving hours of expensive studio time.

Having yet more time off work brought the conflict with my employers, Bearing Service Ltd, to a head so I handed my notice in. I had longed for that moment, but when it came I felt quite saddened. Those guys had been good to me but it was like history repeating - I had done the same thing five years before with Black Gorilla. When the time came to say my goodbyes I was quite sorry they had been very supportive and lenient regarding my woeful time keeping. Rob Brown and Phil Reader saved my bacon on a number of occasions. But now all I had to worry about was the music, and that felt good.

Martin and Steve assured me that a deal with WEA was coming to fruition, and they told me not to worry. Again the dilemma was leaving a secure job with prospects, but all I really wanted was to be involved in the music world. When the chance came along to turn my back on a cosy future for an uncertain risky fate for the second time, there was no contest. I find it staggering now that I managed to live that double life for as long as I did. I don't know how I carried it off; the job was a very demanding one. At least now I could devote all my energies to something that I really wanted to do, and I was grateful for the chance.

Moles club in Bath played host to us - Hugh Cornwall of the Stranglers was in the audience - it was a good gig. Afterwards we took the opportunity to relax a bit on the coast at Weston-Super-Mare. Not having to race back to Leicester and get up for work was absolutely brilliant; it was all like one huge extended holiday. We were like four big kids on the funfair at the end of the pier. Four demented Laurels played the penny cascade machine in the amusement arcade and tried in vain to win cuddly toys from one of those impossible crane machines. In Bath we ventured into a real ale bar and we all ordered obscure sounding ales. Mines a Badgers Sphincter please serving wench! Steve ordered a lager and was bemused to have a dog biscuit placed on the bar in front of him. 'Why?' He queried. 'Lager is a dirty word,' the barman told him. They didn't sell it at all. The dog biscuit showed contempt to any poor soul daring to ask for it. Steve settled for a pint of Transvestites Arse and no more was said. That's what I call a real ale pub!

After the show Martin took us to a club frequented by people of a gay persuasion. He hadn't noticed that the place was full of mincers. The penny only dropped when a chap with a Village People moustache propositioned him at the bar,

'Oh, I dooo luuurve your glasses'

Martin wore large Joe 90 bins. Spooked - he put on a gruff voice, thanked the man for the compliment, and pathetically scurried back to where we were sitting.

Things on Fun Boy Three front moved quickly - we received white label copies of the 12" version of the single and when we played Nero's club in Cardiff - the DJ blasted it over the sound system for us before the gig. We stayed over in Cardiff and I shared a room with Mark O'Hara. Mark was into all things Eastern and esoteric and he spent a good part of the night trying to project himself to the astral plane. Whether he managed to project his spirit that night I never managed to establish. He was still in his bed when I woke up in the morning. Mark later spent time in India doing what is known in the business as a 'George Harrison.'

The next morning we headed to the BBC Television Centre at Shepherds Bus, London to record our first television show with the Fun Boy Three. It was a BBC2 programme called Something Else. Dean and I hadn't been to the BBC since our Black Gorilla days four and a half years before but for Gaz it would be his first television appearance. Mark came along for the ride, as did the 10% brothers. Being back at the Boob brought back great memories. The show was recorded on Sunday April 18th to be broadcast the following Friday night and repeated during the following week. It was a nice feeling - we were afforded 'special guest' billing which got the Swinging Laurels name over to a much wider audience. Alex

Peach, Mark's friend from Leicester (Later to become Porkbeast in a future incarnation with Crazyhead) was in the studio audience proudly sporting a loud, pink Swinging Laurels T-shirt.

Also on the show was a band called Southern Death Cult who later went on to make a big noise in the business as the Cult. We left Shepherds Bush on a real high, very tired, but the experience had been invaluable.

Back at home we did a number of live brass sessions for fellow Leicester outfit the Apollinaires who had just signed to 2-Tone Records. They asked us to play on their first single for the label. The song The Feelings Gone, had become a live favourite during our sporadic live appearances with the band and this gave us a unique opportunity to work with both factions after the Specials split, having already worked with the FB3. Jerry Dammers elected to produce the track himself and we were delighted to find that the recording was scheduled at our old stamping ground, Woodbine in Leamington Spa.

Woodbine had re-located across town to larger premises and when we arrived the track was already recorded bar the brass parts and some vocals. The 2-Tone label had an enormous reputation and I was incredibly excited to record for them and work with Jerry Dammers - the driving force behind the label and its success. The Apollinaires were not the sort of band that you would normally associate with 2-Tone because their success had come through Ska influenced bands such as the Specials – Madness - Selecter and the Beat. We recorded brass parts that should have taken two or three hours, but under the stewardship of Mr.Dammers they took two days! Jerry was a fascinating and complex character, but he was one of those pedantic perfectionists that insisted on twenty takes to record a line that was perfect on take one. For a brass player this constant repetition plays havoc on the lips. Rhoda Dakar, ex-Specials vocalist did the backing vocals. Rhoda had provided the eyrie backing vocals on the classic Specials No.1 Ghost Town in June 1981. This was my first meeting with her and our paths were destined to cross again in the future. We left the studio with the promise that the release would feature a Swinging Laurels 'appear courtesy of WEA records,' name-check on the sleeve.

Brass sessions popped up thick and fast; we were approached MCA Records to play on a single for a hit youth band Musical Youth. They were later to register a big selling No.1 with a song called Pass the Dutchie. They were Brummie kids who dished up a distinctive brand of commercial lovers rock reggae. The track we recorded was called Youth of Today and was intended for the follow up to Pass the Dutchie. MCA Records asked the Fun Boy Three to produce, who in turn asked us to supply the brass. The journey down to London and TW studios was memorable only for the fact that Dean was sick. He barfed up out of the car window on Putney Bridge causing pedestrians to side step the oncoming Technicolor torrent. We met the Fun Boys at the studio and the first thing Terry said was, 'I hear you've been working with Dammers?'

The tone of his voice left no doubt that there was no love lost between the two separate ex-Specials camps. The split must have been acrimonious and we were anxious not to rock the boat and spoil the opportunity that we had forged.

Musical Youth had already recorded the track and all that was required was our brass input. It all went well, but I still haven't heard the finished recording to this day. For some reason MCA Records rejected the Fun Boy Three production of the track and remixed it elsewhere. When the single was released it was a hit and climbed to No.13, but sadly minus our brass parts.

The Telephone Always Rings was released on April 26th on Chrysalis Records and the sleeve and label credits announced, 'Featuring the horns of the Swinging Laurels.' In its first week of release the record made a chart debut at No.68, which was what Terry predicted. A whole series of promotional exercises to promote the single were arranged. Chrysalis arranged a video shoot, recruiting Ultravox vocalist Midge Ure as producer. This was our first ever video shoot - we arrived late and in a bit of lather and it was two very anxious managers that greeted us as we stepped out of our cab. The video was epic in every sense of the word and the finale was a big party scene sing-a long, in a mock up of a living room, furniture and all. Every way you turned there were name faces. Included in the proceedings were members of Madness - Ultravox, and Bananarama with Alexi Sayle, David 'kid'" Jensen and Marilyn Monroe and Humphrey Bogart look-a-likes.

Mark was down for the ride and was roped in as an extra. He was blacked up and dressed as Al Jolson which ticked him off, because when the video was broadcast, no one recognised him! Also there was a real horse with a cowboy astride it. The final scenes had us all crammed into the makeshift living room, the Funboys and Bananarama gathered around an upright piano and Gaz, Dean and myself standing on a sofa miming horns. It was fascinating to see how it was put together technically.

Making a promotional video might sound exciting in the same way that recording can sound glamorous. But there are hours of tedium and hanging around while shots are set up. In one scene I was featured in silhouette with my sax behind Terry as he mimed and although the scene was short there were many dry runs to get camera angles right. During the long periods of waiting the Laurels found the props. cupboard and tried silly hats on and false noses. Boys just wanna have fun! My sister Ann was a big Specials fan; she was even a member of their fan club. When I told her that we were working with the Fun Boy Three she pleaded with me to get their autographs. Now this isn't as easy as one might imagine. When you are working with someone you can't just say, 'Oh, by the way can I have your autograph?' It just didn't feel right to me somehow. I didn't want to disappoint her so when I did eventually pluck up the courage, I said to Terry,

'Can I have your autographs please? It's not for me - it's for my sister.' He burst out laughing saying, 'Yeah, sure it is!' I got a signed a copy of the album and she was well pleased.

The video was originally recorded with Top of the Pops in mind, but was eventually shown on Saturday Superstore on BBC1 and also on Riverside on BBC2. I only saw the video for the first time recently - it surfaced on You Tube. Chrysalis

Records released a picture disc that featured a still from the shoot with Bananarama and members of Madness looking on. In the background standing on a sofa were the Laurels, blowing like our lives depended on it.

With May came yet another session opportunity. Neville Staples of the Fun Boy Three had set up his own record label called Shack Records, and he asked to record brass on a single by his protégés Splashdown from Coventry. We were to contribute to the A side It's a Brand New Day and the B side Actions Speak Louder Than Words. So it was back to TW studios for the recording. The record didn't exactly set the world alight, though it was on the jukebox at the Hope and Anchor for a time.

Exciting news came that we were on alert for a possible Top of the Pops appearance, depending on how well the FB3 single fared in the next chart run-down. The single had climbed to No.37, but we needed a top 30 entry to be certain - it was getting played to death on the radio.

Martin phoned to say that the Fun Boy Three and Bananarama were off on a foreign excursion to record a television programme called Generation 80 in Brussels, Belgium, and they wanted us to go along to mime to the single. They were also to perform It Ain't What You Do It's The Way That You Do It and Really Saying Something, both had been hits from Fun Boy Three/Bananarama collaborations. We travelled by road with the Funboys while the girls flew. Our mode of transport was a luxury Len Wright coach complete with bar, bunk beds and video and we caught the ferry at Dover for the channel crossing.

Our destination was Ostend and after a couple of drinks in the bar we decided to grab a bite to eat and settled down in one of the restaurants. As we ordered a growing crowd of school kids pressed their faces up against the window close to where Terry was sitting and to anyone under any illusions of how hard it could be being a pop star, what followed brought it home. Eventually the intense attention got to him and manager Rick Rogers organised a private cabin for him. Poor Terry spent the entire crossing in total solitude. I suppose fame has some payback but being recognised and pestered everywhere you went wouldn't be my cup of tea. Seeing how hounded Terry was opened my eyes to the pressures he had to endure daily, just doing the ordinary things that we all take for granted.

Once in Brussels we booked into the plush Brussels Sheraton Hotel - we off loaded our gear and went into the hotel bar to unwind. The drinks cost a fortune, but we discovered the Fun Boy Three's Belgian record company, Ariola Records were footing the bill. So we lounged in luxury, listening to a pianist in a white tuxedo, as drink after drink came over from the bar. Each time the waiter came over with another tray of drinks, Dean would gleefully announce,

'This one's on Ari' - in reference to Ariola records. Eventually the 10% brothers told us to calm down before we ran up a ridiculous bill.

The trip encompassed a three-day period, which meant a two-night stay at the Sheraton - we could certainly live with that. At the television studio I was struck by how antiquated it looked compared to the good old BBC. The cameramen were doddering octogenarians and the place exuded a cool sterile feel. Our part in the proceedings was miming to one track so much of the day was spent loafing around, availing ourselves of beer provided by the studio hospitality.

We mimed for all we were worth. Most people imagine that miming is easy, it isn't. It is simple enough for an instrumentalist, but for a vocalist it is a different - watch any edition of Top of the Pops to see that for yourself. With a saxophone you just take the reed out of the mouthpiece - it is the reed that makes the sound so you can blow to your hearts content and all you hear is wind. It is still an unnatural feeling having a television camera a foot away from your face, and only a weak, barely audible soundtrack to mime to. Also on the same show were the band Classix Nouveaux. Generation 80 was a sort of poor mans Top of the Pops - Belgian style; it was transmitted on a Saturday night and then repeated in the week.

After the recording we were dropped at the Sheraton to freshen up and then were taken out for a meal, courtesy of Ariola records. Good old' Ari. It turned out to be quite a meal too; we were all seated around a huge table in a Chinese restaurant. The tab came to in excess of £700, a hefty sum in 1982. I bet that made Ari's eyes water a bit! Much vodka and orange flowed, a habit that was to set the scene for the rest of our night. After the meal the Fun Boys, Bananarama and our entourage went on to an exclusive night club for yet more drinks.

After three or four drinks I realised that I was the only one getting free drinks. I assumed that they were on the tab and everyone was getting theirs free gratis too. Each time I went to the bar one girl in particular made a beeline for me; she served me with a broad smile and didn't ask for money. The other guys who had been shelling out for their drinks soon noticed this, and after 'You're in there' type jokes, Gaz said, 'Yeah, but have you noticed the Adams apple on her?' I hadn't but it was rather pronounced! It began to dawn on me that my friendly barmaid was a transvestite. It has to be said that this was a stunning specimen of man/womanhood. On subsequent visits to the bar I lowered my voice two octaves and slapped my thigh a lot. I am very fussy about who I share my razor blades with and I don't look good in stockings!

All in all we had a rather spiffing yahoo time. Two professional dancers latched onto us. In truth, they had originally homed in on the Funboys but had been given the cold shoulder - they then turned their attentions to us. At kicking out time we got our transport back to the hotel - I don't know how but I ended up with a bottle of vodka, which at the time seemed sensible to despatch. The Fun Boys went to their rooms, but we carried on drinking until the early hours.

Dean and I paired off with the dancing girls and judging by the state of Dean's back the next morning; he'd enjoyed a torrid night. Deep scratches criss crossed his skin, it looked mighty sore and I'll never know how he didn't feel it at the time. Perhaps it was the anaesthetic effect of the vodka. I must admit to being pretty drunk myself. Gaz collared some extremely naughty scenes of me on his super 8 cine camera in 'Electric Blue' mode with one of the girls. At times he was a real pain with his 'fly on the wall' filming - he ended up with some real blackmail material. I paid for it big-time the next day because I felt wretched. We were all pretty well gone; Mark crashed out fully clothed on his bed with a salad roll in each hand which he'd ordered from room service but flaked out before he could remember why! Fun Boy Three manager Rick, was wandering around the hotel corridors starkers, vainly searching for his room. The next day when the dust had settled we all looked pretty tragic.

On the coach back to London I made full use of the bunk beds on the coach, and the Channel crossing was painful in the extreme. That weekend is up there among the best laughs I have ever had and when I occasionally meet up with the rest of the Laurels, it always gets a fond recall.

Chapter Twenty Five

TOP OF THE POPS - REVISITED

On the Monday following our Belgian blow out we anxiously waited for the new top 75. A top 30 entry would signal a definite Top of the Pops appearance. When the new chart was released The Telephone Always Rings was straight in at No.28. I was ecstatic at the prospect of doing another Top of the Pops - this time with a band with credibility. It was still the big one, even though it has now been sadly shelved, but make no mistake, then, it was the show that most recording artists would bend over backwards to appear on.

We travelled to London on the day before the show to supposedly re-record the track for transmission. With Black Gorilla we recorded the whole song from scratch but things had blessedly moved on since then - now everyone cheated. The Musicians Union representative came to the studio but nothing was actually recorded - the studio was prepared, microphones were set up but nothing happened until the inspector entered the room. We then ran through brass parts as if we had been recording for hours and when he left, we swapped the master tapes. The whole process was a farce, but at least we were spared the agony of re-recording the whole thing, a process that would have been well nigh impossible in the allotted time, and expensive to boot.

It was May 12th 1982 when we returned to the BBC Top of the Pops studio, the same day Martin and Steve were overjoyed to have got our first Smash Hits feature in print, it was the top teen magazine of the day. They printed a photograph of us posing alongside the FB3, a shot that was taken at the BBC during a break in filming when we recorded Something Else.

The day was a big day for Gaz; it was his first Top of the Pops. When we first met as seventeen-year-olds the very idea would have seemed fantastic. Dean and I knew what to expect and we were delighted to find that very little about the set up had changed. On the same edition were: - Duran Duran with Hungry Like the Wolf - The Associates with Club

Country - Hot Chocolate with Girl Crazy - Simple Minds with Promised you a Miracle - and Siouxsie and the Banshees with Fireworks. The presenter was Radio One disc jockey Dave Lee Travis.

We did a dry run for camera and lighting purposes, followed by a full dress rehearsal before piling upstairs to the good old BBC bar. In the bar we settled down with our Ruddles County beer. I hadn't spotted any one from Dad's Army this time but on the next table were Siouxsie and Budgie from Siouxsie and the Banshees. As we enjoyed our drinks Martin and Steve were busy formulating a plan to try to get Dave Lee Travis to name check the Swinging Laurels in his introduction. They planned to mingle with the studio audience and nobble him in between takes.

We filed into make-up for our obligatory tarting up and took our places on the set, forgetting what they had planned to do. A camera zoomed in on Dave Lee Travis for his introduction piece and the red light on the top of the camera lit up signalling that it was live. He stuttered,

'Give a big hand for the Swinging Laurels, together with the Fun Boy Three!'"

Hearing this from the other side of the studio made me gulp. I thought, 'They've only gone and done it!' Then the track issued from those tame monitors. It was the best publicity imaginable - Travis announced the names the wrong way round - all I could think was 'Now we're for it'

We mimed our way through the track before returning apprehensively to the dressing room, scared of the reaction from the Fun Boy Three camp. Manager Rick Rogers seemed irate at first, he bawled,

'That's worth ten grand at least'

He calmed down later. Top of the Pops was screened the next day, a Thursday and like the Black Gorilla edition, I watched it at home with my family. Afterwards I went to my local pub for a pint; the landlord had seen the show. He said to me,

'Have you made your first million yet?'

Little did he know? I was still living on the meagre savings I had put aside before quitting my job.

If Top of the Pops was the pinnacle in terms of exposure on pop television shows, then the children's pop show is wonderful for a whole set of different reasons. The day after the Top of the Pops broadcast we caught a train to Manchester to the BBC studios to record the kid's pop show Cheggers Plays Pop. Host Keith Chegwin had hosted a number of children's programmes, perhaps the most notable being Swop Shop with Noel Edmunds. On our arrival Cheggers greeted us warmly - he came over as a genuine chap, despite his over the top, in your face image. On the same show were Malcolm McClaren protégés, Bow Wow Wow performing Wild in the Country and Tight Fit with Fantasy Island. Tight Fit were a syrupy boy and two-girl outfit and Dean was letching after the blonde one - no surprise there; Dean never missed an opportunity. The set consisted of a studio audience full of noisy kids who were seated in banks opposite each other - half wore in yellow t-shirts, the other half wore red. Cheggers got the kids to play games and quizzes and in between a band mimed to their latest platter. The cacophony that issued from the throats of those kids was painful to the ears, but it was great to see them enjoying themselves. The poor kids had to hand the t-shirts back at the end! The next day, back in Leicester, I was stopped by a guy in the street, who said,
'Hey, I saw you on the telly; I bet you are rolling in it!' If they only knew.

When the next chart was announced Telephone had moved up a respectable seven places to No.21. Top of the Pops played the track on the show play out; Blondie vocalist Debbie Harry introduced it. In those days the policy was that no record was featured on consecutive weeks - unless it was No.1.

After all the glamour and hob knobbing it was time to get back down to business on the Swinging Laurels front and back to the good old Hope and Anchor. After the gig serious talks were had with solicitor and good ally Nigel Pearson relating to the deal that had been tabled by WEA records. The deal called for three singles in an initial nine-month period or first option. A stand off had developed between CBS and WEA records for our signatures. CBS said to Martin, 'Don't sign to anyone else before talking to us first' but their offer didn't seem to have any substance or specifics attached and Tarquin Gotch of WEA showed the most serious commitment. Anyone, who could dance as badly as Tarquin had my vote anyway! It was nice to know that contracts were on the table - the secret was all in the timing. You can only play two companies off against each other for so long. The great danger was overdoing it and seeing both interested parties pull out.

One upsetting incident occurred for me at my brothers wedding. He was married on a Sunday; the Swinging Laurels had been featured in the Sun Day magazine from the News of the World that morning. They printed the photograph of us with the FB3 and publicised our forthcoming UK tour that went under the banner of 'the Swing the Cat Tour.' This was a great coup; the circulation of the Sun Day magazine was the largest in the country at around three million. At the wedding reception a succession of kids came over to the table where I sat with Kim and asked for autographs. I felt acutely uneasy at the thought that I might be stealing the thunder from my brother on what was his big day. At the end of the day a slightly worse for wear wedding guest tried to pick a fight with me for no reason, other than I'd been on television and he'd been jealous of the attention I'd been getting - another example how people's attitudes to you can inexplicably change.

On a sweltering hot bank holiday Monday the first leg of the 'Swing the Cat' tour took us to the Horsefair in Leicester market. Excuse the pun but inside there wasn't enough room to swing a cat - it was rammed to the rafters. That day also brought the news that we would be making another Top of the Pops appearance on the coming Thursday which was to be a live show due to the bank holiday. The single had eased up four chart positions to No.17 - its eventual peak.

The Horsefair gig was epic. The punters even stood on tables to get a glimpse of three musicians sweating profusely (Mark didn't sweat of course.) Some days after, the owner Vince, moaned to me about a Leicester Mercury review by their intrepid pop reporter Duncan Hopwood. He had written about the ridiculous number of bodies in the venue and Vince was panicking that it could cost him his licence. They must have infringed every health and safety regulation in the book. What he didn't moan about were the considerable door takings he must have pocketed!

For our live edition of Top of the Pops, Sounds features writer Karen Swayne was along for the ride. Being a live broadcast there was a tangible difference in the studio atmosphere. Live meant no room for error and the tension and urgency was very evident from the cameramen up. This day was also special because our contract with WEA was ready to sign. We were to head to the WEA offices in Broadwick Street after the show. After the dress rehearsal run through we were under strict instructions not to stray far, so we escaped to the sanctity of the BBC bar to unwind before transmission time.

Other bands on this edition were; Echo and the Bunnymen with The Back of Love - Madness who were at No.1 with House of Fun - Adam and the Ants performing Goody Two Shoes - ABC with The Look of Love and Junior with Mamma Used To Say.

In the bar the booze flowed a little too easily and when we left we were quite squiffy. Presenter for this edition was David 'kid' Jensen who we had met on the video shoot a few weeks back. We thanked him for his support - he had been playing our instrumental track Disco Laurels on his Radio One show as a talk-over. We also became briefly reacquainted with ABC singer Martin Fry. When we last met we were trying to secure recording deals for our respective bands - now there we were on the Top of the Pops set! It really is a small world. In the dressing room Gaz discussed the implications of filming live with Terry. Once the cameras rolled you could do virtually anything and no one could stop you. This seemed to impress Terry and when it came to filming our spot he flashed a rebel V sign at the camera. The 10% bros pulled the same stunt as on our last appearance by getting Jensen to give the Laurels a name check in his introduction. It didn't go unnoticed in the Fun Boy Three camp.

During the transmission, Dean spun his trumpet and this caused his mouthpiece to shoot across the stage and land perilously close to feet. He desperately tried to retrieve it before it was trodden underfoot. After our slot we stood at the side watching the rest of the acts go through their paces, but Gaz, who was still glowing courtesy of good old Ruddles County, mingled with the studio audience for a dance. A studio technician singled him out and hauled him up onto the podium where David Jensen was about to introduce the next act. He stood behind Jensen grinning inanely in a white beanie hat, in a 'Hello mum' sort of way. Martin was horrified, he said to me,

'John, for God's sake stop him!'

There was nothing I could do about it. I said, 'Leave the poor lad alone - he's enjoying himself' I have a video copy of that show and that sequence never fails to make me smile. The show culminated in a live satellite sequence from Japan with Madness who were celebrating their No.1, House of Fun.

Straight after the show we met Tarquin Gotch at Warner Brothers head office to sign our lives away. It was strange and almost anti-climatic - after working so long towards the deal, it was hard to believe that we were about to sign. The signing took ages because each page needed to be initialled by each of us and it was as thick as a New York telephone directory! What a day it had been, especially for Gaz and me. From the days when as seventeen-year-olds when we'd skive off work at the Gas Board, we'd dreamt of signing a major recording deal and here we were inking to one of the biggest labels in the world. In football terms it was like signing with Manchester United or Chelsea.

WEA records had huge profile artists on its roster - Prince - Frank Sinatra - Eric Clapton - Rod Stewart - The Pretenders - Elvis Costello; the list appeared endless. In the WEA office there was a large cupboard containing copies of current releases and every time we visited we plundered the stock. On one occasion I struggled away with more than twenty albums under my arm. When the signing was done Tarquin took us to a fancy Cambodian restaurant in the West End for a slap up meal and we had photographs taken for music industry trade publications. To this day - apart from seeing my sons being born and marrying Kim, it is one of the best days of my life.

The deal with Warners had an initial option of nine months during which time we were expected to release three singles. We received an advance of £21,000 and were to be paid a weekly retainer of just £40 each. Contrary to what people imagined I was financially much worse off. £40 was only a third of what I was paid in my former day job. We deliberately opted for a small advance because advances are recoupable, so in effect you end up paying it all back out of your record royalties - IF you sell records that is. It was possible to survive on £40 - just. When we were on the road food and lodgings were supplied. Also there was usually a rider in the dressing room consisting of food and copious amounts of fire water.

It was a five year deal and if all the options were taken up it was worth in excess of £400,000. We needed to get a single in the shops as quickly as possible. People have short memories and we knew that we had to be quick to capitalise on the publicity we'd attracted with the Fun Boy Three. We met one potential producer, Hugh Padgham at the Town House studio complex in London. He was probably best known for his hits with the Police and Phil Collins but when we met he spared us only cursory attention and more significantly he couldn't even remember the names of any of our tracks. This didn't impress us. It was imperative to find a producer that we felt would be good for the Swinging Laurels - someone we could feel at ease with and could work with. We wanted to record at Woodbine with old mate Johnny Rivers, but this was overruled by WEA - in my opinion it was because it was outside of London. Rodeo was the track that we wanted to be our first A side. It was a great favourite live and featured a fine extended trumpet solo by Dean. It was also an apt choice because the lyrics, which had been penned by Gaz and me and were about our struggles to get on in the music business.

The Telephone Always Rings hung around on the chart for three weeks before fading into pop chart oblivion. It registered a respectable nine weeks on the chart in all - helping us towards our deal and promoting our name.

Fun Boy Three manager Rick Rogers summoned us to a recording studio in Birmingham to record brass for the follow up single, which was to be a cover of the classic George Gershwin song - Summertime. We were only required for the B side this time and the song was called Summer of '82. It was a Sunday as the intrepid blow monkeys headed for Birmingham to a studio owned by members of the Electric Light Orchestra. The track had a quaint French B film soundtrack quality, and was peppered with sharp brass punctuation. The middle eight segment featured a Laurels brass frenzy - Dean blowing manic trumpet over layers of saxophone swells. I liked this song and although it was only a B side it has recently surfaced on a number of Fun Boy Three compilation albums including; Best of - Fun Boy Three (Disky/EMI Records 1996) and Really Saying Something - The Best of Fun Boy Three (EMI/Chrysalis Records 1997)

Summertime reached No.18 in the national chart, one place lower than its predecessor but unfortunately this was to be our last liaison with the FB3. A world tour was talked about but that never came to fruition.

An interesting kick back that our Fun Boy Three liaison produced was how we were now advertised. Some venues billed us as 'The Fun Boy Three's backing band,' which didn't please us much. Outside one such venue - Xtreems in Brighton, some poor kid had waited hours so that he could get his Fun Boy Three album autographed. We landed in a Ford Escort estate hire-car with our all our gear in the back. I bet that impressed him! The Xtreems gig was not only memorable because of the solitary autograph hunter, but because it was a God-awful disaster. It was a shame because hoards of Warner Brothers staff came down to Brighton to get a look at their new protégés for the first time. Typical - the sound was abysmal; the sound man was a club employee, so we had no control over the out-front sound. It was so bad that we had to leave the stage half way through the set and that can't have left a very good impression on those that had travelled from London only to see us fall flat on our faces.

The music industry has a real happy knack of slinging up little gems like that. One moment you appear to be riding the crest of a wave, only to have the rug pulled from underneath you, bringing you back down to earth with a sickening thud. Manager Martin had his work cut out to placate the club promoter who was only concerned that we hadn't played for our contracted time, but on the bright side, we WERE at the seaside!

We undertook a series of live engagements that took us to, Cardiff - Neros / Huddersfield – Star bar / London - Thames Polytechnic / Cambridge - Sound Cellar. WEA meanwhile, suggested another candidate for producer - Adam 'skipper' Kidron. Adam's production credits included work for Scritti Politti and Orange Juice - both chart acts at the time. He came along to Cardiff Neros, and we hit it off. Along with him was the distinctive figure of Scritti Politti drummer Tom Morley, instantly recognisable for the mass of dreadlocks that crowned his head. It was unusual to see a white man with dreadlocks and Tom caused quite a commotion wherever he went.

Tom came on board to help us programme the Linn drum computer for our forthcoming recording. He visited Leicester to programme two songs Rodeo and Beating Heart and was billeted at the Holiday Inn. No bed and breakfast dive for him mate! Here was a fundamental difference that being signed to a major label brought. Before signing to WEA staying at places like the Holiday Inn would have been a wild extravagance but with Mr.Warner and his brothers picking up the tab - what the heck! Give the cat another goldfish!

WEA records wanted a single in the shops as soon as possible and so booked us into Eden studios in Chiswick, London on 20th/21st/22nd and 23rd of June. The only problem from our point of view was that the only available time was the graveyard shift. This meant that our four sessions would start at 10pm and go on until the morning. We gladly went for this option, Adam Kidron had recorded some of his best work there, and Eden was well rated. Spandau Ballet were one of the top groups that recorded hit records there.

When we arrived at Eden there was a monstrous American car parked outside and inside another band were just finishing their session. When they emerged it was none other than Shakin' Stevens. The American car suddenly made sense; good old Shaky was a hugely successful recording artist at the time, milking a quasi-Elvis image. I was struck at the size of his pot belly and pronounced Welsh accent but he seemed nice enough.

Recording through the night took some getting used to. It wasn't easy trying to give a sparkling performance at 5 'o clock in the morning. We got back to our hotel each morning just in time to catch breakfast, then struggled to catch up on shuteye during daylight. We were not convinced with the results of that session and came away with a master tape that we were unsure about. Warner Brothers agreed and we decided to re-mix the track. Perhaps Adam's lavish, layered style didn't suit us although it was a production style that had been very successful for Scritti Politti.

Steve Short was called in to beef up the track at the legendary Trident studios, London. Output from Trident included classic, timeless albums, some of which were among my all time favourites. These included: The Rise and Fall of Ziggy Stardust and the Spiders from Mars by David Bowie - Transformer by Lou Reed and many classic hits by Marc Bolan. Setting foot inside Trident was one of those 'pinch me - am I really here' moments when I thought I'd died and gone to heaven. The thought of occupying the same studio space that Bowie's Hunky Dory was recorded in energised me.

Huge paintings of Marc Bolan and David Bowie in his Aladdin Sane incarnation decorated the walls. By coincidence also there that day was Marc Almond and David Ball of Soft Cell. They were viewing a promotional video for their latest release - What. A kind of strained relationship existed between us. Whether this came from the one-time management link with Some Bizarre - I was never sure. Marc Almond appeared to be a prickly character. I once saw him spurn an autograph-hunting fan at a party at the Columbia Hotel. He theatrically bemoaned the fact that he wanted privacy and didn't want to be pestered at a party. Surely that was what fame was all about. Signing the odd autograph comes with the territory. Also that night at the Columbia Hotel I saw the then Soft Cell manager Stevo rolling on the reception desk with a toy gun, threatening to shoot passing guests. The elderly night porter looked genuinely distressed.

The Rodeo re-mix was an improvement and the drum pattern sat better after Gaz added an additional snare drum pattern. Warner Brothers were starting to press and enough precious time had been wasted. Our problem was finding a producer that could transfer our live energy onto vinyl. This dilemma was to plague us throughout our recording career. A good band/producer combination is not to be underestimated. Some bands hit upon a successful partnership early on, but for those who struggle to find the right chemistry, it can be frustrating. You need to forge a creative relationship and a climate that allows both parties to breathe.

Rodeo was scheduled for release on September 3rd, a month later than we'd have ideally liked, but Warner Brothers set about putting the whole major label promotional band wagon into gear. We were packed off on an expensive photo shoot with top lens man Mike Owen. At his studio they supplied us with togs, which they said echoed our image - IMAGE? Five days before I was told not to shave until after the shoot. They saw my image as Latin; a sort of Italian itinerant, travelling musician. I thought - 'Oh no - not Jean Paul again!' A few days stubble would enhance my swarthy looks - they said. When we got to the studio on the day of the shoot, the make-up artist said,

'I thought we asked you not to shave?' - 'I HAVEN'T!' I replied rather indignantly. Well - I was young for my age.

On a sweltering hot day we were plonked on decrepit old barges moored on the River Thames. I was given a string vest and a brown leather jacket to wear; it was incredibly hot and uncomfortable. Even at this stage there was an element of the major label taking over and dictating to us - hi-jacking our artistic freedom. Someone got paid for coming up with those shit ideas! Did they think we were Haircut 100 or something? Some of the photographs turned out quite nicely, particularly the ones of Gaz but we decided that in the future

- we'd decide what our 'image' should be. Large companies are image obsessed - before then we'd done very nicely because we hadn't consciously dwelt on it.

Photographs from that session were used on the Rodeo 7" and 12" sleeves and the music press used them quite extensively. Teen magazines Pink - Oh Boy - Blue Jeans and Jackie featured shots coupled with features heralding our forthcoming single release. The sleeve photo featured Gaz in his white beanie hat made famous from its Top of the Pops exposure. My string vest took some living down.

Pressure was put on us to write more songs so in an attempt to find solitude and inspiration, we booked a week at a studio high on a mountainside in Wales at a place called Abergorlech. It might as well have been in the middle of the Amazon rain forest; the nearest pub was miles away! Not good. Every which way you turned there were trees and then even more trees. Gaz had been there before with Wendy Tunes, and thought that the isolation would provide song writing inspiration. The place was a farm come recording studio; one of the owners, a Mr.Trimble, had played with hit psychedelic prog rock band Hawkwind.

Meals were home cooked and came as part of the overall package. I must admit that the food was excellent. Mark loved it, but then he did enjoy the great outdoors. Ideal astral projection territory - perhaps? Talking of projections, a couple of days into our stay I was propositioned by one of the domestic staff. One night, when everyone else had gone to bed, she barred the way on the stairs when we were alone and I had to barge past to side step her advances. She was an older woman with not many teeth and the ones that she had were black - but by the end a week, stuck out there in the middle of nowhere, even she was starting to look attractive. See what isolation does for you.

Tom 'Scritti' came over for a couple of days to help with the drum programming and we rehearsed during the daytime. It was the first time that we had deliberately set out to write songs to order, and it wasn't easy. NME despatched reporter David Dorrell to interview us and he stayed over for a couple of days. We took him down to the local pub - the only pub for miles, and the locals looked at us as if we were Martians. Just like in those old Wild West films when a stranger walks into the saloon - the juke box stopped and all heads turned our way. Then the gaffer said, 'It's ok - these folk are from the recording studio' From then on they seemed to more-or-less accept us. David Dorrell was a nice chap, we had some laughs. He actually later went on to achieve success for himself in the pop world, chalking up a No.1 in 1987 as M/A/R/R/S with a track called, Pump up the Volume. There was no escaping the insular, close knit feel to that place. It was definitely a case of - 'Stay off the moors - Stick to the main roads!'

One day Dean was playing pool with one of the locals in that tiny pub. The 1982 World Cup was being held and a match was on the television - Italy were playing. Dean made some disparaging remark about Italians - one of the locals was half Italian/half sheep and took great exception. Poor Dean spent two or three hectic hours being chased around the hillsides by irate, cudgel wielding inbreeds on mopeds. He eventually made his way back to the farmhouse in a sorry condition - muddy and out of breath. When we left that place and came across living things that walked on two legs - not four, it was sheer heaven for me. Back in the real world, where there were telephones, people and no sheep.

The Clash asked us to support them live at Leicester's De Montfort Hall. They'd specifically asked for us and we were flattered. We said yes although we did have misgivings but we were glad that we did the gig; the night went much better than we could ever have hoped. People still mention that night to me to this day. Joe Strummer watched us from the wings as we played that night.

Chapter Twenty Six

RODEO - NAME THE GUILTY MEN

More live dates kept us occupied as the release date approached,
Swindon - Brunel Rooms / Canvey Island - Gold Mine / London - Dingwalls / Deptford - Albany Theatre / Leeds - Warehouse / Dudley - JBs/Doncaster - Mainline / Bath - Moles Club / Bradford - Star bar.

Terry Hall showed up to lend his support at the Dingwalls gig and Lemmy of Motorhead was in the audience. I was taken by how clean and neat he looked close-up. How illusions can soon be destroyed. At Bradford Dean and I killed time before sound check in a little run down pub. The regulars looked like Rampton inmates. I went to the toilet, leaving Dean at the bar and when I came back he was playing dominoes with the biggest bunch of bruisers imaginable! He never saw danger of any kind and I left him to it.

Press exposure was building up nicely; we did interviews for, London Event - Poppix - City Limits - the Face and also recorded a live version of Disco Laurels for a cassette magazine publication called SFX. With the Rodeo release just a couple of weeks away David Jensen and John Peel were already playing white label promo copies on Radio One - which was a good sign. The powers that be at Warner Brothers assured us that it would make 'at least top twenty' and we were more than happy with those shallow assurances.

We did a Radio One session for John Peel at the BBC studios at Maida Vale, bringing back memories of the Sinatras session that I'd done the previous year. Blessedly no one brought their girlfriend along. Nothing much had changed, the organisation and format was the same. The four tracks we recorded were; Beating Heart - Murder Mile - Rodeo - Swing the Cat.

We were not that happy when the session was eventually broadcast, it sounded sort of lifeless somehow - we recorded the session on the back of an exhaustive live

schedule and we were knackered but I heard the session recently and It wasn't as bad as we imagined at the time - Peel repeated a couple of weeks later too. He also gave us a good mention in his introduction saying,
'The Swinging Laurels, currently of course a terribly hip name to drop into your conversation.'

During a break in recording we did a photo shoot for Sounds. We didn't have a lot of time, so we went into a children's playground where we were photographed cavorting over climbing frames and swings. When the feature surfaced the pictures made us cringe.

In London the 'New Romantic' movement was in full swing. The whole thing revolved around a club culture with an anything goes attitude - specialist club nights sprang up across the Capital. Steve Strange and Rusty Egan of the band Visage ran one of the clubs to be seen in - the Camden Palace in Camden Town. The Palace was formerly the Music Machine, a venue that I'd played before with Black Gorilla. Other hip clubs at the time were the Beatroute - the Wag Club - the Escape Club, (Another Black Gorilla haunt, formerly known as Gulliver's club, off Park Lane) - Blitz and Billys.

The new romantic movement spawned a number of bands that went on to chart success - Duran Duran - Spandau Ballet and a character ever present on the club scene with his larger than life persona, Boy George. We visited the Camden Palace a number of times when we were recording in London from our usual base at the Columbia Hotel in Lancaster Gate. After a full day recording there was no better way to unwind than to pop to the Palace for a lig and a beer or two. One such time we were there with journalist / musician pal Dave Henderson, and we bumped into Tom 'Scritti' who introduced had just entered the album charts at No.12. Green said rather arrogantly, 'Oh yeah, what album is that then?'

He knew damned well what I was talking about. Unfortunately his arrogance didn't go unnoticed - Dave Henderson was editor of top pop magazine Noise and he us to Green Gartside the Scritti Politti vocalist and leading light. During a bout of small talk I said, 'Congratulations on the album.' The new Scritti Politti album Songs to Remember heard it all. In the next issue he printed a damning account in the magazine's gossip column. I don't know for sure, but I got the impression that Green didn't much like the fact that Tom had been helping the Swinging Laurels out on our recordings.

Regulars at the Columbia Hotel were Scottish band the Bluebells, best known for their No.1 hit Young at Heart. We had a few good boozing sessions with them at the Palace before limping back to the hotel. They have the dubious honour of being the only band to get barred from the Columbia and that must have taken some doing!! The Columbia was a unique. They played host to many bands and had a bar manned by a night porter that stayed open all night. It was not unusual to see two or three other bands slumming it in the bar at any one time. On one stay, we saw punk band Dead Kennedys and Pete Wylie of the band Wah! - He was also signed to WEA records.

One particular night Vince Clarke and Alison Moyet of Yazoo were waiting for the lift, so we shared it. They were staying on the same floor, and we thought we saw them enter the room next door. Later that night we heard shrill female orgasmic screams. They seemed to be coming from the room next door. Dean and I looked at each other and said, 'No, it can't be!' - Vince was very slightly built and was dwarfed by Ms.Moyet who was more generously proportioned. I'm sure it wasn't them but someone was having a good time; the noise went on for ages.

Capital Radio asked us to record a live session for one of their popular flagship programmes called Thank God its Friday. The station had been very kind to us, play listing all our released material to date and we had already recorded a studio session for the station, but this was a live one, consequently the pressures weren't quite the same. It was a chat show with celebrity studio guests who were interviewed with live music in between from the guest band. We performed four songs in all.

There was pressure involved with a set up like that - Capital Radio had the UK's biggest listener ship next to Radio One, so it was big. At least on the live Top of the Pops we were miming - on this we'd be playing live to radio land. We tried to put the thought to the back of our minds, but the way the whole thing was set up made that impossible. WE WERE ALL IN THE SAME ROOM! The star guests were all seated around a large circular table with a microphone at its centre and we were set up just feet away.

Because of the way that we were wired for sound it meant that the only sound that they could hear as we played, were the saxophones, trumpet and vocals. All the keyboards and drums were directly injected through to the mixing desk and monitored to us on headphones. It must have sounded mighty strange. We were made even more nervous when we were introduced to the special studio celebrities; they were all well-known faces. The guests were: John Junkin, veteran television pundit, actor and comedy writer. David Putnam, film director, who had just picked up an Oscar for the film Chariots of Fire. Kevin Godley and Lol Creme, ex- of hit band 10cc and just making a name in the world of promotional video production.

As you can imagine, seeing those people a few feet away as we performed made it really nerve-racking. The studio producer marshalled the sound from his control room. When the show started all the guests were introduced, as we stood in our positions, totally silent. There was some chat about Chariots of Fire and some questions about John Junkin's latest situation comedy then a number from the Laurels. It all went swimmingly at first, although it did seem unnatural performing that way.

As we stood motionless waiting for our next cue, there was more cosy chat from the presenter and her guests. Then it was, 'Now it's time for another track from the Swinging Laurels' The track was Go Out and Find Her, a song on which I started the vocals and which was introduced by an eight beat count in on the bass drum. The studio producer hadn't got the drum tape synchronised, so when it came in we had no idea where the count in was.

SILENCE - PANIC - TRY AGAIN - WRONG.

The delay, which in real life probably lasted about 30 seconds felt like a million years on live radio. John Junkin made some totally unfunny quip about technology while we stewed in our own juices. It must have sounded terrible, but there was nothing that we could do about it and it wasn't our fault. When the producer finally got his act together, we lurched into the song proper - a bag of nerves. The worst of it was having Godley and Crème, who were highly successful musicians, sitting just feet away. We couldn't get out of that radio station fast enough. We were always on our guard for the unexpected, because it always seemed to happen to us.

With the imminent release of Rodeo we racked our brains for an off the wall method promote the record. Something that would attract as many press column inches as possible. The idea that came to the fore was a progression of previous crazy schemes that we had used to promote Peace of Mind. A BUSKING TOUR! After WEAs attempt to mould a visual image for us fell flat; we came up with our own idea of chic - Black bri-nylon skiing pants, cool wrap around shades and sixties style polo necked shirts, all very beatnik. It looked very striking and when we were all dressed in our new gear, we looked like a real band. A whole series of dates were co-ordinated many of which involved playing outside chart return record shops which were crucial sales-wise for a position in the charts. Only certain record shops were designated as chart return outlets. Their locations were supposed to be secret, but record companies soon sussed the retailers with this status, because they had specially adapted tills that fed sales information directly into a central computer. Other shops didn't have these terminals, so it didn't need the intellect of an Einstein to determine which shops counted.

This system was put into place to cut out chart rigging, but it seemed to encourage more. Since the first pop charts there has been chart fixing. Compilers of the charts took national sales figures from the terminals and from this data a weekly chart was put together. Years before this, it was possible to send a runner to different shops to buy a record into the charts. Time consuming - yes, but if it helped a band achieve their first hit, then it was well worth it in the long run.

There is always a way to circumvent any system. A common way to fool the terminal was to give away free singles and albums in return for logging extra credits. Releasing several different mixes of the same song in the same week, counted as a separate sale, thus giving a distorted sales figure which could hype a record into a chart position. Frankie Goes to Hollywood released several 12" versions of Relax and Two Tribes in this way. Some methods were not illegal; Beatles manager Brian Epstein carried out the most famous hype of all time. He bought thousands of copies of their first hit 'Love Me Do' in 1962, which resulted in a Top 20 chart entry, but left him with thousands of surplus copies. In those days it was perfectly above board if you had the money to do it. With the crucial first hit under their belts; the rest as they say is history. This blatant method was soon sussed out and systems were designed to spot irregular sales patterns and average them out, but even this can be unfair, because some bands sell a lot of records in localised areas - Scottish bands for instance. The secret is to sell as many units over a wide an area as you can.

    We rehearsed three numbers for our busking jaunt, Disco Laurels - Rodeo and Lonely Boy and we used small practise amps and backing tapes played on a ghetto-blaster. The horns were played live and just one microphone was needed for Gaz's vocals - Mark played a small Casio keyboard. It sounded very effective in the open air.

    Camden Palace put on a series of showcases for 'bubbling under' bands and they asked us to make an appearance. The Swinging Laurels had built a reputation through the expediency of slogging around small venues and clubs - we generated a play anywhere, anytime attitude. I loved playing live, but Mark, thought that we ought to be more selective. He once said to me, 'You'd play in a toilet!' He was right. If I thought it was right for the band, I would have played anywhere. We never did want to be a mainstream pop band - we wanted to be as versatile as possible.

    We visited Camden Palace to watch another band play a showcase, to see if we could pick up any tips. They were the Eurythmics a band just starting to make waves - they were superb. Vocalist Annie Lennox gave a stunning performance while Dave Stewart moved around the stage taking photographs of the audience. When our night came the place was absolutely heaving. From the stage the venue was quite breathtaking - two balconies leaned over a dance floor area in front of the stage. We sang and played horns live, but drums and keyboards were on backing tape. Just as well because Mark didn't make it to the gig! He broke down on the M1. Had this been a conventional gig we wouldn't have been able to do it, but because Mark was only going to be miming anyway, it didn't matter.

The gig went down surprisingly well - we sat on high stools in our beatnik garb and Gaz crooned Hair by Mantini while percussionist Pete Harriman pretended to cut his hair on stage. Hair by Mantini was an instrumental dedicated to a rather exclusive hair salon in Leicester. Giving the establishment a name check was a wise move - we got our hair done free whenever we wanted. It was gratifying to see that many Warner Brothers staff had turned out to see us and it made up for the disastrous gig at Brighton Xtreems. When Mark recounted his nightmare day spent on the hard shoulder with his stricken car, Gaz quipped, 'You should have popped over by astral projection!'

Warner Brothers did try to promote us. We were offered an appearance on The David Essex Showcase, a talent show in the New Faces mould. No Thanks. It was hosted by singer/actor/heartthrob - David Essex. The show went out on Saturday evening primetime television, but I was dead against it. I remembered too well my experiences with Sister Big Stuff at that god awful New Faces audition - fortunately the others agreed with me, so we declined the offer. The show did have its successes -Toto Coelo and Belle Stars both went on to chalk up hits after appearing on the show. I always felt that achieving success through this medium stigmatised an act - Leicester's Showaddywaddy came through as New Faces winners, and I'm sure that they were sick to death of being reminded of the fact.

As we practised for our 'busking tour' the publicity machine at Warner Brothers asked us to perform at a birthday bash - it could do us some good they said. It wasn't a conventional birthday party. It was on a riverboat on the Thames, and was the fortieth birthday of the producer of Crackerjack - the long running BBC children's show. They featured a pop band each week and an appearance carried a fair amount of kudos - our people reckoned that this could be a way through the back door, and onto the show. As a kid I remember seeing some great bands on Crackerjack - Thin Lizzy performing Whiskey in the Jar and Chicory Tip hamming it up with Son of my Father. Both classics of different kinds.

On the boat we met the Crackerjack birthday boy - he was a chubby rather camp man and also there were luminaries in the world of television production. Television ventriloquist Keith Harris was there but had thankfully left Orville the duck at home, electing instead to bring along a glamorous leggy blonde. This prompted a whole series of Laurel jokes of the 'I wonder how he makes her lips move' variety.

The booze was free and flowed freely and we played as the boat chugged slowly down the Thames to Greenwich. Party guests became increasingly more and more inebriated. There was a lot of 'lovey - lovey' and "darrrrling" type banter flying around. It was bizarre to see the Towers of London glide by - stage left, as we played Lonely Boy. The whole experience was a wheeze. We never did get a Crackerjack appearance though. Straight after our nautical jolly we went to Peppermint Park - a restaurant next to Stringfellows club, to perform a semi-cabaret set in front of diners. We wore our black beatnik stage gear and sleazed a set of instrumental versions of our songs. It was an incredible and weird experience. Cabaret a go-go - good practise for the forthcoming busking jamboree, but it was wacky playing while people noshed away. The owner of the restaurant wanted to re- book us but we decided that once was enough.

As we approached the busking extravaganza Rodeo was getting played to death on Radio One. Simon Bates had taken a real shine to the record and played it at the same time each day on his prestigious morning show. It also figured at No.4 in the New Muzak chart in Melody Maker and Hair by Mantini, appeared at No.1 in a chart in City Limits magazine. It got to the stage that whenever you turned on the radio, Rodeo was playing. It was also on some Jukeboxes - one being my local pub. It always seemed to come on after I walked in and I found that mildly embarrassing.

Our busking tour kicked off on September 30th in Sutton-in-Ashfield; and the final stint was on October 10th at Battersea Park in London. The full itinerary consisted of dates in Nottingham - Leicester - Kettering - Corby - Cardiff and London - with several appearances at each location. Warner Brothers really pushed the boat out and placed a full-page advertisement in Record Mirror, probably to forewarn the middle aged shoppers of Corby that we were coming. Lock up your Grandmas! We turned up, set up, and performed three songs at each site, to the total bemusement of passers by.

We opened with our trusty instrumental Disco Laurels and when the audience were putty in our hands, we launched into Rodeo and Lonely Boy. It took a couple of performances before we relaxed - then we enjoyed the bizarre experience for what it was. When we played outside the Virgin Megastore on Oxford Street in London we nearly got arrested, a flustered, red-faced bobby approached, vainly waving his arms like a windmill at us. Our cabaret was prematurely halted because the crowd had spilled onto the road, causing the traffic to grind to a halt.

At some sites, outside chart return shops, it was hilarious to see fifty-year-old women, fully laden with shopping carrying away their 12" copies of Rodeo. I mused. 'These women will buy anything!' Outside HMV Superstore, on Oxford Street Adam Sweeting, a Melody Maker reporter who was with us for the day, heard one character in the crowd ask another,

'What are they called?' The other chap replied confidently, 'The Singing Lorries!' Just like the blessed are the cheese maker's sketch in the Life of Brian.

We played Carnaby Street - coincidentally outside the offices of Smash Hits, and then moved on to Covent Garden we were photographed in action by the press. Lugging the gear around was incredibly tiring, but we were right about one thing, it got us masses of press. By the end of these pantomime

performances, we were thoroughly enjoying it; Gaz was imploring throngs of shoppers,
'Buy our single and make an old man very happy' I was shouting 'Buy our single and make a happy man very old'

We did three shows in our native Leicester, which for us were the scariest of all. I actually recognised faces in the crowd. At one I saw ex-Sister Big Stuff vocalist Melda - at another I saw the beaming face of my Dad, bless him. I could lip read him saying 'That's my lad.' Thank goodness for my shades! The two morning shows were fine, but after we had spent our lunchtime break in the pub, things went a little bit awry. We played outside the Clock Tower in the very centre of the City and then moved on to the Market Place, which was packed on what was a Friday afternoon. When it came to Dean's trumpet solo on Rodeo he sounded like Les Dawson! Split notes all over the place.

We trudged around Cardiff for what seemed like days - but it was the same story - we were eyed by suspicious shoppers, but they still bought the record! The highlight of the tour was a huge benefit for Oxfam on Battersea Park in London. It was an event sponsored and organised by the News of the World's, Sun Day magazine. It had been trumpeted in the magazine for weeks prior to the day and provided us with some very valuable high profile publicity. Also appearing were chart duo Dollar and hit band Classix Nouveaux - together with a number of television and show business celebrities.

The park was packed when we arrived and we were ushered into a VIP marquee where we could chill before it was our turn to take to the stage. The bar was free, so vodka and oranges started to flow. There were some well known faces availing themselves of the free plonk, West Ham and England footballer - Match of the Day soccer pundit, Trevor Brooking, Slade drummer Don Powell, television impressionist Faith Brown and fashion guru Jordan.

Jordan was a famous designer noted for her punk fashion. She had a huge mane of spiky orange hair and wore a corset bra over her T-shirt, prompting Dean to say to her,

'S'cuse me love, you've got your brassier on all wrong - it should go underneath your blouse!' Dean had quaffed a few drinks by then. Jordan gave him a contemptuous scowl. It was a good day.

A conventional gig took us to the Beatroute club in Greek Street London. This club was ultra trendy and was frequented by a whole galaxy of hip people including the lads from Spandau Ballet. After our show I stood at the bar talking with Gaz, from where we noticed Dean engaging in conversation with Jake Burns, lead vocalist of the band Stiff Little Fingers. Gaz said to me, 'I bet you any money that Dean doesn't realise who he is talking to' Jake complimented Dean on his trumpet-playing prowess and went on to mention our connection with the Fun Boy Three saying,

'I am signed to the same label as the Fun Boy Three, Chrysalis records.' Dean said, 'Oh, are you in a band then?' to which Jake replied 'Yeah, Stiff Little Fingers.' which prompted Dean to say, 'Oh, I think I've heard of you, you've been getting a little bit of press lately, haven't you?' When Dean came back over to us, Gaz said,

'Who was that you were just talking to Dean?' Dean said 'His name is Jim Bunns - I think he's in a band!'

I took the train to London to do a radio interview for the BBC World Service, coupled with a series of press interviews. Manager Martin Patton collected me at St.Pancras station, and delivered me to BBC Broadcasting House. I was led into the studio reception area, given a coffee, and introduced to the producer. The interview was to be conducted by Radio One disc jockey Tommy Vance, but I had to wait while he finished interviewing Sheila Ferguson of the Three Degrees. I was well used to radio interviews, but the producer let it slip that the show had 20 million listeners world wide.

The enormity of this hit me - SHIT - 20 million people. By the time I was put in front of Tommy Vance, I was a quivering wreck. The interview lasted about twenty minutes, Rodeo was aired and we chatted about forthcoming projects. I have a recording of the interview, and at the start there is a nervous tremor in my voice. The producer made no false claims about the far-reaching effect of that programme, my friends in Berlin - Joe Keaveney, Tony James and Mick Mooney had heard the show.

Afterwards I was driven to WEA records head office to conduct a series of interviews for teen magazines by telephone. These were a vital bridge in getting the name of the band across to young girls - they buy a lot of records. The interviews were very tedious, in the same way that local radio interviews were tedious. They asked the same banal questions and it was a chore so far removed from music itself - but it was a treadmill that you had to get on, to promote your record.

I did lots of such interviews, there was no doubt at all that Gaz was our main man but he absolutely abhorred doing interviews. Mark came over as an articulate character on radio, but we didn't dare let Dean loose - certainly not unsupervised. Once we did an interview for BBC Radio Lincolnshire and were kept waiting for an age in the reception area. When they finally sat us around a studio table they gave us nametags, which we promptly swapped around. We changed identities, and when the interview went out live on the radio; we did impressions of each other. We did so many radio interviews that we got used to the same standard stock questions that would be thrown at us, so we had the answers ready. Dean became me and he put on an absolutely hilarious display, answering questions in the style of John Barrow. It was a little bit too accurate for my liking.

After I'd done interviews with My Guy - Blue Jeans - Patches - Jackie, I had lunch with Colin Collinwood a journalist from Music Maker a weekly music paper. I'm not the most outgoing character, and meeting a complete stranger for lunch was incredibly difficult for me. I know a lot of musicians who are crazy and animated on stage, but are quite reserved away from the live arena.

To finish the day I was whisked to the home of a Capital Radio presenter to record an interview for radio. Her home was lovely and littered with antiques and taking pride of place in front of a raging open fire was a tiger skin, head and all. She explained that she'd interviewed Iggy Pop the previous day, and he was so out of it that he was wrestling with the tiger skin on the floor as she fired questions at him!

When the interview was over I was deposited at the train station for my journey back to Leicester - completely worn out. It was a typical of days spent courting the media. Releasing a record is only the tip of the iceberg because you also have to promote the product. It's all a part of the game that you have to play if you want to compete in the market place.

Chapter Twenty Seven

BOY GEORGE - MAKE WAY FOR THE LONELY BOY

Rodeo enjoyed saturation Radio One airplay but didn't trouble the chart statisticians so now the urgency to produce a follow up single became paramount. Our working relationship with producer Adam Kidron never really gelled. After several re-mixes of Rodeo we came just short of a vital, definitive mix and it just goes to show that blanket radio coverage doesn't guarantee record sales. Boy George requested Rodeo when he appeared on Kid Jensen's Radio One show, and Janice Long featured it in a 'records that should have been hits' feature. But the record buying public are not that fickle - if they don't like the product they won't buy it. I personally believe that delays cost us dear - we should have rush released the single to capitalise on the publicity from our liaison with the Fun Boy Three.

We decided to record Lonely Boy which was one of our earliest self penned songs, for the follow up and Steve Levine, who had been producing the fledgling Culture Club, was brought in to oversee the production. He had already enjoyed chart success - most notably with China Crisis. We'd been to see Culture Club live at Leicester Polytechnic and after the gig Gaz went backstage to chat with Boy George. George had already proclaimed himself a Laurels fan on national radio and in the Daily Star. He used to put his hand under his chin and wiggle his fingers, mimicking Gaz's trademark goatee beard. He announced proudly,

'Hey, I bought your single.'

George had been on the periphery of celebrity for some time, and figured in an early incarnation of Bow Wow Wow. He was a well-known face on the London club scene with his outrageous image. He was the perfect pop star commodity - he was intelligent and articulate and he came across brilliantly in the media so it was no surprise that his rise to fame was meteoric.

We met up with Steve and immediately forged a rapport. He was an affable, laid back character and was genuinely interested in our songs. He was based at Red Bus studio in London, a studio used by the likes of Spandau Ballet, Bananarama, David Grant, Culture Club and Tears for Fears.

We started the recording on October 22nd booking Red Bus through to the 28th. The recording went very smoothly, a lot of pre-production work made the process easier and Levine got an excellent brass sound and coaxed a stunning sax solo out of Gaz. Backing vocals were needed on the tail end of the song and although I generally did the backing vocals I couldn't get the phrase to work. Eventually Steve said that he knew someone who would be perfect for the part and he would contact him for the evening session.

After a break we lumbered back into the studio to meet our guest vocalist - It was BOY GEORGE! We were knocked for six. George was one of the most instantly recognisable faces at that time and was soon to become a global phenomenon. The implications were potentially enormous; George was dressed in his trademark finery - large black hat, make up and braided locks. He rattled off his vocal part off to perfection in double quick time, as we watched through the studio control room window. It was pretty surreal and the realisation of what this could mean started to dawn on me.

George is one of those rare vocalists with a pure voice quality that requires very little in the way of treatment from the producer's rack of effects. His part fitted perfectly and there was no mistaking his distinctive voice. Levine told us to stay stumm about George's spot of moonlighting fearing that his label, Virgin, would blow a fuse if they found out that their golden boy was working without their express permission. Culture Club drummer Jon Moss came into the studio before the end of the session and loved the track. Jon was an astute businessman and was behind much of the packaging and promotion of Culture Club.

A few short weeks after the recording we sat with Culture Club in Red Bus studio as they watched their Top of the Pops appearance when Do You Really Want to Hurt Me hit the No.1 slot in the national chart. I felt like pinching myself to see if I was really awake - there we were rubbing shoulders with arguably the biggest pop sensations of 1982. George was picking himself to bits as we watched the show. In the next few months there would be few places on the face of the planet that would not be familiar with the image of Culture Club, and in particular, Boy George. We were certain that his involvement would help to make Lonely Boy a sure-fire hit. He had legions of young fans eating out of his hands and it was hard to imagine a more influential ally.

Clients of Red Bus studio were a who's who of pop stars. It was not unusual to see Tears for Fears or Imagination coming and going. One day, US soul legend Isaac Hayes of Shaft fame interrupted our recording session to view the facilities. He looked a cool cat with his shaved head, shades and long black leather coat. The studio also recorded film soundtrack music and one particular haunting song that we heard over and over was the theme to the box office blockbuster, ET.

As 1982 drew towards its conclusion we busied ourselves on the live front. We supported Mari Wilson, beehive hair do and all, at the Hammersmith Palais in London. She registered hits with Just What I always Wanted and Cry Me a River and her backing vocalist Michele Collins later became better known as Cindy Beale in the soap East Enders. The Palais was packed and the gig was good all round. 1982 had been a phenomenal year for the Swinging Laurels, we'd done so much in such a short space of time and as we steamed towards 1983 we had everything to look forward to.

We got wind of the fact that Mick Mooney, our mate in Berlin, was throwing one of his legendary toga parties so we pleaded with Martin and Steve to let us go. They knew how hard we had worked throughout the year, and finally relented. We flew to Berlin and turned up at Mick's flat unannounced. We got digs over a seedy looking bar, near the Kantsrasse that had the novel idea of employing young girls in short skirts as doormen. Let me tell you, they weren't that good at the job. They would be forever climbing into the cars of strange men - they can't have gone far because they always came back after a few minutes. They seemed very friendly. Perhaps they were helping them to find a parking space?

For Mark and Dean it was their first visit to Berlin. Gaz and I were determined to show them everything that this unique place had to offer and we had four days to cram it all in. When we dropped in on our friends they were flabbergasted to see us. Berlin is desperately cold in winter, so a toga party was not a great idea, but the flat was heated by a huge edifice of a coal fired boiler that stood against the wall. It threw out so much heat that you couldn't bear to stand too close to it. Booze flowed all night. It was a typical Mick Mooney extravaganza; his flat was piled to ceiling height with crates of beer. His parties were known to last for a whole weekend and we all paid for it when the effects of our excesses began to wear off.

We made the obligatory visit across the Berlin wall to the East on a Sunday and we were staggered to see literally thousands of people promenading down the main street, Friedrickstrasse. It was a customary pastime on a Sunday in East Berlin. We stood out big time in comparison with the native East Berliners and their colourless uniformity. Their clothes were drab, the surroundings were drab, and we stuck out like sore thumbs. Queues of people lined up to gawp at us, as if we were some freak show curiosity. We looked like a band. Dean had a carrot coloured Eraser head, hair do - Gaz had his trademark goatee beard and balloon baggy trousers - and I had had a jet black barnet - courtesy of Mantini, and my leather trousers - Mark never went anywhere without his flat tram drivers hat. We were a huge attraction to the natives.

We went to a top-notch hotel for dinner. It was obviously a place frequented by wealthy East Berliner diplomats and they eyed us enviously. Again people went out of their way to stare at us, as if we were some sort of exhibit. To those poor impoverished people we were something they could never hope to be. Dean suffered a panic attack and begged us to take him back to the West - it really got to the poor guy. A coach full of Russian soldiers pulled over in the road, just to get a better look at us.

We couldn't visit Berlin without experiencing the seedier side. Mick took us to Big Sexy land - no points for guessing what went on there. We went into a peep show where there were a number of cubicles facing each other in a circle. Through the window of the cubicle, when the shutter was up, you could see the faces of guys opposite peeping through their respective slots. Inside was a revolving platform, on which a girl posed like crazy. A coin was required to the lift the shutter and see inside, and when the money ran out, it unceremoniously clattered shut.

As my shutter came up, I looked across to see which of my mates I could spot in the cubicles opposite. I saw Gaz raise his camera - CLICK - and quickly lower it again. The photograph actually turned out when it was developed. One night in a dark club Dean took a shine to girl - there was a lot of eye contact going on but he got the shock of his life when he visited the toilets to answer a call of nature. Standing at the next urinal with mini skirt hitched up, fishnet stockings exposed, there she was, using what was definitely a male appendage to urinate with. That cooled Dean's ardour, and illustrated how sexual boundaries in Berlin were blurred. We revisited Café Central but Jayne County wasn't there with Gaz's money! The trip was real fun and we all let our hair down but I needed a week to recuperate when we got back to Leicester.

Do You Really Want To Hurt Me was a massive world wide hit for Culture Club, topping the charts in many counties. A rivalry had developed in the UK for the teen market between, Wham! Duran Duran and Spandau Ballet. But it was Boy George who became the darling of the media - it became almost impossible to open a newspaper or turn on the television without seeing his image. All this augured well for the Swinging Laurels of course; we'd kept Boy George's involvement with our single a closely guarded secret. The people at Warner Brothers were telling us that THIS TIME we were definitely staring a top twenty single in the face. Now, where had we heard that one before?

Such was George's public-profile, that even without a credit on the sleeve, we knew that his voice would be instantly recognisable. The 12" version of Lonely Boy featured George's vocals prominently on the slow fade at the end of the mix.

To capitalise on the meteoric success of Culture Club a tour was arranged for the spring of 1983, through the Derek Block agency and we were thrilled to bits to be asked to join them as special guests. Such was the importance of this tour that Warner Brothers delayed the release of our single to coincide and maximise on potential record sales. The tour was one of the hottest of 1983; some record companies would have paid a fortune to get one of their bands on it.

All was not well at Brothers Warner though - in a behind the scenes coup, Tarquin Gotch who had signed us to the label, was moved on. This meant that he no longer had the overall control of the label which was bad news for us. One of the major factors that convinced us to sign was his unswerving support - he was a real fan. Now we were faced with the prospect of a newcomer controlling our careers. Max Hole was brought in as his successor and from the off we got bad vibes. A new man, keen to impress was bound to want to bring in new talent and it was unlikely that he would devote as much of his attention to acts he had inherited.

I went to Warner Brothers office to conduct more interviews. I was introduced to people several floors up that I'd never met before. I was amazed; there were promotional people responsible for radio and television exposure that I'd never been introduced to. We had been signed to the label for six months, and there were people crucial to our advancement, that we'd never met! This angered and saddened me and highlighted one of the drawbacks of being signed to a multi-national concern. When we were signed to Albion Records, we knew everyone in the organisation from the directors down and that was the crucial differential.

A new photographic shoot was set up with the record release and tour publicity in mind. This was to be our first session with top photographer Jill Furmanovsky. Jill is an incredibly intuitive artist - very well respected in her chosen field. She has photographed many icons from the rock field. Among them are Debbie Harry - Stevie Wonder - Bob Marley - Mick Jagger - Sex Pistols - Police - Pretenders - Oasis and more recently fellow Leicester band Kasabian. Photo shoots with her were relaxed; she had the great knack of getting the best out of her subjects. Our sessions with her are, in my opinion, the best that we ever commissioned.

First we had a series of shots in our black 'beatnik' gear and then a series of shots for postcards, publicity photographs and also for the Lonely Boy record sleeve. At this session she took shots of Gaz for the sleeve that were to receive much critical acclaim. Jill produced a mock up of the famous Van Gogh self portrait for which she had painstakingly hand painted a stunning back drop with single brush strokes. Gaz sat motionless for hours, while his plain white jacket was painted, to match the backdrop. After hours of preparation the effect was staggering. The picture was featured on the Channel 4 television show, The Tube, when presenter Muriel Grey interviewed Jill. They have also featured in an exhibition of her work.

With the Culture Club tour confirmed we felt that it was high time that we recruited a real string bass player. Dean was playing more and more trumpet live, which meant he wasn't able to cover as much work on synthesiser bass. Also from a visual angle it made sense to free Dean to join us at the front of the stage. We auditioned several bassists, but no one seemed to have the playing acumen or personality to fit in.

Until one day we auditioned a batch of hopefuls at Archway studios in Leicester. One applicant was so obviously a Laurel that it hurt. He was tall and spindly with a haircut that suggested that he'd just taken a huge bolt of electricity. He didn't even have a case for his bass guitar and after a couple of numbers it was patently apparent that he was our man. His name was Kevin 'Reverb' Bayliss. I asked him afterwards, 'How long have you been playing the bass?' He said, 'About two hours!' He was previously a guitarist in cult Leicester band Rockin' Ronnie and the Bendy Ruperts. He borrowed a bass guitar that morning and practised on the

BUS on the way to the audition. Reverb was a humorous, wacky character and there was no doubt at all that we had made the right choice. There was never a dull moment when he was around. We played a series of gigs to get up to speed and very soon Reverb fitted in famously. These were: the Asylum Club / Nottingham - Goldsmith College / London - Leicester University and Lonsdale College / Derby.

Just prior to the Culture Club tour news filtered through that the majority of dates had sold out and an extra matinee had to be added at the Dominion Theatre. The full tour itinerary was:
Cardiff / Top Rank - Manchester / Apollo - Newcastle / City Hall - Liverpool / Royal Court Theatre - Bristol / Colston Hall - Poole / Arts Centre - Portsmouth Guildhall - London / Dominion Theatre (Three consecutive dates.)

The Swinging Laurels were paid fifty pounds a night. Not each, the whole band! This may shock some people, but support bands on major tours are routinely treated in this way. People assume that just because they have graced the same stage as the star act they reap similar financial rewards. This is a complete fallacy. Many support acts actually pay for the privilege of playing on a major tour and five figure 'buy on' fees are not unheard of. Supporting on the right tour can elevate a bubbling under band to the top flight in a short space of time. From a business point of view it is easier to play ten 3,000 capacity venues, than to slog around the small clubs for months to reach the same amount of people.

I have heard of instances where the headlining band have hardly passed the time of day with their support, treating them as some sort of underclass but we knew Culture Club and they were gracious enough to treat us with respect. At the end of the day, it is always the headlining act that the majority of punters have paid to see - so it is a case of winning over as many people as possible in the forty minutes that you are on stage.

The 10% brothers named their management company Swinging Stars and the contract that we signed with them kept everything legal and above board. We were just a couple of weeks away from the Lonely Boy release date and the portents were good. The powers that be at Warner Bros were predicting success and were trying to gear everything up to coincide with the tour. We had just taken delivery of white label test pressings and that was when you knew that your record was imminent. I only played the test pressing to a couple of people; we still wanted to keep Boy George's involvement under wraps for fear of legal repercussions. People raved about it saying,

'How on earth did you manage to get Boy George to record for you?'

I tingled with anticipation and expectancy. The single sounded as good as anything else that was around at the time, but the ace up our sleeves was our very special guest and the fact that we had secured a slot on one of the most eagerly awaited tours. Warner Brothers even commissioned a television ad for the record. It featured a snippet of the track, showed photographs of the band and was introduced by David Jensen.

It was then that a blunder of monumental proportions robbed us of a certain hit record. Our management team and publishers Albion Music crafted a press release to promote the tour and the single. It didn't mention Boy George by name, but the way it was worded would have prompted any dullard to suss out what we were trying to conceal. Here is the press release that was printed in all the major music publications,

'The Swinging Laurels the Leicester band with a passing 2-Tone connection although they eventually signed to WEA, will be supporting Culture Club on their forthcoming British tour. The band will be unveiling their new line up for the tour, which consists of six people and a Revox for backing tapes. The new recruits will be adding 'real bass' and percussion to the line up. The band have a new single called "Lonely Boy' released on February 25. It features some guest vocals by someone who must remain anonymous due to contractual reasons but whose voice should be instantly distinguishable and may not be unconnected with another band mentioned earlier in this story.'

Doh! This is called shooting yourself in the foot! It got worse; the Record Mirror made it lead story in their gossip column Private Lives. They printed a photograph of Boy George and wrote,

'What a naughty Boy George is... I know he doesn't make any money out of the wonderful Multi-cultural club, but I wouldn't have thought he need resort to moonlighting in order to scratch up a bob or two to squander at the Boots No.7 counter. You see the golden throated crooner will be singing backing vocals on the new Swinging Laurels single which comes out this week. But keep it under your hats folks, as they'll be no credit on the cover, to avoid any possible hassles with his record company. Whatever next? TV ads for Harmony Hairspray perhaps...' that career wrecking piece was courtesy of Simon Tebbut!

The phone lines to Max Hole at Warner Brothers all but melted. By the time the ink was dry on those articles George's record company Virgin Records were crying foul, and talking of serious litigation. To be fair to George, all this was nothing to do with him, he had done the recording as a genuine favour and now he was innocently embroiled in big legal shit. Virgin records demanded an undisclosed up front payment and a ridiculous percentage of the profit from the sales of the record. It got pretty ugly, so eventually Warner Brothers agreed to erase George's contribution and Gaz had to re-record George's parts.

Sales were certain to be boosted significantly with George on it. An army of little girls would have bought anything even vaguely connected to their beloved heartthrob. This also forced a delayed release date - everything had been primed to co-ordinate. All the carefully integrated promotional work no longer synchronised and the release no longer coincided with the tour dates. It could only happen to us. I still have a couple of those rare test pressings and I suspect that one-day they may become very collectable items.

This debacle clearly shows how crucial decisions are in the pop business. One lapse of judgement can cost and talent isn't everything. A huge slice of good fortune is needed to make it to the top and without that element of luck, you've no chance. The threat of litigation did little to endear us to the new head of A&R at Warner Brothers but we just wanted to get on with the music. All this meddling and stirring by outsiders had nothing to do with music at all and it left a bad taste in my mouth.

As a part of the pre-release promotion Gaz and I travelled to Southampton to record a television interview with David Jensen for his Coast to Coast pop programme on TVS television. We were interviewed on camera then they played our single. He was genuinely interested in what the Laurels had been up to and he had an extensive musical knowledge. In the canteen after our interview sat none other but comedy sit. com actor and writer John Junkin. The last time we met had been on that embarrassing Capital Radio show, where we bungled our intro, live on air. He eyed us suspiciously.

Afterwards we travelled along the coast to Portsmouth to conduct an interview for Radio Victory. Independent local radio stations all seemed to be manned by loud people who think that they have their finger on the pulse - most of them hadn't. Harry Enfield's 'Smashy and Nice' is a stunningly accurate window on the world of local radio and we've seen loads on our travels. There were exceptions. John Shaw at Radio Trent in Nottingham knew his stuff as did Jay Cooper at Leicester Sound. Others tended to ask the same limp questions. To address this problem our publicist at Albion, Julian Henry, cleverly compiled a biography booklet which told the Laurels story in semi-fictional form. It embellished each of our characters. It was a great idea - radio presenters and regional press lapped it up and after reading it they tended to ask more interesting questions.

After the full realisation of the opportunity we'd lost kicked in, we busied ourselves practising hard for the tour. When the first leg of the Culture Club tour came around we were pretty apprehensive; we had done big support slots before but never anything as substantial and protracted as this. We travelled to Cardiff for our first date at the Top Rank.

When we got to the venue a sizeable crowd of Boy George clones were already assembled outside the stage door. Support acts traditionally get the briefest amount of time to sound check. Generally they are looked on as a hindrance by the sound technician, who is more interested in creating a good sound for his paymasters - the headlining band. Sound men have been known to give support bands an inferior sound - meaning that the star band sound so much better. For example they would leave the master volume low and then crank it up when the headlining act came on.

We were wise to this, so we bought a bottle of liquor for the sound technicians and lighting men. It is amazing what a bottle of plonk can do for you - after that they couldn't do enough for us. It was vital to have these people on our side because we were totally in their hands. For ten important shows they had the power to make or break us so a bottle of fire water was a small price to pay.

Unfortunately this little spot of subterfuge did us no good on the opening night; everything was running late, so there was no sound check for us at all. We sat in the dressing room as the auditorium filled with hysterical teenagers. When show time came we stepped onto the stage dressed to the nines and raring to go. The sheer power of the vocal onslaught from 3,000 high pitched screams was awesome and knocked us back. Gaz reached down to activate the reel to reel tape machine with our drum tracks on it, and turned it on.

ZAP-ZIP-SHOOOOM-ZUP-ZUP-ZUP-ZAP ZUPZUP-ZIP

It was a while before we realised what was going on. THE DRUM TAPE WAS ON THE WRONG WAY ROUND! It was a problem that could have been easily ironed out at sound check - had we had one. Yet another of those curl up and die moments that seemed to visit the Swinging Laurels on a regular basis. 3,000 screaming pre-pubescent girls were wetting themselves at the thought of seeing George & Company, and there we were standing like lemons. As Gaz rewound the tape to feed it back on to the machine, I made a pathetic attempt to communicate with the audience by saying something really crass, like,

'Hello Cardiff, are you allllrrrright?'

It cut no ice, so I quickly buggered off, stage left. It seemed to take an age for the tape to rewind but when we nervously filed back onstage, the reception if anything was even louder.

Those girls would have screamed at anything. A stray dog would have brought the house down!

We went down superbly despite our earlier faux pas, but our reception was nothing compared to the one that Culture Club got. There was such a cacophony it was a wonder that the roof of the arena wasn't blown clean away. Dave Henderson, working for Sounds, was with us for the first three dates to write a feature. In a review he wrote,

'If Freud could have analysed the meteoric rise of Culture Club, he would surely have some explanation as to why hordes of pre-pubescent girls go ape over a man dressed as a woman. It was scream and scream again.'

There was a steady stream of lifeless female bodies being passed over the heads of the audience to the first aid area, which incidentally was a place that Dean liked to hang out. He liked to be on hand when they finally came round! Easy pickings! Culture Club were very good - their live sound was much harder and more substantial than on record. George had the audience exactly where he wanted them and they screamed themselves blue in the face to show their approval. The thing is with George is, what you see is what you get, and that is one of the reasons that I admired him. I admired his honesty for daring to be what he wanted to be.

Despite our little technical setback the experience was exhilarating, but there was one little surprise that we were not prepared for. Culture Club had got this part of the proceedings off to a fine art. Before the last scream had faded in the auditorium, they were spirited out of a back entrance, into their limousine and away to their hotel. We made the mistake of hanging around too long before making our exit and when we attempted to leave, we were swamped by hundreds of young girls. Reverb was pinned against a wall and systematically relieved of his shirt buttons. Some of those girls appeared much older than their years and had developed girlie parts and tongues like ferrets. Having missed Culture Club, they focused their attention on us as next best things. Anyone that had been up on that stage was fair game. It was a real eye opener in every sense; we signed autographs for ages before we finally managed to break away. When we made it back to our hotel we were shattered, but the adrenaline kicked in and we retired to the bar for a real session. I didn't even make it to breakfast the following morning.

The following gig was at the Manchester Apollo Theatre, which was an entirely different show altogether. For one, we actually got a sound check, proving, if proof at all were needed that bribery really does work! The Apollo was a huge, impressive all seater auditorium with three tiered balconies and a huge stage. Our set went really well and there were no mishaps this time, prompting an excellent live review from Sounds, part of which read,

'The Swinging Laurels staggered on to the stage dressed to the nine and determined to succeed. Like an anarchic ballet, they moved with grace and agility and received rapturous applause. New songs alongside old faves simply underlined their top pop status and with front man Gary Birtles gyrating like a crazed helicopter, they were a magnetic revelation. There are no half measures with the Laurels; it's straight-down-the-line accessible and endearing pop. The crowd lapped it up.'

With Culture Club again long gone, an enthusiastic crowd accosted us outside. Stepping onto that stage in such an emotionally charged atmosphere really did take your breath away and the deafening roar that greeted us almost stopped us in our tracks. Being the support we only performed thirty minutes of material, so the time soon passed. The only song I dreaded in the set was Go Out and Find Her because I started the main vocal part. I never really felt at ease singing solo parts, but in front of thousands of screaming kids, it was really taxing.

After the Manchester gig the Laurels entourage headed for the trendy Hacienda club, along with Dave Henderson and lens man Steve Pyke of Sounds. Steve, like Dave was another Leicester ex-pat who had been in the band RTRs - today he is, like Jill Furmanovsky, world famous for his portrait photos of iconic figures. Our people managed to blag us a free entrance. I found the place seriously lacking in atmosphere, but we made the most of it. The Hacienda was one of those clubs that had a national reputation; people travelled miles for a night out there. The powers that be at Factory Records owned it. Factory records were a hip Manchester indie label that bought bands like Happy Mondays and New Order to prominence and Leicester music legend Kevin Hewick was signed to them for a time too. Sounds later featured a Pyke shot of Dean and me enjoying a cocktail and pulling silly faces.

On to Newcastle City Hall and the usual mayhem awaited us. By now we'd started to gain more stage confidence, so it was a lot more relaxed and we could let our hair down. At this show we sent Steve Pyke onto the stage and into the lion's den to introduce us. He seemed quite up for it until he actually stepped out into the limelight. As the spotlight picked him out, he stood frozen like a frightened rabbit caught in the beam of car headlights. A huge scream engulfed him and he looked absolutely terrified as he fumbled for the microphone. Finally he stuttered,
'LADEEEZZZ AND GENNELMEN - GIVE A BIG WELCOME TO THE SWINGING LLLL-LLLLL- LLLLAURELS!'
With that he scurried, shaking to the sanctity of the wings. Poor chap - he was ashen - I don't think I've ever seen anyone quite so frightened.

As the tour wore on we all became quite used to the circus that surrounded us. We used to call the phenomenon 'tour frenzy.' There is a point in the middle of a tour when you look forward to its finish and getting home to sanity. But after a few days at home, you start pining for the road again. When we played the Southampton Gaumont theatre, after sound check, I nipped to the pub next door to unwind and to kill time before our show. As I entered four girls leapt on me. They scratched, pulled my hair and tugged at my clothes - my only refuge was the gent's toilets! The landlord came to my rescue and ejected the girls from the pub. It was a very red faced John that ordered his drink. You wouldn't believe how vicious girls can be when they gang up! Back at the venue, when I told the lads about the incident they said, 'You poof!'

One bizarre aspect of the Culture Club live phenomenon was the debris that littered the stage before each show. Vast amounts of red roses and piles of 'Care Bear' cuddly toys were tossed onto the stage by adoring young fans from the audience. Most of these offerings had poignant little messages attached; written in a hand barely capable of doing joined up writing. In his hey day Tom Jones got ladies underwear thrown at him on stage, George got cuddly toys!

By the time that the bandwagon had rolled into London for the climax of the tour and the final three dates at the prestigious Dominion Theatre, we could perform our set on auto-pilot. Gaz still rates one of those Dominion gigs as one of his finest moments in music. Now that we had acclimatised ourselves to all the madness that followed Culture Club around on the road, we were more accomplished and relaxed. Although they left the scene quickly after each show, the lads in Culture Club had lots of time for their fans and signed hundreds of autographs in their dressing room. They had good reason for escaping like they did, if we caused pandemonium with our exit, imagine what the fans would have done to them.

Culture Club's tour manager allowed absolutely no photographic gear backstage. Even as part of the overall show package, we were not allowed to bring cameras into the venue. When the staff from Sounds were with us, we had to get express permission for their photographer to operate around us. The reasoning was sound because each night shady characters were pitched outside touting illegal forged merchandise. Boy George was such a saleable commodity, that his image was used everywhere. So it was little wonder that the band resented illegal merchandising. The perpetrators were costing them big money. A major tour can gross huge revenues from the merchandising products associated with it. Counterfeiters sensed the chance of a quick buck and muscled in, selling inferior products to young fans who blindly snapped it up.

Backstage at the Dominion Theatre Dean made a discovery that had us all in stitches. In the toilets as he took aim he noticed a small hole in the frosted glass window in front of him. Peering through the hole he saw hundreds of girl George clones congregating down below outside the stage door. On seeing his shadow through the frosted glass, a large section of the girls began to peer upwards. Dean stuck an index finger through the hole and what started as an excited murmur grew into a full-throated scream. Dean ran into the dressing room and said excitedly, 'Quick, come and look at this' He led us to the position at the urinal and slowly poked his finger through the hole in the window ...SCREEEEAAAAM! Mark said, 'Come out of the way. Let me try.' Mark duly poked his finger through the hole, once - then twice in quick succession. Each finger flash was greeted with a loud scream. We were in tucks; we took turns until we tired of the game. The girls outside would have kept it up all night. I wonder if they thought it was George's finger or even something else thrusting out of the hole.

We got some glowing live reviews for our performances at the Dominion. Jim Reid of the Record Mirror wrote,

'In the days before pop was processed, packaged and sent along to grin at Mike Read (former Radio One disc jockey) there were bands like the Swinging Laurels. The Laurels are pop craftsmen, pure and simple. Theirs is a pop full of personality and character, a music that escapes the studio and inhabits the real world. The Laurels- a brace of synths, a clutch of brass and one very resolute bassist- are a bag full of infectious, idiosyncratic pop tunes. That's the game. Here's the full time result. Gaz caterwauled, Dean played trumpet like no one since the Hendon Brass band and I desperately searched in vain for a reason why the Laurels shouldn't be in the top 20-right now'

The Dominion shows provided a fitting climax to the tour, which had been a marvellous experience. It was such a shame that Lonely Boy was released too late to benefit from the exposure that the tour had given to us. During our dealings with Culture Club on tour none of us had an incline of the affair that was going on between George and drummer Jon Moss. There was no real doubt about George's sexual orientation but they managed to keep the chemistry between them well under wraps from the outside world.

Our relationship with Max Hole at Warner Brothers deteriorated; he seemed to devote more of his energies to his newly signed acts, Matt Bianco, Modern Romance and Howard Jones. We recorded two more tracks at Red Bus with Steve Levine at the controls. Steve had recently acquired an Emulator computer sampler, a sophisticated piece of kit for its time; it was capable of recording stunning samples. We were the first band to try it out and boy did we try it out. The two tracks we tackled on that session were Going Nowhere and One Of Our Saxophones Is Missing.

Going Nowhere was a ballad of epic proportions, a band composition filled with lush string arrangements; real harpsichord parts, we even drafted honorary Laurel Nick Murphy in to play brush parts. It was lavish and over-the-top. Max Hole was expecting a bouncy three-minute pop single and made his dislike of the track obvious. We were several months into our first option on the contract and with the initial nine months calling for the release of three singles, it was looking increasingly unlikely that we'd have time to fulfil it.

We then recorded one of Gaz's compositions called Give Me Strength, a catchy pop song with memorable hook line. We became convinced that given the right promotional push, Give Me Strength could be a contender for chart action. This song was a particular favourite of Culture Club drummer Jon Moss.

Around this time too the Swinging Laurels recorded a brass session for Steve Levine again at Red Bus for Charisma Records, hit French band 24hrs. They didn't speak much English and we never did hear the finished track and have no idea if it was subsequently released. This was one of the strange, disjointed aspects of session brass work sometimes. There were times when you would turn up at a studio, record your parts and not even meet the band you were working for. Often we never even heard the track all the way through because we would only be played a specific section where the brass was needed.

Steve Levine also asked us to play on an album that he was expecting to produce for Graham Parker. This job unfortunately didn't come to fruition, which was a shame because we had been fans of his work from the early days and I had been to see him live years earlier. His album Heat Treatment had been a particular favourite of mine.

When Lonely Boy was released at the end of the Culture Club jaunt the timing was completely wrong. It was a situation that was completely out of the control of the band. The reviews for the single had on the whole had been good. Radio One's Janice Long gushed about us on her radio show after seeing us on the Culture Club tour. But in general the record didn't attract as much Radio One airplay as its predecessor Rodeo. Simon Bates played the record on his morning Radio One show in a series of records back to back - but he didn't introduce the track, so he might as well have not played it at all for all the good that it did us.

Lonely Boy fared rather better airplay wise on the ILR (Independent Local Radio) networks, gaining play listing status on several and being selected as a 'hit pick' on three - including Radio Luxembourg. Directly on the back of the Culture Club tour Jeff Craft at the Cowbell Agency set up a headlining tour for us. This was great because tour frenzy was starting to kick in. We were beginning to get restless and anxious to go out on the road again. The dates included,
London - the Venue / Portsmouth - Polytechnic / Torquay - 400Club / Coalville - Bensons / Hull - Dingwalls / Glasgow - Nitemoves / Newcastle - Dingwalls / Sheffield - Polytechnic / Manchester - University / Bristol - Dingwalls / Liverpool Polytechnic / Loughborough - University.

Some of the gigs on this tour were absolutely great, lots of young punters who had seen us on the Culture Club tour turned out to say hello and it was back to good old bed and breakfast accommodation. The Venue gig in London was perhaps our biggest headlining live show to date and we went to town with the stage set up. We hired industrial ladders and placed lighting strategically to create the right ambience. The gig itself was more sparsely attended than we would have liked but by the end of our set some of the audience clambered on to the stage to dance alongside us as we played.

Carole Linfield of Sounds wrote,

'The achievement of making the cavernous impersonal practically empty Venue come alive with dancing bodies and tapping feet is not one to be underestimated. The achievement of making the initially distant and self-conscious crowd actually STORM THE STAGE by the end of the set is virtually unbelievable. Such is the power of the Swinging Laurels; Power to enthuse, enjoy and engage. Their bounce, overwhelming energy and happy-go-lucky attitude penetrates and permeates even the darkest, dankest corners of the room: a refreshing surge of pure ENJOYMENT (remember that?) which grabs you by the scruff of the neck and throws you onto the dance floor.'

The next batch of gigs meant that we would be away from Leicester for a few days with gigs in Portsmouth, Torquay and Bristol. I caused a major stir by FORGETTING MY SAXOPHONE! We were a few miles out of Portsmouth when it suddenly dawned on me that I couldn't remember packing my sax with the rest of the equipment. How on earth was I going to break the news, Portsmouth is approximately 160 miles from Leicester so turning back was not an option. You can imagine the reaction when I told them - comments stronger than 'Oh, you twit!' came my way. We had to hire a saxophone from Bristol, stumping up a hefty deposit - I've never lived the incident down to this day.

At Bristol Dingwalls we got bladdered in a real ale bar before the show. We were discussing rumours that George Michael and Andrew Ridgeley of Wham! put shuttlecocks in their shorts pockets onstage, to make their todgers look bigger. At the venue management had generously provided lots of fruit in the dressing room - a nice touch. When we took to the stage we placed bananas and apples down the front of our trousers. You may think that this would create a great impression with the girls in the crowd. The truth is - NOBODY NOTICED! Manager Martin had his attaché case stolen in Hull and lost the fees from several gigs, credit cards and tickets for a David Bowie concert in London. Losing the Bowie tickets was the thing that hurt him the most. Amazingly the thieves were eventually caught. Police waited for the robbers to take their seats at the Bowie concert and nicked them. The resulting trial got prominent coverage in the Hull local rag - but they spelt the name of our band wrong! Never did like Hull.

After the gig at Nitemoves in Glasgow a fan handed me what turned out to be a huge lump of cannabis. I didn't use drugs and he seemed a little put out by this. The Laurels were, with the exception of Mark, drugs free. Mark indulged only in the occasional smoke and was anti hard drugs. A lot of people believe that all musicians are major drug fiends but it isn't the case; there are probably more merchant bankers into drugs. In Glasgow some of our Glaswegian friends from Leicester travelled up to keep a close eye on us. Norman, Tommy and Angelo introduced us to a number of their friends and relatives who were great - that is until they'd had a few drinks. Then you needed an interpreter because there was no chance of understanding the dialect when they got excited.

After our sound check at Manchester Boardwalk we took time out to have a look at Granada Television studio and the set of Coronation Street. In those days the set was clearly visible through a wire fence at the end of the lot but nowadays you have to pay to go an official guided tour. It was strange gazing through the fence at that legendary set - Rovers Return and all. The houses were only facades, there were no backs to them and huge wooden staves supported them.

After the show in Southampton, Dean, Gaz and I were invited back to the flat of a fan who turned out to be an erotic dancer. After we demolished her liquor stash she treated us to a private show which was all very steamy - there are some perks to the job after all! Her flatmate had the hots for me - I fended her off but for months afterwards she sent me photographs of herself in basques, suspenders, high stiletto boots and brandishing a bull whip - scary.

The worst gig of the tour was at the Torquay 400 Club. I had played the venue twice before - with Sister Big Stuff and Black Gorilla and I had some good memories of the place. That night the place was packed to bursting with drunken students. Nothing wrong with drunken students, but this was an ambivalent crowd in no mood for a live band. We were on to a loser from the outset. Some of the more drunken specimens were aggressive and Gaz started giving as good as he got. We could sense the growing hostility and left the stage early before trouble kicked off. Verbal threats had been levelled at us, so we stayed in the dressing room. Eventually Reverb and I could stand being cooped up no longer and we crept out to the bar. Gigs like that were a rarity - thank goodness. All things considered the tour was a success. We met some great people and had some great laughs. It was impossible not to have a crack with characters like Dean and Reverb around. The banter in the tour van was priceless. Once Reverb brought along a thick telephone directory of a sex manual full of bizarre case histories relating to unusual fetishes. Every so often he would giggle to himself and say 'Listen to this one,' leaving us in fits. One case caused much merriment and took on a life of it's own in the band humour for weeks afterwards. It was about some poor chap who got an erection every time he passed a wet fish shop or fish market! His first sexual conquest had been with a girl who worked on a wet fish stall and afterwards he couldn't get aroused without the presence of a strong fishy smell! Hey, anything to detract from the boredom of travelling.

Chapter Twenty Eight

GOODBYE MR.WARNER - AND HIS BROTHERS

Lonely Boy sold reasonably well in its first weeks of release and made a lowly showing in charts used by record companies to register 'bubbling under' records but we suspected that the record had been wilfully under promoted. The record had some successes; Boy George told us that he'd heard it in a Tokyo bar, while he was on tour with Culture Club in Japan. Also I did hear that it was featured on a far-eastern compilation album featuring other Warner Bros. acts including Rod Stewart, but I never saw a copy.

Confirmation came from the plush offices of Max Hole, with gold discs on the walls that Warner Brothers were not taking up the next option on our contract. Now that Tarquin Gotch was out of the frame we weren't convinced that we wanted to stay with a label that was not a 100% behind us anyway. It seemed inconceivable to me that Warner Brothers were prepared to drop a band that in little more than a year had played on a top 20 hit, made Top of the Pops appearances and had recorded with some of the biggest names in the business. Our records been played to death on Radio One and we had completed a highly successful sell-out tour with one of the hottest acts of the time, whose lead vocalist Boy George was a Laurels devotee. It just goes to show how fickle the industry is. Despite this we were pretty upbeat - we still had lots going for us. Martin and Steve of Swinging Stars assured us that finding a new label would be no problem and at least publishers Albion were standing full square behind us.

The backlash from the press had not yet materialised but we knew that inevitably at some point it would. The UK music press is notorious for building up and lionising an act only to shoot it down again. The British record buying public have incredibly short memories, any absence from the scene and you are soon forgotten - you become yesterday's news. In the States bands seem to live off the back of a hit for years

- Americans seem to respect success. It can also be difficult for a band that has been signed to a major label to attract an alternative deal. In a sales oriented environment which is reliant on shifting units, the harsh reality was that the Swinging Laurels hadn't sold enough. Steve Levine brokered a deal for us with Polydor Records but we ran a mile from it because they wanted us to commit to seven albums.

We started to wonder whether our management team was pulling their weight, we felt very strongly that Lonely Boy should have charted - even without Boy George's contribution. If the mighty Warner Brothers had wanted to chart it, with their muscle, they could have done it. Perhaps Martin and Steve weren't forceful enough in fighting our corner and one of the supposed benefits of being signed to a label giant was to utilise their considerable power to promote your product. Otherwise what is the point of being signed to a major label?

The whole ethos in the 80s seemed to have changed from what it was in the 70's. A record company in those days would let a newly signed act cut its teeth on a couple of albums before really pushing them for success. This strategy often paid off in the long run because the act was better poised to deal with sustained success and longevity. Overnight success is a rare.

We threw ourselves into yet another series of live gigs of colleges and Universities. Silly summer ball season meant one thing - pissed students. One remarkable gig was at a young doctor's summer bash in Cobham. The event was an all night affair and those hardy enough to last the alcoholic assault course until day light were served strawberries and cream. There was a fun fare, dodgems, a bouncy castle and several marquees where a variety of acts performed. The bouncy castle was a big mistake.

Guests were young Maximillians and Priscillas, dressed in dinner suits and ball gowns. These were privileged progeny and I found their haw-haw-haw attitude nauseating. A jazz band fought for attention while jugglers mingled with the audience and there was a man on stilts! When the Tobys and Henriettas were sufficiently lashed the bouncy castle attracted them like a magnet. What a spectacle - there were bow ties askew and ball gowns tucked in knickers. It really was quite pathetic. We made the most of the night; I had a ride on the dodgems with Reverb who was not only a crazy guy but also a crazy driver. What the heck, we were getting paid a small fortune for our services but the hooray Henrys weren't interested in live music that night.

We played Warwick University with Dead or Alive whose larger than life vocalist Pete Burns was helping to propel the band to the top with his gender bender image, in a similar way to Boy George. They reached No.1 in 1984 with You Spin Me Round (like a record.) We also played at the Birmingham University summer ball with Big Country and the Lotus Eaters. We were supported by One the Juggler and King. King comprised of ex members of Coventry band Team 23 who we'd gigged with a couple of years earlier. Within months they went on to mark up a No.2 hit with Love and Pride on CBS records. We chatted backstage.

Things came to head with Swinging Stars in June 1983 when, out of the blue, we each received a £2,000 VAT bill. It was not our job to handle this sort of thing. We were signing on the dole since we parted company with Warner Brothers and it was only our passion and belief in our music that drove us on. Signing on for me was particularly embarrassing because a girl who worked there was a Laurels fan and she recognised me.

We decided that enough was enough and we caught the train to London and parted company with Swinging Stars. The split was amicable - we'd been through so much together, but perhaps business relationships shouldn't be conducted on such a basis of familiarity. Without management we were leaving ourselves wide open - most record companies prefer to deal with managers as intermediaries. Often the artist is too subjectively involved to make objective career decisions Martin and Steve stayed on in management and took on another Leicester band called New Age. Martin later went to work for PWL, The organisation piloted by 80's production phenomenon Stock Aitken and Waterman. He told us some years later that, they'd sampled our brass sound and used it on some of their hits - allegedly - we never managed to verify that. Martin later managed Underground and Mc Almont and Butler and more recently, Catatonia. Steve went on to be the road manager for Jools Holland. In the 90s Gaz saw Steve driving a Roll Royce - he drove a Vauxhall Viva when he managed us!

Before the split they'd laid on a Dutch tour and a Radio One session for Janice Long so we had plenty of work to get our teeth into. The Dutch tour was a festival tour that took us to: Vlissingen - Apeldoorn - Amsterdam - Rotterdam - Groningen and Emmen. It was August, very hot and perfect festival weather. Nick Murphy came along as road manager and our first gig was at the beautiful coastal town of Vlissingen, where we supported hit African band Osibisa. It was an excellent night and we found the Dutch to be friendly and laid back.

In Amsterdam we played the famous Milky Way venue. Mark's eyes were out on stalks when he saw cannabis growing wild in the courtyard outside our dressing room and Feelabeelia keyboards player Andy Povall came over to see us. Reverb got totally rat arsed after the show and knocked a counter display over in a shop while he was trying to order something to eat.

To conclude the tour we did two festivals on the same day at locations just miles apart. The first was in a park with a huge lake at Groningen in front of 25,000 punters and the show was broadcast live on Dutch national radio. It was a beautiful setting, and beautiful day. From the stage we saw a carpet of bodies spreading out into the distance and it was gratifying to see many Dutch fans singing the words to Lonely Boy. Nick Lowe was the headliner but we missed his performance as we sped off to the second festival in Emmen which also was a memorable show. Dutch girls seemed incredibly accommodating and friendly. While we were on stage I spied Nick disappearing backstage with a young girl fan. GREAT! We were playing our little hearts out while the road manager was stealing OUR groupies! The Laurels didn't attract groupies in quite the same way that Black Gorilla did. You would have to have been a one-eyed monster not to capture in that band. We even had league tables! Perhaps it was because Gorilla played night clubs and the Laurels played universities and colleges where the girls were more worldly wise. We got lots of fan mail though and it was staggering at times what girls sent to us. Provocative Polaroid photos were not unusual and they were not at all afraid to say what they wanted to do to you. We kept a collection of the best ones.

The Dutch tour was tremendous but realistically it did little to further our career - but we enjoyed it for what it was - fun.

The day after our arrival back in England we travelled to Manchester to record a Radio One session for Janice Long. The studio was the old Playhouse Theatre and it was quite the strangest recording studio that I had ever worked in. It was surreal because it was a living theatre with a stage and rows of seating - it was used for radio broadcasts with live audiences. The producer's control room was tucked away at the back of the theatre and you could barely see him from the stage.

We recorded four numbers but the session was a nightmare for me. We all have days when nothing goes right and we felt pretty jaded as a consequence of our Dutch bonanza. Tuning had been an ongoing problem for me but a lot of it for a brass player is psychological - once things go wrong it seems to get progressively worse the harder you try.

On one occasion at Woodbine in Leamington, I was set up to record my saxophone parts and on the practise run I played a phrase that had the control room jumping up and down. Thumbs were up and I thought, 'What did I do?' A tinny voice over the intercom said, 'Perfect, just do that again.' Because I was improvising I hadn't a clue what it was I'd played and we spent ages trying to re-create the phrase but I couldn't get it. After several failed takes you start to worry and a sort of paranoia sets in because you can see the wagging tongues in the control room but were unable to hear a word that they were saying. Eventually we settled for a part that was almost there because I was taking up so much valuable studio time. There is a good argument for recording everything - even practise runs. Some producers routinely do this because often the first take is the best of the lot. You can sometimes feel very isolated and vulnerable with your headphones on - peering at studio staff through the control room window. Your only form of communication is an intercom system - I call it 'the goldfish bowl syndrome.' Also very often I recorded my parts after waiting around for hours, so it could be difficult to inject life into it.

Recording block is one of the worse feelings that there is. No musician is immune to it and when it kicks in it is best to leave it and come back another day. No amount of trying will put it right. I didn't have that luxury because Radio One sessions had to be wrapped up in a day. The reverse can happen too - occasionally a session goes like a dream, when everything you play is perfect and you put your parts down in one take. I remember recording Hair by Mantini and the sax solo on Falling and Stranger than Fiction like that - it is a brilliant feeling when that happens. The Janice Long session was made all the worse because of the distance between the stage and the producer. In the end I wrote it off as a bad day and the producer patched up some of my suspect tuning.

As we cruised to the end of 1983 label-less and manager-less our confidence was as low as it had ever been. Reverb decided that it was time to move on and I can't say that I blamed him - our collective sense of purpose and direction had faltered. I missed Reverb a lot; he was great fun to have around, especially on tour. But there was one annoying little habit that he had on stage. He waited until I played a sax solo and he'd sidle up and stick his tongue in my ear! He knew that I could do nothing about it without screwing up my playing. It always tickled him no end. He had one of the most grotesque, crevice ridden tongues that I had ever seen - it looked as if someone had attacked it with a cheese grater!

Gaz and I visited Dai Davies and Mark Anders at the headquarters of Albion Music to discuss ways to raise the profile of the band again. They suggested that we release an album on the Albion label, but a lot of our best recorded work was languishing in the Warner Brothers vault. Dai suggested releasing Falling, a track we had recorded at Woodbine. In my opinion Falling was one of the most instant pop songs we'd ever recorded and we jumped at the chance to release it as a single.

Right on cue the stroke of luck that we had been praying for presented itself. Boy George contacted us to see if we would like to be special guests on the Culture Club Christmas tour. We didn't have to think too long about it. This came at just the right time, certain sections of the press were labelling us 'almost made its,' which was a little disconcerting. We brought in a new bass player Ciro Buccheri - an excellent bass technician from the jazz / funk circuit. When Albion got wind of our good news they started to prepare for the release to coincide with the tour dates - many of which had already sold out. We gained more useful music press exposure on the announcement of the tour but it was to hit me in the pocket hard. At this point we had no income and were signing on the dole but with a high profile tour looming, people immediately thought that we were coining it. A few weeks prior to the tour I went to sign on. The girl behind the counter said,

'I see that the Swinging Laurels are to tour with Culture Club again' I said, 'Yeah, that's right, I'll notify you of the dates when they are confirmed.' She went into the office at the back saying, 'Oh, there's no need. I have a list of the dates here!' She actually knew the tour itinerary before I did! She refused to believe that the band were to be paid just £50 a night. As a consequence I had my dole payments suspended for a month which left me penniless over Christmas. To an outsider it must have been difficult to believe that we were getting peanuts for playing on such high profile, sell out tour.

Albion records steamed ahead getting our release ready for the tour. Julian Henry showed us proofs of the sleeve artwork which featured a striking elongated version of one of the Jill Furmanovsky shots in black and white. But again events forced us to totally re-evaluate our plans. Culture Club drummer Jon Moss had expressed a desire to produce us and when he heard of our plans for the Albion release, he advised us against it. He said that he could get us a deal with Virgin Records and that he'd booked studio time for after Christmas. He said releasing a record on another label might prejudice the deal. Jon wanted us to record a hybrid version of two songs Give Me Strength and Swing the Cat - he seemed so upbeat about the project that his enthusiasm took us along with him. It sounded too good to be true, but Jon was sincere and there was no doubting his faith in the band - so we agreed. I noticed Jon in the wings watching us perform several times during the previous tour. When we told Albion records that we wanted to shelve the single they were not happy, the sleeves had been printed and a fair amount of pre-selling had been done to prime the market for the forthcoming release. When the Culture Club tour dates were announced we learned that we were to play,

Southampton / Gaumont Theatre - St.Austell / Leisure Centre -Gloucester / Leisure Centre - Leeds / Queens Hall - Leicester / De Montfort Hall (Two shows) - London / Hammersmith Odeon (Three shows)

The most appealing dates of the tour for me were the two shows at the De Montfort Halls in our native Leicester. We played a warm up date at Leicester Polytechnic which was a sell out. While we sound checked Central Television filmed us miming to Lonely Boy for transmission on a pop magazine programme called Popwatch, and afterwards they interviewed Mark and Gaz. Ironically the technical crew used the version of the song that featured Boy George. Gaz mimed to his vocal parts. George's management would have had a blue fit if they knew that this unauthorised version had been used on television.

The Culture Club tour was accompanied by even more hysteria than the previous one - if that were possible. One of the Leicester dates was a tea time matinee and was probably the most subdued of all in terms of audience reaction. It is a recognised fact that Leicester audiences are notoriously difficult to please. Booking agents told me how they would blood a new act in Leicester - because if they could get the crowd going there, then they would go down well anywhere. On the other hand crowds in Newcastle and Glasgow are brilliant in their appreciation.

The largest venue was Leeds Queens Hall, a cavernous disused tram shed with a standing capacity of 10,000. It was so capacious that juggernauts carrying the stage and lighting equipment drove right into the main body of the hall. Undoubtedly the highlight were the three dates at the Hammersmith Odeon which had sold out weeks before. In the time since the last UK tour Culture Club had become a massive world wide pop phenomenon, chalking up huge hits across the globe. It was no surprise that the London dates were so eagerly anticipated and they went to town with lavish stage settings. The final night was beamed to the States for a live MTV transmission. Also drafted in was a fully-fledged string section and Judd Lander on harmonica. It was his distinctive harp playing that helped Karma Chameleon to the No.1 spot just before the tour kicked off - it stayed on the chart for 20 weeks.

The stage set was a giant mock up of the Sphinx that opened up to allow Boy George to make a grand entrance. Brilliant vocalist Helen Terry also lent her talent to the proceedings and it was a privilege to be associated with the whole enterprise. As special guests we went down very well too - many young fans sang along, and screamed out for specific Swinging Laurels songs.

Just prior to the show on the final night, I was standing in the stage door area when George Michael arrived accompanied by a couple of young nymphets. He tried to blag his way in. Wham! were one of Culture Club's deadliest rivals for the hearts and minds of the young teen market. George Michael stood right next to me and I thought, 'There is no way that suntan is real!'

The Hammersmith Odeon gigs were a massive success - footage from that final night was later released on video. Culture Club were brilliant it has to be said. Jon Moss popped into our dressing room to reassure us that our little enterprise was still on course and we went into Christmas in a really optimistic frame of mind. Poor but optimistic! With my dole money suspended - I was penniless but the thought that we were to sign to Virgin Records and work with Jon Moss made up for it. After a series of sell out dates to an aggregate crowd of 35,000 people, we drove home to Leicester in a rusty hire van, with dreams of what might be.

Christmas of 1983 came and went. In January the devastating news came that the deal brokered for us by Jon Moss with Virgin had fallen through at the last moment. It couldn't have gone any closer to the wire; he had even booked the studio time. Without a label and having spurned the Albion offer to release Falling we were left with feelings of what might have been. Had the record been released on the back of such a major tour there was every chance that it may have charted - again we were thwarted and deflated. We also learnt that it was option time on our publishing deal with Albion Music and we needed to write nine songs to fulfil our obligations on the contract. This meant composing nine songs in as many weeks, and given that we were not exactly prolific songwriters, the task seemed gargantuan. Before we signed a publishing deal our writing seemed less self-conscious - almost effortless. Our early writing seemed to flow naturally - largely through experimentation. Writing to order seemed to be so much of an ordeal. When we signed to a major label we were aware that they wanted commercial three-minute pop songs and our more radical ideas were consigned to b-sides or extra tracks on 12" releases. We were anxious to stay with Albion, they had supported us through thick and thin, and we enjoyed a great working relationship with them. In the time we were with them they never turned down a reasonable request for funds or assistance to further our careers - they must have spent a lot of money on us. Gaz acquired a 4-track Portastudio and we grafted together nine new songs. We met daily in Gaz's bedroom to thrash out ideas and then record them. There was never a set formula to the way that we wrote songs. Sometimes they would come from a jamming session, other times Gaz would come up with a song complete, as with Beating Heart and Give me Strength. Many times we would match my chorus with his verse or visa versa to create a complete song - we did this many times we to good effect.

This process also applied to lyrics. We each kept notebooks and kept words for future reference, sometimes

Gaz wrote a complete set of lyrics, sometimes I did. It may seem an odd way to work but it worked for us. Now and again we were asked about the meaning of our lyrics but often they were a succession of words that sounded good together. It was great when someone said,
   'I know just what you meant when you wrote that line'
       Don't get me wrong - our lyrics meant a lot to us. It was tough working to such a strict deadline, but we were pleasantly pleased with some of the results. We packaged the songs together and duly despatched them to Albion Music but our efforts had been in vain, they decided to retain the songs but decline the next option on our contract.

Chapter Twenty Nine

HAPPY RECORDS

We were now left without a recording contract and without a publisher to fight our corner, and it was an incredibly demoralising sensation. For the two or so years that we had worked with Albion they had offered us total support and I will always be grateful for that. It made me wonder if our decision not to release Falling at the last moment had anything to do with their decision. While we were signed to them we had worked with big names in the music world but somehow the pop stardust had not rubbed off on us. We had to seriously consider where to turn next.

Things had all got a bit too much for Dean and he decided to leave the band - reducing us to a trio. Dean's contribution can never be underestimated. Apart from being a great guy, he was a very talented musician and I for one was gutted at his decision. I'd worked with Dean since my Sister Big Stuff days, so it was a bitter blow to me personally. Poor Dean never quite grasped the workings of the business side like the rest of us. He never understood the machinations and nuances of the music industry - he climbed on stage and did his bit but the non-musical side went completely over his head. Unfortunately the business is about more than turning up at a venue and playing - performing is the tip of the iceberg. In a matter of months Dean went from performing in front of 10,000 screaming kids back to the Desford Colliery brass band. He was by now a little too old to return to his paper round!

The remaining Laurels held a crisis meeting. It would have been easy to throw in the towel at that point. After all we'd been through and coming so close to making it, we owed it to ourselves to carry on. We still believed that we had something to offer - we were now much wiser and had a better grasp of the industry than at the start of our adventure. The best thing to do was to come out fighting. Looking back I find it very difficult to imagine how we survived - we were all so broke. In some ways I could understand why Dean had decided to call it a day - trying to survive on such limited funds was a truly humbling experience. It was hard to reconcile the differences - on one hand we were still a pretty high profile band and still got good service from the national music press. We were playing large prestige venues to thousands of screaming girlies, yet we were all stony broke. You can only live on adrenaline for so long - one thing is for sure - it doesn't pay the bills.

A radical change was needed to bolster our flagging morale and to give us something to work for. We had become increasingly disillusioned by trying to secure another recording contract by conventional means; the Warner Brothers experience had left a bitter taste in our mouths and it was for this reason that we decided to form our own label identity. It seemed like the right thing to do - a natural progression. By being in control of our own destinies, we wouldn't have to be so reliant on other people and all decisions would be ours alone.

Running our own label meant that we would be able to control every aspect of the process, from writing and recording, to packaging and marketing. It was an exciting prospect; we felt that for too long that our careers had been dependent on external forces that often left us powerless and impotent. Setting up an independent label in 1984 was more difficult than it would be today. Today pressing plants handle the whole package - you supply the recorded master and sleeve artwork and they do the lot for you. Technology has moved on in leaps and bounds, CD burners / MP3s / I pods, make everyone a potential recording artist. Back then you had to arrange all the procedures separately. The labels and sleeves had to be printed, the master had to be cut and the lot had to be co-ordinated. Not an easy task - timing was of paramount importance.

We named our new label Happy Records. We realised that we would be small time players compared to the EMI's of this world. There was paperwork and registration to complete and we logged our name with the independent label register, which gave us copy right. It also seemed appropriate to signal our fresh start by a name change so we dropped the

'Swinging' and became the Laurels. There was also an underlying reason for this change, at the time there were a number of 'swing' revival bands on the scene and we found that we were being wrongly typecast. Bands like Roman Holliday were at the forefront of this movement.

Now that we were in business it was time to select a song to record and we chose Zoom (Take the test) a song penned by Gaz during our frenzied efforts to write those last songs for Albion.

The decision where to record our first Happy Records offering was easy - there was only one studio in the frame - Woodbine in Leamington Spa. We had come full circle because our first tentative efforts were recorded there and we had built up a tremendous working rapport with producer John Rivers. Our rebirth began with change from the name up and we became tremendously excited at the prospect of striking out on our own.

For the recording we enlisted the able assistance of ex Newmatics guitarist Rich Barton and Ciro Buccheri on bass. The recording session at Woodbine was fun as usual; John Rivers was on his usual ebullient tip-top form. There was one small problem that we hadn't had to worry about for a long time - footing the bill. This focused us on using the time to best effect. Long gone were the days at Red Bus studio with Steve Levine, when we'd stop recording for a couple of hours while we waited for a harpsichord to be delivered. Time didn't matter when Mr.Warner and his brothers were picking up the tab!

Our plan was to release Zoom and to promote it on the club scene and also aim for the independent charts. The 12" version included a 7" radio mix and we hoped that this would help to get us radio airplay. We kept to our trusty instrumental formula on the flip side with a track called Ramsi Ramsi Ramsi, which we recorded live in a couple of takes. I played piano on the track - though 'played' is a description that could be disputed! A Chimp in boxing gloves springs to mind! With finite funds we had to limit studio time to a minimum but we were pleased with the final results of the session. Zoom had a catchy pop song quality, with Gaz producing a stirring vocal performance and Rich laying down some nifty guitar work. John Rivers mixed a radio version of the song with a hi-fidelity, radio friendly feel. Some recordings sound mighty impressive in a studio control room when booming out of large speakers but the same track can sound completely different on a transistor radio. For this reason, many producers like to mix on small monitor speakers, to get a better idea of how it is likely to sound on air. Radio play was crucial to the success of any record then so it made sense to mix a track that sounded good on that medium.

Now the tracks were recorded we needed to secure a distribution deal to get it into the shops. After the problems experienced at Warner Brothers we realised how crucial good distribution was. A number of distribution companies expressed an interest in handling our product - ID, Pinnacle and the Cartel among them. The deal worked like this. The distributor took copies of the record and guaranteed national distribution for a percentage fee against sales. We finally opted for Pinnacle because they had an established track record. They handled the distribution for a number of the larger independent record companies like Mute and Rough Trade, helping them to achieve chart success. Like record companies they employed a pro-active sales force to pre-sell your record so that when it was released it would be on the shelves of record outlets. Before the release of any record it is of vital importance that the market is primed weeks in advance. Press, poster campaigns and radio airplay ahead of the official release date help to create the all-important demand for your offering.

For a small label such as Happy records it was purely down to finance as to how far we could stretch ourselves on promotion. Major labels would have thought nothing of spending vast amounts to break an act into the mainstream chart and they recouped initial outlay on sales if the act attained chart longevity. Major labels routinely dished out nice little freebie titbits to dealers - T-shirts, posters, caps, and free records - all were sweeteners. One of Warner Brothers better promotional ideas for Lonely Boy was to give Radio One DJs anti-static turn table mats, with our name on it.

Innovation and clever marketing is a must when limited to a small promotional budget as we were. When you consider that there was an average of 200 singles released weekly, it was essential to make your release stand out from the rest. Anything that set the product apart gave a real advantage. For the Zoom project we screen-printed nifty white carrier bags to present the record in, they really looked the business. Also we screen-printed t-shirts with matching artwork.

One animal at the heart of record promotion without which very few records would ever make it to the charts is the plugger. All record companies either employ them or hire them to do the job. Smaller independent companies often hire pluggers for a pre-determined spell at the start of a sales campaign, paying them a set fee for the work that they do. The job of a plugger is to get radio plays and some are paid for the amount of plays that they secure. Record companies such as Warner Brothers have in-house pluggers, who are rarely out of the BBC Broadcasting House building, where they court the favours of producers. Contrary to what a lot of people think, it is usually the producer of the show that decides what records will be play-listed, so the power lies with them and not the DJ. Some DJs have a bigger influence on play-listing than others, but the majority concentrate on putting a show together rather than selecting the music that is played. Sweeteners were of course frowned upon but invariably happened. Ever since the first pop chart was introduced the power of radio has been recognised as vital component for promotion.

Some independent pluggers were high profile and commanded large up front fees to market and promote a record. For a large record company desperate to break an act the fee was almost immaterial, without Radio One plays in the 80's there was little chance of selling units. We were well aware that we needed help in the plugging and promotion areas. We signed a distribution deal with Pinnacle Records at their head office in Orpington and then set about getting quotations from record pluggers. The big boys were way out of our league, but we did find a much cheaper outfit run by an ex Polydor A&R man who offered us a special rate.

Chapter Thirty

THE RADIO ONE ROAD SHOW

Our plugger did achieve some degree of success although it was very difficult to validate and confirm airplay figures. One beneficial area that our guy introduced us to was the Radio One road show. These shows were held in theatres by star DJ's, to augment their meagre earnings. We appeared on two - one with Peter Powell and the other with Adrian John. The basic ingredient of these shows was - One Radio One DJ – 2,000 screaming teenagers, a multitude of road crew receptive to Mr. DJ's every beck and call lots of 'Come on, put your hands together?' - 'Come on, you can do better than that Basildon?' and lots of free records and T-shirts. The people grafting the hardest were the poor road crew. The prima donna Radio One jocks were on stage for an hour at most, during which time they were barely audible above the noise created by thousands of young throats. They didn't even spin their own records for Christ sake; one of their servants performed that menial task.

We mimed to our record in the most obvious way imaginable, but it didn't make one iota of difference. It was scream, scream and yet more screaming. We didn't even have microphones, but it didn't matter - no one noticed. It is debatable whether these events do help you to sell your record; the whole exercise was all so false. The only obvious winners from all of this were the Radio one DJ's, who no doubt left the scene of the crime with a fat cheque. It's tough at the top!

After the Peter Powell show, Peter 'Mr.Sincerity' Powell approached us in the dressing room and said,
'Oh, the Swinging Laurels. I've played a number of your records on my show.' He was one of the few Radio One disc jockeys never to have played one of our records; he had even gone on record as saying that he didn't even like the band.

That is fair enough, but not having the courage to admit the fact face to face spoke volumes.

Zoom got good reviews. Music Week said,

'The Laurels have come up with a great, bubbling track boasting memorable smooth vocal melodies and uplifting horns.'

Zig Zag magazine trumpeted, 'The Laurels boom and toot away as if their valves are fit to burst. Like Spandau on a hub cap nicking spree-HUGE-Hugely enjoyable.'

The record was a limited success but the chances of it creating more than a minor splash were remote. It was all a learning process and there was still an awful lot to learn. We steamed ahead with a series of live shows to support our release. Sounds printed a full-page photograph of Gaz in their gig guide section to advertise the Phoenix Theatre show in Leicester. The live shows, in the main, were still going down very well. An outstanding gig at Upstairs at Eric's in Bournemouth elicited a brilliant live review in Coaster magazine, but an indifferent performance at Camden Dingwalls drew these comments from rock journalist Andy Hurt,

'Sadly the Laurels horizons seem to have been reduced (temporarily we hope) to the level of charming the pants off the gaggle of giggling girlies surrounding them. The almost inevitable invasion of the stage by the post-pubescent nubiles thankfully does not occur until late in the day, but happen it does. The dynamic duo of John Barrow and Gary 'Wild Bill' Birtles have lost none of their verve, but a lack of direction. When they've retired to a neutral corner for the magic sponge treatment, I trust we'll see those Laurels come out swingin' once more.'

That piece mirrored a disappointing night and it was one best forgotten. The best tonic was an excellent all day event which we headlined at the Abbey Park music festival in Leicester. It was an eagerly awaited annual occasion and at its peak it attracted crowds in excess of 20,000. The success of the festival was in no small part due the hard work of music promoter Teri Wyncoll whose contribution to the

Leicester music scene over many years can never be underestimated.

Before we could consider our second Happy Records enterprise Pinnacle went into receivership. When we signed the deal there was not even the slightest hint that they might go bust. More bad news, But there was a small chink of light to give us a psychological boost. We acquired the lease on a building that would be our base for future musical endeavours. Eagle eyed Gaz noticed empty premises on the old cattle market site and made tentative enquiries. He established that it was Council owned and the lease was up for grabs. We longed for a permanent headquarters - finding rehearsal space had always been a bind. The building was a former BBC Radio Leicester studio used for recording sessions and interviews in the fledgling days of the station and although it had been empty for a number of years, the control room and studio trappings were still there. It needed a serious make over but it was perfect for our needs and we signed a three-year lease.

Our grand plan was to base the label there and offer recording facilities and rehearsal space for local bands, in the hope that we could raise enough money to supplement the rent. The beauty was that we could leave our equipment permanently set up and could practise whenever it suited us. For continuity we named the studio Happy House but there was another reason for the name; in the 1960s the building had been a morgue! Physical evidence of its previous life was still much in evidence. In the back room, white tiles covered the walls from floor to ceiling and drainage sumps criss-crossed the floor - weird to imagine that autopsies were carried out there. As we renovated the premises I was often in there alone late at night, and at times it got mighty spooky. Local press had a field day when they found out - prompting one wag of a hack to write,

'I know that the Laurels have died a few times on stage but this is taking things a bit too far!' - I suppose they've got to earn a living somehow!

With a permanent base we set about trying to find new publisher facilitated by the ease with which we were able to rehearse and write new songs. Several name publishing houses had expressed interest, only to pull out at the last moment. At times we seemed like a rudderless ship - drifting from one let down to the next, but still we persevered.

Soon a whole host of bands were making use of the rehearsal space. Shift-work was the order of the day and we took turns to be on hand to help the bands set up. In time the back room was completely re-vamped, thus removing the last vestiges and visible signs of the old mortuary. Some excellent bands surfaced in Leicester at this time and many of them went on to sign recording contracts - a few even came close to cracking it. Gaye Bykers on Acid - Feelabeelia - Hunters Club - Bomb Party - Sister Crow - Chrome Molly - Dirty Boppers - A Lifestyle - Saquii - Yeah Jazz and Just Like Jane, to name a few.

Probably closest to hit the pay dirt were the Gaye Bykers on Acid and Feelabeelia. The Bykers were led by charismatic front man Mary Mary. They signed to Virgin Records and scored a near thing with their record Git Down (Shake your Thang) which reached No.54 in 1987. Vocalist Mary has more recently performed on hits by Apollo 440. Feelabeelia featured Joe King and old sparring partner Nick Murphy on drums - occasionally they were joined by Rich Barton on guitar. Leading the line up was vocalist/guitarist Mark Price and on keyboards was Andy Povall. One of their singles, Feel It featured a distinctive trademark harmonica solo by legendary Motown artist Stevie Wonder. The record only bubbled under in the UK charts but it was a top ten hit in Italy. They appeared on the Friday night cult pop show, The Tube presented by Paula Yates and Jools Holland. I actually played live with Feelabeelia on one occasion and recorded on a demo for them at Q studios in Loughborough.

We liked to think that the Happy House promoted an ambient atmosphere and it certainly seemed popular. The money that we collected for rehearsal time barely kept the place afloat financially but we were helped out in many ways by the patronage of Council backed music project Multiplex. Multiplex was the brainchild of and co-ordinated by Teri Wyncoll, assisted by her partner, journalist Dave Davies. The project helped a lot of kids that wouldn't otherwise have had access to recording facilities and musical instruments. A lot of excellent results came out of those sessions and some of the kids were very talented. Gaz recorded them with our gear and I even gave basic sax lessons for a time too. Lots of the kids from that project went on to join bands of their own in later years. Once a party of profoundly deaf people visited the studio and they had a fantastic feel for music - it was all very humbling. We set up different types of instruments and let them bang and toot away - they loved it and so did we.

In 1985 with no developments on the contract front, we talked of disbanding. We were in Brighton to play the Zap Club, which was built right into the beautiful old promenade that runs along the sea front. Before the gig we sat in a pub discussing our game plan - we were sick of the near misses and being dubbed the almost made its of pop. We began to feel that in the eyes of some we were past our sell-by date, but each time that we talked of calling it a day, something else came along to keep us dangling for a little longer. We decided to honour our existing live obligations and bow out with one last blow out of a gig, 'The Laurels last stand.' Once the idea had been outed it took on a life of its own but I'm sure that privately we'd all considered it.

Highs and lows permeate the life of a struggling musician. When we were suffering the depths of depression, something usually came along to snap us out of it and give us a much-needed leg up. One time this happened to me.

It was one of those dark, damp, miserable January days that so typify the English winter and I was finishing my Happy House shift alone. For some obscure reason I felt incredibly depressed and morose. I can never remember feeling that low before. After my stint I locked up and headed for home. Going home to Kim in that frame of mind didn't seem a good idea so I deviated from my usual route and found myself walking randomly down a long street of dingy terraced houses - it was almost dark even though it was only four o' clock in the afternoon. I suddenly became aware of loud music blaring out from the bedroom of one of the tiny houses further down the street. As I drew level I was staggered to hear Lonely Boy thumping out from a dimly lit bed-sit. I stood there for a moment and listened. The curtains were drawn and I had no idea lived there. It was a profound experience for me and the black cloud of depression lifted immediately. Someone, a stranger, was listening to our music. I'll never know why I happened to walk down that street that day but they do say that some things are meant to be.

The Laurels 'last stand' was at the Leicester Polytechnic - a fitting venue, because it had been the scene of some fantastic nights in the past. It was a sell out and was a mega event in every respect. Helping us out were Rich Barton (guitar) - Steve Cooke (bass) and on guest vocals, Wendy Christian. Erected on the stage were two scaffold frames on which Gaz and I stood during our opener, Disco Laurels. Mark stood on a platform opposite at a considerable height above the heads of the packed throng and powerful spotlights picked out three shaky Laurels perched precariously above the crowd. Not being a lover of heights, I couldn't get down off of that platform soon enough but it certainly was a night to remember.

After the gig we held a party to end all parties at the Happy House which was attended by many friends. Johnny Rivers came over from Leamington, Mary of the Gaye Bykers on Acid and Kev Reverb were DJs, stand up comic/musician Martin 'Arnold Bolt' gave a rousing impromptu set, and it was an all night affair. It was a night of mixed emotions and it was tinged with sadness but it was a fitting, raucous end to what had been an amazing set of experiences during the lifetime of the band.

Once the dust had settled it was time to get the new outfit Happy House up and running. We decided to use a real drummer this time, so we recruited Gaz's brother Phil Birtles. Phil had been an evergreen on the Leicester music having played in a number of different outfits. A drummer made a huge difference to the way that we performed and wrote new material. Steve Cooke stayed on as bass man and occasionally we were treated to a guest live appearance on guitar from Reverb. The new unit attracted interest from publishing companies immediately as we put an entirely new live set together. Morrison Leahy Music were one of the early interested parties and they came to see us play a number of times without really committing themselves. We would have been happy to sign with them; they had name artists on their books, George Michael being the biggest.

Having our own studio space was a real bonus, although rehearsals were never that straight forward, Steve lived in Brighton and had to commute 160 miles by coach to Leicester!

Chapter Thirty One

RHODA

    A huge vote of confidence for the new project came in the shape of Rhoda Dakar, the ex-Bodysnatchers and Specials vocalist. We had first become aquatinted with her when recording the brass on the Apollinaire's 2-Tone single The Feelings Gone. We got on great with Rhoda, or 'Rodge' as Gaz called her. She is a lovely girl. She hadn't done a lot musically for a while; her harrowing No.35 hit The Boiler with the Special A.K.A. was her last high profile recording. The experience of working with the Specials had unfortunately dulled Rhoda's appetite for the music industry; she'd had some bad experiences. 2-Tone supremo, Jerry Dammers, had a reputation of being a perfectionist in the studio - nothing wrong with that, but some performers suffer more than others when subjected to endless, repetitive takes. Rhoda was one such artiste, but we were delighted that she had decided to walk back into the pop world with the Happy House.

    We played a showcase at Legends in London. It was a big night for us, big cheese industry types turned out to give us the once over, including publishers Morrison Leahy. In the final event, not everyone who promised to turn up, did turn up - in time honoured fashion, although Mr. Leahy stayed on to see us limp on to the stage at 1.30 am! Legends was a trendy gaff, it was not unknown for the likes of David Bowie to show up for a late watering. It was the venue where Mr.Geldof and the great and the good from the Live Aid entourage loosened up after that momentous day at Wembley. The gig wasn't an entire waste of time. John Best of Music Week turned out and gave us a great live review.

    It was around this time that my partner Kim and I discovered that we were with child. Coincidently a few short months later Gaz and his partner Ann discovered that they were in a similar condition. Babies for the old men of rock, I ask you? I once promised that there was no way EVER that I would climb onto the stage once I had reached the decrepit age of thirty. I had reached that milestone and I was still bopping. Gaz had a great answer for journalists who asked his age he would say, ' I'm a year younger than whatever John said he is'

The Morrison Leahy deal was on and off. Mostly off! They came out with the old chestnut,
'We'd like to hear some more material - we are not sure that we can hear a hit.'

We recorded several demos, some produced by Joe King, some by Gaz on our new 8-track recording equipment, but publishers were still dithering and keeping us hanging by a thread of hope. It seemed that a change of name hadn't radically altered our fortune.

At 8.10 am on February 26th 1986, my first son Rhett was born. I was fortunate enough to be present at the birth feeling useless and surplus to requirement, as all fathers do. But the experience was emotional and profound; it was without doubt one of the most exhilarating days of my entire life. After the birth I went straight to Happy House to record demos - I was there in spirit only. I hadn't slept for two days, but that didn't matter - I felt ten feet tall. Being a father was to affect my whole way of thinking - for the first time in my life I had another tiny life to consider, a little soul totally dependent on me. It drove me on and perhaps more than ever it was now imperative that we made the music pay.

Producer Steve Levine got in touch with us to tell us about the fabulous studio complex that he was putting together in Fulham, London. He had recently returned from the States where he'd produced a Beach Boys album. This was the production job he had dreamt of - he was a life long fan, but the recording went anything but smoothly. The eccentric behaviour of Brian Wilson has been well documented, but it beggars belief to imagine musicians of their stature, arguing over whose vocal harmony parts were loudest in the mix. Steve was glad to see the end of the project.

He named his new studio Do Not Erase and asked us to be the first band to record there. Our plan was to record a track and then find a record company to release it. How could we possibly fail - a world name producer recording our music, and paying for the privilege. This project actually represented a significant financial outlay; the rates at Do Not Erase were approaching £3,000 a day!

We had a couple of months to prepare for our session so we made a short list of songs and rehearsed different formats. Steve listened to eight new songs and eventually selected a track called The Shelter. It was a band composition, but I was particularly thrilled because I had written the lyrics. Steve allotted us two precious weeks of his studio time - precious is right, at his rates the package was worth around £30,000!

On seeing the studio for the first time we were dumbstruck to a man - it was like a high-tech musical instrument showroom with every conceivable top of the range technical outboard effect imaginable. Mark's eyes were out on stalks as he inspected the banks of keyboards. Steve Levine was managed by Tony Gordon who was Boy George's manager, so we knew that we were in good hands. The recording was rather a painstaking process, but The Shelter had an unusual time signature, and to some extent Steve and arranger Julian, were finding their feet with the new equipment. The song had a nice laid back lilt and it hung on a bass line peppered with harmonics. Rhoda helped out on backing vocals and because this was the first recording in the new studio, we benefited from some useful press coverage.

While we were at Do Not Erase the tabloid press seized on Boy George's heroin dependency and Steve was bombarded by calls from the slimy element of British journalism. Because of his association with Culture Club, hacks seeking sleaze pestered him to death, but to his credit he said nothing. He was more than a little miffed when they approached his family though. Steve was still in touch with members of Culture Club, although the band had all but imploded by then. Guitarist Roy Hay popped by while we were recording.

George's drug problem came as a great shock to us. When we were working with him, only two years previously, he was fiercely anti-drugs. We figured that there had to be outside influences at work - the crowd of hangers on that he was associating with. It just goes to show that the pressures of stardom can easily push an individual over the edge. The pressures that George felt must have been enormous - he was constantly courted by the media. I for one was delighted to see George come through that drugs hell and re-build a successful career.

When the recording was complete Steve's manager Tony Gordon came in to listen to the finished recording. Tony didn't strike you as a manager type - he looked more like a city gent. He cut a dashing vision in his long black Crombie overcoat and mirror shiny shoes - not at all like someone that had helped to steer a band like Culture Club to super stardom. After listening intently to the fruits of our labour he uttered the words that I never ever expected to hear in real life - they were words that you would expect to hear in a 1960s Cliff Richard film,

'IT'S A SMASH'

I stifled a giggle. The Shelter wasn't a smash, in fact it wasn't anything - despite our best endeavours, we couldn't find a label to take it on. Back to the drawing board.

Despite the leanest of times we still firmly believed that we would be able to laugh at all the adversity one day. We got a couple of mentions on the Central television Popwatch programme and we played a couple of Red Wedge benefit gigs. Rhoda was into the Red Wedge movement and had worked on benefit gigs with Billy Bragg, Paul Weller and her mates from Madness. We played a showcase gig at Zeetas in Putney, London. Steve Levine even mixed the sound for us, but nothing came of it - except that we were even more out of pocket. Another publishing deal so nearly came off for us through a guy called Derek Savage who had previously worked at Albion, but like the others it bit the dust. One of the lowest points came when we played a place in Leamington Spa called the Hod carrier. The gig was held in a pub function room and there were no more than ten paying punters - disastrous because we were getting the door take. So anxious were we to escape the scene of the crime that we left the venue before we realised that we hadn't been paid. I went back in to collect the money and the manager, presented me with a handful of loose change. I thought, 'Has it really come to this?'

We spent a few weeks mooning about in a depressive state of mind until a couple of our mates, Steve Hawkins and Nick Wastell from rock band Chrome Molly convinced us to reform the Swinging Laurels. With one year still to run on the Happy House studio lease, we thought it was at least worth having one last stab.

We penned a song called Push and Shove and recorded it at Nightfall studio in Nottingham with Joe King in the producers' chair. I even managed to coax Dean Sargent out of retirement to play trumpet and he didn't disappoint. We sent new material out for review and were pleasantly surprised to see good reviews. Underground magazine wrote,

'Where have they been? We don't know. But it must have been somewhere nice, as they're now sounding deliciously relaxed and modern as a result. The Laurels were never a band to stand still for more than a moment. Perhaps their time has come.'

Our old mate Steve Turner from our Emgas college days put up the funds that allowed us to release Push and Shove on Happy Records. We pressed the record on 7" vinyl format and things started to pick up for us again. Neil Mather, who was the entertainment secretary at Leicester Polytechnic, put together a University tour for us to coincide with the release. We practised hard and were firing on all cylinders but lurking in the shadows was another real body blow. Just as the tour dates were finalised, Mark O'Hara decided to throw in the towel and it was the biggest body blow since Dean jumped ship. Mark had been disillusioned for a long time and who could blame him?

Gaz and I held a crisis meeting to decide whether to call it quits. When you have tasted a slice of what things could be like, you crave more. We decided carry on. After leaving the band Mark went to India to search for God, I don't think he found him because he came back to England with a runny bottom and opened a carpet shop. He later opened a night club but that venture unfortunately hit the skids. When we meet up occasionally we still laugh over the 'what might have beens.' Mark now has a high flying job in the financial sector and travels the world.

It was weird not having Mark in the set up. Six years is a long time to work with someone, especially in the intense creative atmosphere of a band. It may sound a bit twee, but you do forge special relationships with fellow band members. It is difficult to describe it to anyone that hasn't experienced it. It is more than friendship. There is camaraderie built up through extreme highs and lows. We were lucky to find a quick replacement - Mark Pearson joined the fold and quickly set about learning the keyboard parts in preparation the forthcoming tour. The confirmed dates were:

Leicester - The Cooler / Treforest - Polytechnic of Wales / Liverpool Mardi Gras / Manchester - University / Salford - University / Leicester - University / Sheffield - University / Leicester - Polytechnic / Leicester - College Hall / Scraptoft - College / Brighton - The Richmond.

The tour signalled a real return to basics - we even slept on floors just like the old days. We played a summer ball at Manchester University and were on the same bill as such diverse acts as: the Bay City Rollers - HONEST! - Kenny Ball and his Jazzmen - Pop Will Eat Itself and Jerry Sadowitz. The Bay City Rollers featured only one of the original line up from their hit teeny bop 70s line-up - Eric Faulkner. He was at least three stones heavier than in his knicker wetting days, but one thing had not changed, they were still dire. Hoards of pissed up students pelted them with plastic beer glasses. We shared a dressing room with alternative comedian Jerry Sadowitz. He was booed off stage for calling the inebriated students 'A bunch of c**ts.' Harsh - but I thought he had a good point. It was an all night bash and by midnight the students had transformed into a drunken, baying mob. It was a shame; the entertainment that night was exceptional, they just didn't appreciate it. In the dressing room Jerry showed us some of his conjuring tricks and sleight of hand - the guy was absolute master class. Also on the bill were The Bootleg Beatles. Gaz and I stood at the back of the hall while they played and at times it was hard to believe that they were not the real thing - their covers were so faithful to the originals.

Another wacky night was at Leicester Polytechnic - we special guests for Cleo Roccos, best known for her Miss Whiplash character in the Kenny Everett show on television. She was plugging a record but the students only wanted a flash of her naughty bits - which was a shame because she didn't have bad voice. She was heckled relentlessly. We met Cleo backstage and found her to be really charming. She gave us all a kiss before leaving. I bragged to the guys in my local pub - 'Cleo Roccos snogged me.' In truth it was a peck on the cheek, but I milked it for all it was worth.

The rebirth of the Swinging Laurels was fairly short lived but it was fun. We even managed to recreate some of the early frenzied fun filled attitude that was such a feature in the very early days. Latterly we were managed by Arthur Anderson and David Sanderson, two guys who had previously managed a band called Fire Next Time featuring Jimmy Maddock - they were signed to a major label and came close to making it. Under their guidance we played a series of showcase gigs in London - the Pegasus and the Portland being just two. By this time drummer Nick Murphy had rejoined and our live performances got pretty tight again. We played the Haymarket theatre in Leicester and it was the night that my good friend Tony James took his long term partner, Theresa on their first date. I often rib them that it was the dulcet tones of a Swinging Laurels performance that sprinkled love dust on them!

Ex Wiggly Worms front man and would be porn star, Steph arranged a string of gigs at the prestigious Rock Garden in Covent Garden, London. Steph was a complete loon. He worked for an exclusive men's wear outlet in Covent Garden and supplemented his earnings with occasional male modelling jobs and television ad appearances. Some of those Rock Garden gigs were excellent, the place was always ram packed, mainly because of its trendy location. Tourists flocked through the doors. We took two coaches of Leicester reprobate fans one time and we told them to be at the venue early - it tended to sell out and complimentary tickets didn't guarantee admission. True to form, one contingent led by Gaz 'Ace' Bond hit the local pubs and when gig time came they arrived late and to an enormous queue. The doorman barred Gaz because the crowd exceeded fire safety regulations. There was no way of talking the beefy doorman round and Bondy was stranded at the door. I had a heated conversation with the guy and pleaded with him, saying he'd come a long way. I said, 'If he doesn't come in, I'm not playing.' It didn't cut any ice, he said, 'Don't play then!' With that I went back into the venue, leaving Bondy outside in the chill wind. He hibernated, hamster like in a freezing telephone box until we surfaced at the end of what was a great night.

Nottingham record company No Label records re-released Push and Shove in 1987 and we played session brass on two other records that were released in the same week meaning that we had a hand in three separate pieces of vinyl that were released on the same day. The other records were, Sitting Pretty by The Smoking Hinchcliffes and She Said by Ten Minutes for Doris - none of them did much.

The studio lease was about to run out and I began to think the unthinkable - it was time to find a CONVENTIONAL JOB! We were still going down well in a live capacity but for me there was always the nagging feeling that we had gone on a year too long. It was an agonising decision to make. The plain truth was that Kim and I had battled for a while to keep our heads above water financially and Rhett was still a babe in arms - I had little alternative. For years we'd had hung on in the hope that success was just around the corner. We'd achieved so much in the pop world without ever really reaping the rewards. It was one of the hardest things that I had ever done when I told Gaz. I didn't want to be the one to precipitate a split but if the truth were known, I was sure that he must have considered it too.

I'd been offered a job with the people I used to work with - but there were conditions because I had left them twice before to follow my dreams. It broke my heart to walk away from music but there was no alternative. I had to give my solemn assurances that I wouldn't leave them in the lurch again and I was sure that I would never have to deal with that dilemma again. Not for the first time I was wrong. The first few days in my '"real job' were an absolute wrench, I hadn't been a slave to the clock for years - I was used to my freedom. The first day seemed like weeks. In the seven years that I had been away, most of the people that I'd previously worked with had progressed very nicely thank you. All had nice homes and comfortable lifestyles, but I had no regrets, money couldn't buy the brilliant experiences I had lived through in my quest for world wide fame and fortune.

The break from music wasn't quite complete - the Swinging Laurels still gigged. It just meant that I had to revert back to manic dashes to London straight after work by train. It was harder now that I was older; it made me wonder how I had survived all those years ago with Black Gorilla. One person who was delighted with my new found conventionality was mum. She never understood what I was chasing after for all those years. Even when I told her that I'd signed a £400,000 recording deal and she'd me on Top of the Pops she would say to me, 'When are you going to get a real job?'

Chapter Thirty Two

CRAZYHEAD & THE SPACE BASTARDS

After a spell with a band called New Age, Reverb, our former bassist formed a band called Crazyhead. They quickly got noticed through their early releases and a flirtation with the independent charts. They comprised of Rob (Vomit) on drums - Rich (Fast Dick) on guitar - Reverb on guitar - Alex (Pork Beast) on bass and Ian Anderson on vocals. Pork Beast had transformed from Mark O'Hara's mild mannered friend, Alex Peach, to monstrous leather clad, bass player who looked like he ate babies for breakfast.

Outwardly all the lads looked mean and menacing, but that was just appearances - they were a great bunch of lads. They belted out a brash, hard-hitting brand of rock that soon got them major music press attention and a healthy fan base. Food Records, who saw their potential early on snapped them up. Food later became the home of Blur and Jesus Jones.

Crazyhead were labelled a 'grebo band,' - whatever that was - another example of press terminology that unfairly labelled bands. They wrote gutsy songs that jerked you alive and were responsible for one of my favourite song titles ever, 'What Gives You the Idea that You're So Amazing Baby?' Reverb asked us to record the brass on a demo for Food records at Rick Wilson's 8-track studio in Leicester. Trumpet was needed so I contacted Dean but he wasn't up for it - he had been out in the wilderness for too long and had declined a number of recording sessions since he left the Laurels. So we approached a guy called Tony Robinson who coincidentally, like Dean, came from Coalville. He had gravitated through bands like Munch and The Sole Agents and although his principle instrument was the keyboard he was a more than able trumpet player. We immediately hit it off; it was amazing how similar his sense of humour was to Dean's. Must be something in the water.

We recorded a track called Rags to Riches. Their first release for Food Records, Time Has Taken Its Toll on You peaked at No.65 in the Top 75, a creditable first stab at the chart. Reverb asked us if we would play a number of live slots with them and we were more than willing to oblige. I'd done bits of session work with other bands around that time - Return of the Seven - Wendy Christian and the Last Band and Dog Patch Four and the idea appealed to me.

There is a marked difference between playing as a session man and performing in your own outfit. While the pressure is still on you to perform, it is a different sort of pressure. Not being a band member sets you apart and as long as you do your bit on stage, every thing is cool. We rehearsed six or seven numbers and made our debut at the Trent Polytechnic in Nottingham. This was followed with gigs at Stafford Polytechnic and at The Diamond Suite in Birmingham. THEY WERE LOUD - LOUD AND PROUD and delivered a pulsating set brim full of energy. Vocalist Ian Anderson had a commanding stage presence, pouting and gesticulating as he sang. Reverb and Fast Dick meshed meaty riff work with precise guitar licks. Pork Beast, with legs astride stance, pumped out power bass, while Vom's crisp, driving drumming held it all together. Crazyhead were an exciting live band to watch.

The prestige gig was at the Astoria in London and when we stayed in London with the band we either stayed at the legendary Columbia hotel or a notorious gay hotel in Earls Court - a place that had to be seen to be believed.

Because of my new day job, I blagged a lift from ex Sinatras guitarist Nev Hunt - we were talking again by then. Crazyhead's debut album Desert Orchid had been highly acclaimed by the music press and vocalist Ian had been featured on a number of high profile cover shots. He even had the dubious honour of being voted 'most fanciable man' in a poll for one of the weekly music publications. It was a storming show. Afterwards we met their manager Andy Cheeseman, who asked us to join them on their forthcoming European and Scandinavian tour with rock legend Iggy Pop. Saying yes would mean taking four weeks off work - a massive problem for me because I was only a few weeks into my new job. The offer was too good to pass up. The opening night was to be in Berlin and I'd harboured a desire to play there since my first visit in 1979. But to play Berlin with Iggy Pop was too good to be true. When we saw the tour itinerary we were totally blown away, it covered eleven nations with twenty-one shows in as many major cities. If you could go into Thomas Cook and book a trip like that it would cost a fortune. I had to say yes even if it meant losing my job.

I tentatively broached the subject with my manager - he was totally pissed off but he begrudgingly agreed as long as it was the last time that I put music before business. It seemed that each time I tried to call it quits another golden opportunity reared its head and I had to hang on for fear of missing out. Having a baby son focused my mind into provider mode but inwardly I was in turmoil - I struggled big time coming to terms with my conventional nine to five existence.

The full tour schedule was impressive. The itinerary was, Berlin - Tempodrom / Dienze - Brielpoort / Amsterdam - Paradiso / Copenhagen - Valby Hallen - Oslo - Skedsmo Hallen / Stockholm - Olna Hallen / Gothenburg -Scandinavium / Hamburg – CCH / Offenbach - Stadthalle / Dusseldorf – Phillipshalle / Munich - Circus Kroner / Vienna -The Arena / Zurich - Schuezenhaus / Milan - Rolling Stone / Lyons - Le Truc / Barcelona - Studio 54 / Madrid - Jacara / San Sebastian - Polideportiva Andeta / Bordeaux - Grand Parc / Paris - La Cigale (Two nights)

We flew out to Berlin on the 4th November 1988. An added bonus was a free day there which meant that we could catch up with Leicester friends, Mick Mooney and Joe Keaveney. Berlin Tempodrom was a unique building sited in the shadow of the Reichstag. It was a circular and the audience sat in rows of seats that surrounded the stage giving the place an incredibly intimate, almost claustrophobic feel. When the auditorium was full the atmosphere was sultry and sticky.

Berlin is bitter cold in November, and our changing rooms were trailer caravans parked outside and we were half frozen. The Crazyhead set was well received and as we came off stage I caught my first sight of Iggy Pop in the smokey half-light. He was stripped to the waist with his ultra-lean torso exposed, glistening with sweat. It was great to be back in Berlin, but to be back there in the company of the great Iggy was unbelievable. His live show was full of raw power and energy although he must have been in his forties at the time. He belted out a non-stop ninety-minute set and the crowd lapped it up. It was said that he had recently renounced his drug habit and here was evidence, he showed how super fit he was.

Someone said that David Bowie might show for the concert because Berlin was an old stamping ground of theirs - Bowie had produced Iggy's classic album Lust for Life there which contained the seminal track the Passenger - a song I heard on my first ever visit to Berlin.

That Berlin gig is high up on my list of most memorable gig moments. We had the next day off so we enjoyed the inevitable visit over the wall to the East with Reverb and Pork beast. It was would have seemed inconceivable then that in a little more than a years time, the Berlin wall would be no more - such was the speed of the political upheaval in the Eastern bloc. Mick Mooney arranged to meet us at his local drinking oasis; he called it 'the whores bar!' We should have taken a clue from that description and when we found it we walked by a number of times, not daring to go in. When we plucked up the courage we found that there was a room at the back away from the seedy frontage and we need not have worried.

Food Records released Crazyhead's album across Europe and the tour was a vehicle to promote record sales. Consequently the band were required for press and radio interviews at each location and as it didn't involve us as session players it left us with a lot of free time. As long as we made rendezvous times we were given a free hand. We flew to some engagements but for others we travelled in a luxury Len Wright sleeper coach similar to the one that took us to Brussels with the Fun Boy Three some years before. Also on the road with us were a catering crew called Eat to the Beat who provided musicians and road crews with a hot meal at each venue. We ate in shifts - Iggy Pop's entourage first and then the Crazyhead contingency. Over a period of time we got to be friendly with the two girl caterers - one insisted on calling drummer Rob by his stage name Vomit. It sounded mighty strange to hear a caterer ask,

'More potatoes Vomit?'

The next stop was at The Paradiso in Amsterdam and once again we had time off to explore. I hadn't been to Amsterdam since the Swinging Laurels tour in 1983 and it was great to be back. After the show we hit the bars but on returning to the coach for the overnight haul to the next gig, we were horrified to discover that we had been robbed. It must have been an opportunist thief because only goods close to the door had been stolen; the coach driver was asleep, resting himself for the long drive to Scandinavia through the night.

Poor Tony had his trumpet stolen and a number of personal effects from his travel bag. I would have been totally devastated had my saxophone been nicked but Tony seemed more concerned about a brand new packet of Y fronts that had been lifted - a case of misplaced priorities perhaps?

Copenhagen was our next destination and on our arrival we spent several tiring hours trawling the music shops in search of a new horn for Tony. It would have been a damn site easier searching for Y fronts! I had this bizarre vision that somewhere in Amsterdam there was a chap mincing about wearing Tony's new Y fronts and playing a selection from the trumpet 'Tune a Day' book. Who knows, it could well have been the same stiff that misappropriated the Black Gorilla stage gear in Glasgow all those years before!

We stayed at the Sheraton Hotel in Copenhagen. Gaz and I were rooming together and on arrival we dumped our bags in the room and switched the television on. It was tuned to a pop channel which was playing Jackie's Still Sad by Leicester band Diesel Park West, who were also signed to Food Records. The Diesels featured old mate, Rich Barton in their ranks and were led by the charismatic songwriter John Butler. He was aided and abetted by long time partner and stunning guitarist, Rick Wilson. It was hard to believe that we had travelled all that distance and were listening to our mates from back home. In my opinion John Butler, has always deserved top-flight success and recognition - he is a real and rare talent. He has written many brilliant guitar based songs and done justice to them with of classy recordings but sadly has just failed to reap the rewards he so justly deserves. Diesel Park West's best chart showing was Fall to Love which reached No.48 in 1992.

Travelling through the night often meant surfacing from our respective bunks in a different country each morning. Often we would sit up and watch videos until we were tired enough to crash out. Some of our time was spent avoiding roadie Spike who was a tall likeable skinhead from Coventry who had threatened to 'get' the brass section before the end of the tour - exactly what 'getting' the brass section meant - none of us were keen to find out.

When he wasn't threatening us Spike did an awful lot of graft behind the scenes. He re-strung and tuned guitars, looked after the back line and shifted gear around. He was worth his weight in gold and was a real larger than life character. Road crew are often dedicated unsung heroes and without them proceedings would come to a grinding halt. The Swinging Laurels had a roadie called Penny, who had shifted gear for the best of bands. Such was his dedication that on occasions he'd sleep in the van with the equipment.

One night on the coach between destinations Spike and the others plied poor Tony with copious amounts of Tequila. I thought that they were going to kill the poor lad and I ended up holding his head over a bowl while he wretched it all up. He was a funny colour when he emerged from his bunk the following morning.

A couple of the Scandinavian gigs were in large ice rink stadiums with endless rows of seats tapering away high above the stage area. Before leaving Amsterdam we were warned about the extortionate price of booze in Scandinavia, so we filled to coach with beer from Holland to see us through. Stockholm played host to us on a Saturday night and after the gig we were in party mode so we hit the town. It was a surprise to discover that bars were virtually non-existent - young Swedes spent Saturday nights in coffee bars! WILD! Probably put off by the beer prices.

It was a blessing to hit Hamburg, where we had another rest day. Hamburg couldn't have been more different to Sweden; its nightlife was wild and decadent. We sampled the dubious delights of the Reeperbahn area, which was seedy but had a unique atmosphere and after being out on the tiles all night, we finished up at the squat of a young German who had been showing us around the city. In Dusseldorf Crazyhead shot a video for their forthcoming single release Have Love Will Travel and a film crew flew out from London for the shoot. We weren't involved although the gig at the Phillipshalle was filmed live so that excerpts could be used in the video. Have Love Will Travel was recorded without brass, but we played on the track live. Some weeks before the tour we had attempted to overdub brass onto the original album version, but it didn't sit right in the mix so it was released in its original form. That session was overseen by Food Records main man David Balfe who in his own playing days had been a member of hit 80's band Teardrop Explodes and had played on Echo and the Bunnymen recordings. While we were waiting for studio equipment to be set up, I actually beat him at pool - which was rare; I've only ever beaten a handful of people.

Each band member was given a cine camera to record footage of life on the road as the tour progressed. This was so they could patch sequences together to make a travelogue for the promotional video - in keeping with the Have Love Will Travel theme.

Vocalist Ian began started a serial wheeze on the tour. As he introduced us brass guys onto the stage each night he tired of saying 'Please welcome our brass section,' so one night he made up a name for us and as the tour rolled on, the names became more outlandish. What started as -

'Please welcome DIRTY BIRTY AND THE OVER THIRTIES!' quickly degenerated into,

'Please welcome 'THE SPACE LEATHER RATS!' Then he really plumbed the depths and delivered the best of all,

'Please welcome THE SPACE BASTARDS!' On hearing this one we dissolved into fits of laughter and it was sometime before we could strike the next number up. The moniker stuck. It does have a certain ring to it, don't you think? We were later credited on a Crazyhead CD as 'The Space Bastards.'

Bass player Pork Beast looked menacing and imposing onstage - like a mean Hells Angel from a chapter in San Francisco - but when he made his way to the microphone to roar at the crowd, instead of a gruff Lee Marvin type grow there came a high pitched Peter Shilton whimper and it destroyed the illusion somehow.

The only date of the tour that Crazyhead headlined was in Vienna at a venue called The Arena. As usual we arrived in the early morning after trucking through the night as we slept. It was a great way to travel because we were oblivious to the hassles and long monotonous hours on the road and by arriving early in the morning we had the whole day to sightsee. In Vienna I didn't get up until late, by which time the rest of the guys had taken off for a spot of exploring. It was raining and it was cold, so it didn't bother me unduly.

We met back up with the Iggy Pop entourage in Zurich where they'd had enjoyed a rest day while we had played Vienna. I hadn't been to Zurich since the Black Gorilla dates in 1979, but it was every bit as picturesque as I had remembered it to be. After Switzerland we were glad to leave the cold, inclement climate as we headed to Spain for the next leg of the tour which took us to Barcelona, Madrid and San Sebastian. Barcelona was great - I loved the place. While we were there another Leicester export helped us to straddle the language barrier and cadge a few free drinks into the bargain.

Gary Lineker was born in Leicester and made his name playing for Leicester City before making big transfer moves that took him to Everton and Tottenham Hotspur - at the same time scoring a shed load of goals for England. Now a television soccer pundit and crisp salesman in chief on Walkers Crisps advertising campaigns, in 1988 he played for the almighty Barcelona Football Club. The Spanish are soccer mad. Thousands turn out just to watch their favourite team train and in Barcelona Lineker was nothing short of a God. His image beamed out at you from everywhere - from billboards, news stands and shop windows. It was almost impossible to walk down the street without seeing his face somewhere. Reverb used our tenuous Gary Lineker connection to best effect, in bars he would say,

'Hey, Gary Lineker, Gary Lineker.'

More often than not he would be rewarded with a free beer. We played at a place called Studio 54 and on stage we got a lot of mileage from Lineker's name - the crowd loved it. Again we had plenty of free time to take in the sights and some of the lads went to see the Gaudi village while I explored the waterfront. Afterwards we got together in a restaurant where the owner spoke little English and it was a real effort to make him understand what we wanted to eat. Frustrated by this Pork Beast said,

'The only way to make them understand is to point at what you want. Watch me.' He pushed to the counter where photographs of meals were set out on a display. He grabbed the proprietor pointing at the pictures as he spoke - 'Look, I want that, that and that, ok?'

With a self-satisfied look, he returned to his seat as the rest of us struggled to make ourselves understood. Presently the food started to arrive. It was piled high in piping hot mounds on our plates. When Pork Beast's meal came over all that he had was a plate of runner beans. Rather than complain and admit that he was wrong, he sat and ate the lot, pretending that it was what he had ordered all along. One snigger is all that it would have taken to set us all off.

During the tour we only occasionally saw Iggy backstage, he arrived just before his performance and was spirited away straight afterwards. We saw a lot more of his backing band though and we got on well. Iggy came into our dressing room backstage at the Madrid gig and spoke to us all in turn. What impressed me most was that he had obviously done his homework because he knew our names. He shook my hand saying 'Hi Jaaaahhhn' - It made my day.

Gaz and I got lost in Madrid while taking in the sights. We found ourselves outside a huge bull ring arena and had to ask two non-English speaking policemen for directions. We finally made it back, in the nick of time but I must admit I was a little worried for a time. San Sebastian was a beautiful, picture post card coastal town sited in deepest Basque country. There were very few English-speaking inhabitants and it was easy to see why the Spaniards kept that little place to themselves, it was so pretty.

The tour wound to its conclusion with a date in Bordeaux and two nights in Paris and Spike was still threatening to 'get the brass section' on the final night. What started off as a jolly jape at the beginning of the tour became more worrying as the tour drew to the end. We hoped that Spike might forget - He didn't forget. Each day of the tour we had been given spending money but because we had been to so many different countries, some more than once, at the end we were left with notes and coins in eleven different denominations.

After an adventure that had spanned four wonderful weeks we arrived in Paris for the last two dates. Much as I had loved the whole experience, I was missing Kim and little Rhett and looked forward to going home. We were booked into a hotel close to the Moulin Rouge and some of the guys flew their girlfriends out for the last live show. I was more concerned with avoiding Spike, he was a big strong lad and God only knows what he had in store for us. We got our heads together and devised a plan to appease him. We thought it only fitting that we buy the band a little something to thank them for a really great time and we extended this to Spike as well. It did the trick. As we had found in our Swinging Laurels days, a bottle of plonk by way of bribery works every time. It worked like a charm; Spike was like a kitten. The Paris shows were at a place called La Cigalle. The venue was a lot more intimate than the larger arenas that we had played.

The last night was a real drink fest. Melody Maker sent a reporter to write a feature and there was a bit of trouble that the hotel management took great exception to - just drink fuelled high jinks really. Undoubtedly Spike was involved somewhere. The hotel manager was wandering around the place muttering 'Crazy people - crazy people!' over and over.

Back in good old blighty it was great to see the family again but I had very little time to re-acclimatise - I was due back at work, the very NEXT DAY! What a killer that was - there couldn't be a more marked change in environments. The previous night we had played to a packed hall in Paris and a few short hours later I was back in my mundane day job. If I'd thought at the time that it was the last thing I'd ever do musically, I'd have settled for that. We were close to winding down the Swinging Laurels for good but we still had a few gigs that we were committed to. We played a place in Northampton called the Lig Club, on Sunday lunchtime - it was a function room above a pub. There were around fifty people there when we played. That is what I call coming down to earth with a serious bump - days before I had played in arenas to 4,000 people. Rock n' roll hey?

Chapter Thirty Three

THE TELEPHONE ALWAYS RINGS - THE BEAUTIFUL SOUTH

Not long after arriving back in the UK and as I struggled to find my feet in 'real job land,' Gaz called. On the back of our work with Crazyhead, Station agency offered us the chance to audition for a band called the Beautiful South who were on the look out for a brass section to take out on the road with them. The Beautiful South were formed by ex members of hit band Housemartins, and I was asked to take a couple of days off work to go to Hull for auditions. I had to say no. There was no way that I could get away with bunking off so soon after the Iggy Pop tour. On paper the job looked sound, especially if they emulated the success of the Housemartins, who had a series of chart hits. However I tried to resolve the dilemma there was no chance of pulling it off. I hated the thought of putting Gaz and Tony in such a tricky situation but in many ways it was typical. For two or three years we had really pushed to secure a chance like this and now that I was back at work and tied down again, along it came and there was nothing that I could do about it.

On the recommendation of Joe King, they enlisted the help of a guy called Kev Brown from Nottingham. They went to the audition and got the job. I imagined that the Beautiful South would be another fleeting pop phenomenon - perhaps enjoying a couple of hits and then fading into the sunset. More question fodder for pub pop quizzes - perhaps? Just how wrong can a man be? Thirty plus hit singles and several No.1 albums later, they are one of the biggest selling British bands ever! Gaz and the lads are still supplying the brass for them. We all make errors of judgement but I think that my little blunder must rate right up there with the best. At least I made the decision for the right reasons - with my family in mind. When one door closes, another door opens! If I'd have known then, what I know now, I might have made a different decision but then everything seems clear-cut in retrospect.

The Swinging Laurels played their last live gig at Humberside Polytechnic in Hull, which by strange co-incidence is where the Beautiful South come from. It was sad to see the demise of the band but fittingly the gig was a good one. There were no regrets. When we started out if we had been told that some day we'd be playing on hit records, associating with name acts and making Top of the Pops appearances, we wouldn't have believed it. Perhaps we had been one of the unluckiest bands ever, but then pop is littered with bands that think they should have made it.

In March of 1989 Crazyhead took off on yet another UK tour and Gaz, Tony and yours truly played brass live on seven dates. This time I was able to get the time off work legitimately, by taking holiday leave. What a holiday - other people go to the Lake District and I opt for a college and University rock tour. During this jaunt one of my most embarrassing moments occurred.

We played Nottingham's Rock City and it was a sell out crowd. As on the Iggy Pop tour we played the two opening numbers then went off to come back later for the climax of the set. This meant that we had to keep a close eye on the running order, so that we knew when to come back on.

The first part of the show went swimmingly and we returned to the dressing room, which was in the bowels of the earth. Pinned to the wall was a set list with the running order so we could count off the songs until our next stage entrance. Being so far from the stage and loud as Crazyhead were, all we could hear was a distant rumble. We chatted, helped ourselves to a beer and made occasional reference to the list. Suddenly we became aware that the rumble upstairs had stopped. We looked at each other - we thought that there was another number before we were due back up there. We didn't realise that they had run two songs into each other, so there was no punctuation of applause to tell us that the song had finished. Everything ground to a halt and upstairs in the usually noisy auditorium there was SILENCE. Then there was the thud of urgent footfall in the corridor. It was a red-faced road manager, 'What the f**k are you playing at?'

Crazyhead stood like stuffed dummies in front of 2,000 sweaty punters, waiting for the horn section to arrive! After the gig they were quite understandably livid. In all the years that I had played live, nothing like that had ever happened before. It was one of those moments of pure undiluted horror and totally unforgivable on our part. As professional session players it is a very basic requirement to make your cue on time. In the dressing room afterwards you could cut the atmosphere with a knife and at one point I thought Vomit was going to take a slug at me. Time eventually healed the rift and we even came to laugh about it but I wouldn't want to experience it again.

For a joke, at the Leadmill gig in Sheffield, we came on for the final number in stockings and suspenders. Much like the bananas down the trousers escapade at the Laurels Bristol Dingwalls gig - no one took that much notice! The last gig of the tour was at the Town and Country club in London and for that show we had to make sure that we made it to the stage on time!

In June 1989 we were filmed live at the same venue for a Thames television series called The Concert. I liked the Town and Country club (now the Forum); its ambience was band friendly. On a good night, the venue was as good atmospherically, as any in the Capital. I had never recorded a live gig for television before; the closest had been a live Top of the Pops with the Fun Boy Three in 1982 - but then we mimed - no such luxury this time. The sound was monitored on a mobile recording studio parked outside the venue and the show was broadcast on the ITV network.

This period was pretty satisfying for me, the occasional Crazyhead gig meant that I still felt a part of the scene even though I did have to scamper to London a few times straight after a day's hard work. We played at the Brixton Academy as support to New Model Army. I had to grab a taxi to the railway station in Leicester immediately after a day's toil and then catch a train to London. I got to London in plenty of time, but found myself a victim of industrial action by tube train drivers and I got to the Academy with barely moments to spare.

On August 27th Crazyhead played Reading Festival and took us along with them. I had never played a major festival in the UK before and was thoroughly excited by the prospect. We played a warm up gig at The Mean Fiddler in London to shake away a few cobwebs. Also on the Reading bill were Voice of the Beehive, Wonderstuff and The Mission and each band was allocated a trailer to act as a dressing room. To take to the stage we ascended a huge ramp and when we reached the top we caught sight of a carpet of bodies that stretched way into the distance. It was an incredible sight. Attendance estimates were 50,000 and the gig was an absolute pleasure to play - the vista from the stage was awesome. Ligging in the VIP drinks tent after the show was an absolute must and later we went out front to watch some of the bands and soak up the atmosphere. That is what I call a gig. As the brass section we were only on stage for twenty minutes - at the most. If only all gigs could have been as easy and as pleasurable as that.

Gaz and Tony, along with sax player Kev went from strength to strength with the Beautiful South and came to form the regular brass section and soon they were sitting at the top of the charts with a song called A Little Time.

1990 ushered in a tougher period for me. The realisation that my musical life was ending dawned on me and it didn't help when postcards from Los Angeles and Tokyo landed on my doormat from Gaz or Reverb, as I readied for work on a cold, winters morning. Being away from music depressed me - after all it had played a massive part for most of my adult life.

My second son Nile made his appearance as I started work on another project that I had dreamed about for some time. In my satin jump suit days, as I hauled my sax around the discos of the UK with Black Gorilla, I heard a track called Big Blow in the trendy clubs. It was recorded by African horn player Manu Di Bango - it was never a hit in the conventional sense - more of a cult club hit. Saxophone was the lead instrument and the track had a nice groove. With Gaz's help we recruited a number of musicians to record a cover version

- the plan was to find a record company to release it as a one off single.

After the Laurels folded Gaz formed a fine country / pop band called Yellowbelly and he talked their guitarist David 'Wally' Walton into helping out. Also roped in was Nick Murphy on drums Tony Robinson on keyboards. Gaz did a marvellous job of the production and when the track was complete I despatched cassette copies to contacts that I thought may be interested. We went under the name Mighty Blow but all I got for my pains was a succession of standard turn down letters - even so I felt a sense of achievement in getting the project up and running. Although the project didn't ultimately succeed we got lots of press coverage and among the pile of rejection notes one in particular cheered me up. I sent a package to Go Beat Records, a label run Norman Cook, ex of the Housemartins. Although he turned my enterprise down, he sent me a personal hand written note offering encouragement. A nice gesture, I thought. Norman Cook is now a mega producer/DJ and also known as Fat Boy Slim.

In April 1990 ex Sister Big Stuff vocalist Sammy died after a long illness. He never recovered from a vicious assault that he had suffered when working as a doorman at a Derby club. After the incident he was a mere shadow of his former self. The funeral service was an incredibly sad occasion and the chapel was crammed with mourners and many had to stand outside. Out of the sadness came laughter too. After the service we shared anecdotes about his ludicrous scams and ex Big Stuff members downed a few drinks and celebrated Sammy's memory. All sorts of outlandish escapades came to the fore - not least the side splitting Prince Charles caper.

Former Laurels drummer Nick Murphy had kept himself busy with a number of musical projects. He formed an outfit called Ska Boom who became a popular live band trotting out blistering Ska anthems. Nick vacated his drum kit to take over the mantle of lead vocalist. Ska Boom toured non-stop, stopping only to record an album before hitting the road again. Gaz and I recorded five tracks on one of their albums called Traffic Warden which was produced by Andy Povall, in a manic three-hour session at a studio in Loughborough. Nick assembled seven brass men for the session and we were crowded around a microphone in a tiny studio room and periodically watered with lager brought in from the pub next door. It is probably just as well that we finished the recording quickly, there may well have been suspect notes flying, courtesy of the alcohol.

At a gig to promote the album Nick hired both male and female strippers, dressed as traffic wardens, to appear with the band on stage. He reckoned that by having strippers of each sex would prove that he wasn't sexist! The album itself caused a real stink when it was released - mainly from traffic wardens! It was claimed that title track could incite violence against them - local council suits were up in arms and condemned it - there was even a report about it on Radio One's Newsbeat programme.

In music as in life, the highs are usually tempered with desolate lows and a real low came when got news of the untimely death of roadie Spike. He was killed in a car crash while working for a band called Bolt Thrower in Germany. Reverb and Crazyhead put together a benefit gig at Leicester University to raise funds for Spike's family. It was testament to how well Spike was loved in the business because a number of name bands agreed to play. As well as Crazyhead there was Wonderstuff and the Milltown Brothers. The gig itself was tremendous but tinged with real sadness but we were all more than happy to take part for the sake of Spike's memory.

In 1993 former manager Arthur Anderson called to see if we would be interested in working on a project at his Back to Mono studio in Bedford. It was a CD single being put down by black film and television personality Norman Beaton, who was enjoying world wide success with the Channel 4 sitcom series Desmonds. Beaton had made records in the past and his versatility was such that he was a highly rated character and comedy actor.

We heard a rough demo and crafted potential brass parts for the track. We enlisted the help of trombone player

Adam 'Flymo' Birch, to beef up the sound - he later went on to work with the reformed Specials. I faced the recurring problem of getting time off work but the recording was scheduled and I had no alternative but to 'throw a sicky.' While I was in the studio someone from work phoned my home with a problem relating to a job I was working on. I wasn't there of course. When the phone rang Kim was hanging washing out, so six year old Rhett answered the phone. My work colleague Kev Burns asked,
'Can I speak to your daddy please?' - 'He is at work.' Rhett said "He isn't - I'm ringing from your daddies' work. 'Then Rhett then came out with the classic line, 'Oh yeah, I forgot - he has gone to London with his saxophone!'

You try to teach your kids to be honest and little Rhett was being just that. I was lucky - Kevin sussed out what had happened and covered for me.

When the Norman Beaton CD - Diddly Squat, was ready for release there were hopes that it might be an outside contender for a chart position. Chat show appearances and a Radio One road show were organised to promote the record but unfortunately poor Norman died just as the CD was about to hit the shops. He had suffered ill health for some time and without him to promote the record, it sadly sank without trace.

In 1994 I hit the big 40 year old landmark. It was a milestone that I would have cheerfully let pass by with as little ceremony as possible. I didn't feel down about it, in fact I felt quite at ease compared to how I felt when the big 3-0 hit. I elected to celebrate with a few quiet drinks. Kim and Gaz had other ideas - they colluded to set up a surprise birthday party for me at the Princess Charlotte venue in Leicester. They got me there on some flimsy pretext and once inside I was greeted with a happy birthday chorus from people lying in wait for me.

I was totally speechless. My saxophone had been smuggled in and I was railroaded into playing old songs with former Laurels cohorts Dean Sargent, Nick Murphy and Reverb. I hadn't played those songs in years but was forgiven the for odd bum note. It was one of my best ever nights. Kim had been shrewd enough to arrange a night that included music and my oldest friends - a sure-fire winner. The whole event eased me into my forties in a painless way.

My playing became less as time progressed but a succession of compilation re-issues surfaced from earlier work that I had done. I was delighted to see that The Apollinaires track - The Feelings Gone was featured on the 2-Tone Story- a four CD box set. The Laurels got a nice name check in the book that accompanied the collection. The same track also surfaced on The No.1 Ska Album, a CD set that featured legendary hits by Desmond Dekker - The Pioneers - Harry J All Stars and Dave and Ansil Collins.

Gaz and Tony continued to ply their trade with the Beautiful South who by this time had notched up a lengthy string of hits. I went to a number of their gigs and was mightily impressed with the beefy 'in your face' brass sound that they served up. It was a strange feeling watching Gaz on stage and not to be standing next to him, as I had done for so many years. One thing I do admire is the way that he has persevered all these years - he deserves all the success that is due to him and no one can say that he hasn't paid his dues. During that period he seemed to be on television more than Wogan!

No less than four different Fun Boy Three compilations found their way into the shops through 1995/6/7/8 featuring differing mixes of the tracks we had recorded with them in 1982. Also re-runs some of our Top of the Pops appearances received airings on the UK Gold television channel. You know that you are past it when that happens!

The last song writing / recording collaboration with Gaz came in the shape of a six track CD/EP called Be Someone released on Happy Records in 1996. The CD featured three new songs - Be Someone - Chicago - My Intentions and also for the first time on CD format, three older songs Peace of Mind Swing the Cat - Disco Laurels. The CD garnered good reviews and was later issued via Internet music label peoplesound.com. That wider exposure brought us into contact with fans from the old days - one being Michael

Hemsley from Australia. He sent me some great live photographs that he'd taken at the Hope and Anchor.

I received an e mail from a guy in New York named Greg Fasolino saying that he'd been a huge fan of the Laurels and that our music had been played to death on New York State University radio while he was studying there in the 80's. Through him I was put in contact with another Laurels devotee in Chicago, Ed Rapacki who runs a new wave record distribution company. He thought Peace of Mind was one of the finest 'new wave' records ever made. No accounting for taste! It is very gratifying to know that at least we were pushing some of the right buttons. Ed's record company, Wave Distribution, distributed Be Someone in the USA.

As I settled to my well-earned retirement from live work a chance presented itself to tread those boards again. Gaz managed a band called Molee' who, just when they looked like they were going to do something, sadly broke up. Out of the ashes of that outfit evolved a band called Baby Genius featuring drummer Mark 'TRM' Reid and bass man Moff. Mark is a 'King Blagger,' a fantastic drummer who now works with the Fun Lovin' Criminals. Moff was a solid, tight bassist - quite one the best that I've worked with and vocalist JJ had a voice of rare, pure quality which sounded haunting on the big stage. Under the production stewardship of Gaz they recorded an outstanding debut album called Rockin' Out.

It was on one of our regular Friday night watering hole sessions that Gaz asked me if I fancied playing with Baby Genius at the Marz bar in Leicester. I was a bit apprehensive about baring my soul in a live capacity again but said OK. Gaz had already played several gigs with the band when his commitments with the Beautiful South permitted

More tooting into my wardrobe ensued although by then the old dear that used to live next door to mum was banging out a rhythm on a more spiritual plane. I worked out my parts and met most of the guys from the band for the first time at the sound check! The gig was great and I felt that adrenaline surge that I'd almost forgotten about.

After the gig the conversation turned to a support slot on the forthcoming Beautiful South tour. Paul Heaton had heard the Baby Genius album and really liked it. Gaz said 'if it comes off, I'll play the opening set with you guys and then play the Beautiful South set after.'

The tour became a reality, it was only six dates and by some fluke I managed to swing the time off work - just like old times. The itinerary took in;   Grimsby - Leisure Centre / Bristol - Colston Hall / London - The Forum / Leicester - De Montfort Hall / Blackpool - Winter Gardens / Belfast - Queens Hall.

Time was tight - we had time for just one rehearsal before the tour kicked off, which was to be my first ever rehearsal with the band. At the studio, on a rain lashed Saturday in October 2000, conspicuous by its absence was Gaz's saxophone. He dropped a bombshell,

'The Beautiful South have told me that I can't play with the support band, you are on your own John!'

I had spent ages working out the harmony parts that we'd be playing - because he could no longer play, I had to re-work the lot. I had one day!

More increasingly desperate tooting into the wardrobe followed. It had been a long time since I had taken on such high profile live work. We were driven to the opening gig in Grimsby by 'Large' their road manager - he had the loudest snore in the history of loud snores - once he gets a head of steam up he sounds like a Hippo on heat. I know because, I shared a hotel room with him in Bristol. After that night lots were drawn. Also on board was guitarist Rob Tucker who ran a hairdressing emporium in Leicester and I reckon that he knows everybody in the entire world.

Arriving at Grimsby Leisure Centre on a bleak rain swept October day gave me very mixed emotions. We'd had a real laugh on the journey but for the first time in years I felt nervous. When we walked into the arena Moff said to me, 'I'm shitting myself!' I daren't tell him but so was I. I couldn't remember being as ill prepared for a gig as I was for that one.

The band strode onto the stage and opened their set to generous applause while I stood stage right waiting for my cue to go on. When it came - I screamed inwardly - 'HELP,' -

but there was no help - I was on my own. Strange but sometimes standing on a stage in front of thousands of people can be so lonely! I dug deep and the gig was great and as the tour progressed my confidence grew, as did the stature of the band. High points for me were playing the London Forum - I'd last played there with Crazyhead when it was called the Town & Country Club in the late 80's and De Montfort Hall where Kim and our boys Rhett and Nile came along. I was keen to let them see me on a big stage before I finally hung up my sax sling for good. During one number as I stepped forward to play a solo I caught sight of Nile through the smoky glare of the lights sitting astride Stalky's shoulders. I nearly choked - it was lump in the throat material. It had been a great tour and we had an epic end of tour party in a pub in Belfast.

In December 2001 I played with them on a live national BBC1 television programme for the Children in Need appeal with Louise and Atomic Kitten. Louise stood next to me in the wings as we waited to sound check - I didn't recognise her in jeans and trainers.

Opportunities became less but some session jobs came my way. The Charmers, a band fronted by Andy Sharman, were a band that I'd much admired for a long time and I was delighted to record a couple of tracks on their album, Learning to Cope with Happiness. Great band, great guys and great pop songs.

In November 2002 the Swinging Laurels were featured on Top of the Pops 2 with the Fun Boy Three in a re-run of a 1982 appearance and the Laurels got a great name check from Steve Wright.

In 2003 Gaz and I recorded brass tracks with ex Specials trumpet man John Reid for an album by ambient band Normal Position and took to the road with them on a five-date UK tour. It was interesting because they had a four piece string section, Strung Out Sister, along for the ride. The gigs were, in the main, at art centres where some audiences actually sat down cross legged on the floor to watch the band. Different and all very early 70s. The album was called

Rave killed the Romance and got some great reviews from the ambient music genre publications.

Chapter Thirty Four

ISTIANITY - MAY WE DOMINATE YOU?

In 2004, after a whirlwind twenty seven year courtship, I finally tied the knot with Kim. She'd finally tamed me - well I was never one to rush into things! We got hitched in a pretty, post card chapel in Las Vegas accompanied by a few close friends. Kim's brother and one of my life long friends, Kev Moore was my best man. Sounds pretentious and very rock 'n' roll but it was a very special day in every respect.

In 2005 I received an e mail from a guy called Mark 'Flash' Haynes asking if we would be interested in blowing on tracks for a new album that his band were working on. The band were called ist and had already had a number of critically acclaimed releases under their belts. Mark was a Laurels devotee from years back and coincidentally, came from Coalville - there goes that Coalville connection again.

Ist are fronted by a talented, enigmatic Canadian singer/song writer Kenton Hall whose clever intuitive lyrics sets him well apart from the pack. The band had risen from the ashes of considerable adversity - after seeing bass player Mark 'Detroit' Robbins die tragically at an unreasonably young age and having guitarist Jack Bomb leave the fold, the album was held in limbo while the remaining members took stock. New recruits were drafted in - John McCourt on bass and Brett Richardson on guitar and bassoon. They rightly decided to proceed with the project and Gaz and I were delighted to accept the offer. The album, King Martha, was already almost complete when we met at Cordelia studios in Leicester to record our input. It was produced by ex- Deep Freeze Mice guitarist/vocalist Alan Jenkins and we rattled our parts off in a three hour session. Also featured on the album were many special guests including legendary singer/songwriter Kevin Hewick - it was a great honour to appear on the same album

as him after all those years. Other featured artists were the Have Nots and talented keyboard player Paul Swannell. When the album was released on Pink Box records in April 2005 it commanded exceptional reviews-
Mark Edwards of Skidmark internet music site wrote:
'If ist's last album 'Freudian Corduroy' was the band's puberty then 'King Martha' is definitely their 'coming of age' - this CD still has the fine, zesty, guitar-driven sound of the early offering, but the more mature, reflective angle of the tracks are enhanced with the warm, seasoned sound of special guests, The Swinging Laurels on brass & horns. Independent release-wise I'd say this is the definitive alternative pop CD of 2005 - a 'Sergeant Pepper's Lonely Heart Club Band' for the post-millennium generation.'

We were delighted that one of the tracks that we played on - Here We Go Again was lifted from the album and was released as a single and we were given special guest status, which was great. The single also attracted healthy reviews - Record Collector enthused;

'With an accompanying blurb citing Costello, Cocker and The Kinks as influences, ist (whose followers are called "Istians" - pretty cool) push all the right buttons. Even the saxophone solo at the end sounds bearable (normally we consider the sax a work of Satan), and the fuzz and pop from the vintage amps and Hammond bubbling away underneath makes what could well have been an awful pseudo-Style Council whimper into a strident and, dare we say, sexy, little pop number that doesn't even have the cheek to out-stay it's welcome. Top Stuff.'

To accompany the single release the band arranged a promotional video shoot and Gaz and I were duly asked to make cameo appearances. The shoot was set up at a house in the suburbs of Leicester and when we arrived a huge boom camera straddled the pavement outside which triggered a great amount of curtain twitching from mystified neighbours. At the beginning of the video Gaz and I were filmed walking down the street with our saxes around our necks while the boom camera tracked us. It took several takes and more than once proceedings had to be halted as a member of the public sauntered into shot. As we stood on our marker waiting for the camera to position itself a car backed out of a drive in front of us. Seeing us standing outside his house with saxophones around our necks, the guy wound his window down and said - 'What do you think you are doing?' Gaz said 'We are filming a pop video' the guy retorted 'I bet you feel like right twats' and with that he drove off!

We played the Carling Academy in London with the band and it was a great day because Gaz's son Jordan and my son Nile came along to watch - we stopped for fish and chips on the way back at a shop two doors away from the Hope & Anchor and we regaled our offspring of tales from times past. It looks incredibly up market now - I can't imagine Ian Dury or Hugh Cornwell walking in there for a pint these days! There was also a gig at the De Montfort University in Leicester which was packed full of young girl students. After the gig Gaz, Kev Hewick and myself huddled together for a pint and the conversation turned to how ancient we all felt in that company - the old men of rock! We were staggered that a lot of young girls came over to chat with us when perhaps we should have been at home tucked up in the warm, with our slippers on and sucking on a Werther's Original!

We also played Leicester's Summer Sundae festival at the De Montfort halls - headliners were Patti Smith and the Magic Numbers among others.

In December 2005 my poor brilliant dad passed away after a long and painful illness. It ripped my insides out but he'd stood months of agonising pain with real courage and was as much an inspiration to me in death, as he had been in life. Because of his passing I pulled out of a gig for the first time in my entire playing career. I was due to play the Musician venue in Leicester with ist but I really couldn't summon the strength to do it.

The ist single and the album actually reached the No.1 spot in the Russian download charts - which technically was the Laurels first No.1 since our Indie topper, Peace of Mind, in 1981. Ist have an incredible internet fan base world wide, which is a great testament to the power of the internet - I only wish that sites like My Space had been around in the

80s/90s. We are currently working on tracks for the next album, Toothpick Bridge which is due for release in spring 2007.

All of this brings us neatly up to the present day - As for some of the characters mentioned in this diatribe - Stalky occasionally plays drums for a blues band - Dean Sargent, has a son called Bradley and still plays for his brass band. Three years ago he was the subject of a Carlton television documentary called The Real Brassed Off, which featured photographs of the Laurels. Dean was a real star. Mark O' Hara, after not finding God in India - or anywhere else for that matter and seeing a night-club venture hit the skids, is now a high flyer in the financial sector. Phil Birtles lives in Southern Ireland and Nick Murphy actually taught music to my son Nile at school!

My flirtations with the music industry doubtless cost me in a financial sense. In the twenty or so years that I 'went for it,' I saw many of my friends establish themselves into well-paid jobs and enjoy the benefits of a regular pay cheque. Many of them slogged away in the same jobs - but have any of them played in Oslo, San Sebastian, Vienna, Bannockburn - or even Coalville? Money couldn't pay the stunning times that music has given to me. I persevered for as long as I could and always told myself 'this is the year' - unfortunately, that year never materialised for me. I came close to making it so many times that the law of averages needed re-writing. But how do you quantify success? When I started out in the business, just being in a band was success. Top of the Pops, hit records, big recording deals, major tours, were pipe dreams then. Looking at it from that angle, in my own way I did succeed. The only missing ingredient was the financial rewards that long term success brings. I regret nothing. If I had my time over again, there are very few things that I'd change. That lump of metal that I call my saxophone has been the passport to unforgettable experiences and capers. It helped me to achieve my childhood ambitions and for that I am very grateful.

I have always firmly believed that you have to strike out in life and experience as much as you can - I have impressed that philosophy onto my sons. Both now play guitar - Rhett plays in a band called Burnin' Babylon and Nile is in an outfit called M48 along with Gaz's son Jordan. It's ironic - Can it really be that after all my trials and tribulations, I may have spawned another Von Trapp family - Partridge family - or even worse - Osmonds. You see I believe that if you never try then you'll never know what you are capable of - apparently?

ISBN 141201413-1